Private Property and the Constitution

Private Property and the Constitution

State Powers, Public Rights, and Economic Liberties

James L. Huffman

palgrave
macmillan

First published in 2013 by
PALGRAVE MACMILLAN®
in the United States—a division of St. Martin's Press LLC,
175 Fifth Avenue, New York, NY 10010.

Where this book is distributed in the UK, Europe and the rest of the World, this is by Palgrave Macmillan, a division of Macmillan Publishers Limited, registered in England, company number 785998, of Houndmills, Basingstoke, Hampshire RG21 6XS.

Palgrave Macmillan is the global academic imprint of the above companies and has companies and representatives throughout the world.

ISBN: 978–1–137–37660–2

Library of Congress Cataloging-in-Publication Data

Huffman, James (James L.)
Private property and the constitution: state powers, public rights, and economic liberties / James L. Huffman.
pages cm
Includes index.
ISBN 978–1–137–37660–2 (alk. paper)
1. Right of property—United States. I. Title
KF562.H84 2013
346.7304'32—dc23 2013024873

A catalogue record of the book is available from the British Library.

Design by Integra Software Services

First edition: December 2013

10 9 8 7 6 5 4 3 2 1

For Kurt, Erica, Spencer, Claire, & Meg

Contents

Figures

Preface

Much has been written about private property and the US Constitution. A central focus is always a clause in the 5th Amendment stating: "nor shall private property be taken for public use without just compensation." Most writers, no matter their politics, agree that the US Supreme Court has done a less than stellar job of interpreting and applying this clause. I share that judgment, and offer some thoughts in Chapter 6 on how the Court has gone wrong and what it might do to adopt a better course. But this book is not just about the so-called "takings clause" and the protections it does or does not provide for private property. By examining the historic and contemporary understandings of the discreet powers and responsibilities of government as they affect private property, I hope to illuminate the weaknesses (and occasional strengths) of Supreme Court property rights jurisprudence.

Standing alone, this book is about government powers as they operate to define, enforce, regulate, and sometimes limit or destroy private property rights. A companion volume, *Private Property and State Power*, examines the nature of property, its justifications, the private and social consequences of different property regimes, and the general relationship between private property and government power. Each book stands on its own, but the reader of this book may find the other volume helpful to a deeper understanding of the ubiquitous social institution of private property.

The two books represent the culmination of four decades of learning, teaching, and writing about private property and the constitution. Teaching courses in natural resources law, water law, legal philosophy, legal history, torts, and constitutional law has afforded me the opportunity to consider private property and the constitution from many different perspectives. Though my property law professor colleagues may disagree, I like to think that my never having taught property law allows me some perspective that might have been compromised by mastering the arcane intricacies of the common law of property. To borrow from the first edition of Paul Brest's constitutional law casebook, my perspective is more that of the parachutist than the truffler.

My first serious exposure to the US Constitution came in college courses taught by Richard Sheridan and Richard Roeder at Montana State University. I don't recall that much time was devoted to the constitutional guarantees of property rights in either course, but I do know that most constitutional law courses taught at most American law schools dedicate very little time to property rights. Indeed when I taught for a semester at the University of Oregon I was told that they generally didn't bother with the subject at all. But thanks largely to the expansive regulatory initiatives inspired by the environmental movement, I have profited from an abundance of writing on the subject of the 5th Amendment Takings Clause.

Many people, too numerous to mention, or even remember, have contributed to my thinking about private property and the constitution. Two generations of law students have tested my ideas and taught me that learning is as much about overcoming biases and preconceptions as it is about acquiring knowledge and the tools for analysis and persuasion. Colleagues at Lewis & Clark and faculty from dozens of other schools have reinforced, but more often challenged, my ideas (the academy being what it is in our modern era of liberal dominance). As something of a counter to the generally statist thinking in the legal academy, I have had the opportunity to represent the interests of property owners in court as legal counsel and more often as amicus (friend of the court). All of that and more are the ingredients of a sort of property rights stew from which the ideas expressed in this book and its companion volume have emerged.

I am grateful for the generous support of the Hoover Institution's John and Jean De Nault Task Force on Property Rights, Freedom and Prosperity, and particularly to the Task Force's co-chairs Terry Anderson and Gary Leibcap. Thanks go also to Lynn Williams and Tami Gierloff of Lewis & Clark's Boley Law Library for always prompt and skilled research assistance, to Joseph Westover for editorial assistance and seemingly enthusiastic transformation of my reference notes into proper citations (appearing as endnotes to each chapter), to my daughter Claire for assistance with the chart that graces Chapter 2, and to Claire's siblings Kurt, Erica, Spencer, and Meg, all of whom inspire me in everything I do, and no doubt could have assisted with the chart if asked. Finally I am grateful to my wife Leslie Spencer for encouragement and support, and for helping me to understand that in writing, less is usually more.

Chapter 1

Introduction

Parents and others responsible for the care of young children devote considerable energy to teaching about sharing. But they expend virtually no effort teaching about private property. Nevertheless, very young children are quick to grasp the idea of private property. Given the fact that many things and spaces can be consumed, used, or occupied by only a single person at any moment in time, this seemingly innate understanding of the concept of private property is not surprising. And it is an understanding reinforced by the ubiquitous sharing rule propounded by the adults in charge, which is that each child must have an equal opportunity to use a plaything or occupy a play space.

Children are also quick to take offense when the rules for sharing are changed arbitrarily or without notice. Every child understands that if the sharing rule requires taking turns, it is not fair when one child takes two turns in succession. Even worse is when the adult in charge fails to enforce the sharing rule against a child who refuses to yield possession at the end of his turn.

There is no escaping that sharing usually requires successive or alternating individual use of a toy or occupation of a space. The children might be told that playthings belong to everyone, but the physical reality is that most things of interest to small children (and adults) can be enjoyed only when in the exclusive control of one or a few individuals. When it's Suzie's turn to play with a ball, Suzie understands that she has a right to exclude Johnny from playing with the ball. But when Suzie's turn is over, Johnny assumes exclusive control of the ball for the duration of his turn. While Suzie and Johnny might play catch with each other and thus have joint control of the ball, not all children on the playground can play catch with the same ball at the same time. There is no avoiding that one child or some children will control the ball while others wait their turn, even when all are said to be sharing.

In the companion volume to this book, *Private Property and State Power: Philosophical Justifications, Economic Explanations, and the Role of Government*, this inevitability of private property is explored in greater depth. So too is the inevitability of some set of externally imposed and enforced rules, like those for children in the family or nursery. In the broader society, the state is the authoritative definer and enforcer of the rules of private property. The adults in charge are the elected and appointed officials of the state.

Beyond establishing that private property and the state are inevitable, *Private Property and State Power* also includes a practical, non-technical explanation of the concept of property, a review of the main lines of philosophical justifications for private property, an account of economic theories about the private and public consequences of private property, and an introduction to the role of the state in a modern property rights system. The overarching theme, illustrated by three real-world stories in the opening chapter, is that government is both necessary for and a threat to private property. The state provides the necessary infrastructure of a private property system by defining and enforcing rights. At the same time, the many powers of government threaten the clarity and security of those rights.

When property rights are not clearly defined or rigorously enforced, there are consequences. Resources that could be invested in productive activities will be expended on dispute resolution and rights clarification. Moral values and ethical principles served by private property will be neglected, although competing values and principles may benefit. Scarce resources will be wasted or used inefficiently, leaving net social wealth less than it might otherwise be. Less net wealth will mean a diminished capacity to fund private philanthropy and pay for government services (including property rights enforcement). Finally, other rights dependent upon and facilitated by private property are put at risk.

Because the security of private property is often more at risk from the well-intentioned exercise, not to mention abuse, of government power than it is from nefarious private invasions, the founders of American government devised an array of constitutional constraints on government power and enacted explicit protections for property rights. These constitutional protections, and the nature and scope of the government powers they are meant to constrain, are the subjects of this volume.

The citizens of many nations of the world would likely say that government power is limited only by the goodwill of those people wielding that power. Sadly, goodwill has proven time and again to provide little constraint on the abuse of government power, although even the most tyrannical dictators would insist that they act in the public interest. To be sure, there are and have been benevolent rulers, but even they seem unable to avoid the temptations of power. As the drafters and ratifiers of the US Constitution recognized, even democratic governments conceived in the name of liberty cannot resist compromising the liberties of some for the benefit of others.

To protect against the influence of factions and the tyranny of the majority, government power in the United States is divided vertically among national, state, and local governments and horizontally among the legislative, executive, and judicial branches. At the time of America's founding, it was generally understood that the powers of the national government were strictly limited to enumerated matters of national concern. All other powers not retained by the people were understood to rest with state and local governments. Over the course of two centuries, those understandings have changed dramatically as ever more power has been assumed by the national government. However, understanding how power was originally meant to be divided and what those powers were remains important to the interpretation of the constitutional protections of property.

From the beginning, federal powers, whatever they might be, were to be exercised subject to explicit limits including the Due Process and Takings Clauses of the 5th Amendment. Thus, a gradual shift of power from state to national governments should in no way diminish property rights guarantees. But because most of the powers assumed by the national government, particularly since the New Deal, were among those previously understood to be aspects of the states' police powers, the 5th Amendment's explicit property rights guarantees have been gradually weakened in favor of a balancing approach designed to accommodate the late twentieth-century understanding of the police power.

As explained in Chapter 2, the modern concept of the police power is very different from its nineteenth-century and earlier origins. Historically, the state had authority to "police" private invasions of private rights. The prosecution of offenses such as assault, trespass, and theft was part, but not the whole, of this power. The police power also included regulation to prevent these invasions of private rights. Thus understood, exercise of the police power could not result in violations of property and other private rights. But over the course of the twentieth century, the police power came to encompass virtually everything state and local governments do, including things that limit rather than protect private rights.

Among the state powers now said by some, including even the US Supreme Court,[1] to be a means for executing the police power, if not simply an aspect of that power, is eminent domain. Chapter 3 discusses the historical foundations of eminent domain, the core principles of which are just compensation for property taken and the significant constraint that property may be taken only for public use. Historically, public uses included things like roads, schools and parks (generally owned by government and open to the public) and a few privately owned facilities (like mills, trains and ferries) to which the public had a right of access. However, the dramatic expansion of the police power and the idea that eminent domain could be used to implement broad public purposes have led to controversies like that which erupted after the Supreme Court's decision in *Kelo v. New London*.[2] In that case the Court held that property could be taken by eminent domain from one private owner and transferred to another private owner to promote economic development and increase tax revenues.

A third basis for the recent ongoing expansion of government power in relation to private property is the assertion of claimed public rights. Chapter 4 examines the historic public rights rooted in the common law public nuisance and public trust doctrines. Both doctrines function as preexisting limits on private rights, meaning that title to property is acquired subject to the public's right to be free from public nuisances and to exercise public trust rights (use navigable waters for commercial navigation and fishing). To state the matter differently, no matter when private property is acquired, the owner never has a right to use the property in a way that would infringe on these public rights. By definition, therefore, enforcement of those public rights cannot be an infringement on private rights. Public rights trump private rights not because they are more important, but because they came first. Judicial and legislative expansion of these public rights, as if all public rights date from time immemorial, has enormous implications for even long-vested private property rights.

The creation of new public rights, combined with the expansion of the police and eminent domain powers, makes constitutional protections of property all the more important from the perspective of property owners and those who believe that clearly defined and secure property rights are essential to liberty and economic prosperity.

Chapters 5 and 6 examine the current state of constitutional property rights protection. Rather than increased scrutiny of alleged threats to property rights in light of an expansion of government powers, the judicial response has been the opposite—greater deference to the government planners, managers, and regulators.

The second-class status of economic liberties is the subject of Chapter 5. Coincident with the Supreme Court's general acquiescence to the pervasive New Deal intrusion into the national economy, the Court began to draw a distinction between civil or political liberties and economic liberties. With respect to the former—e.g. free speech, equal protection, rights of the accused—there developed an appropriate presumption that government constraints are invalid. But with respect to economic liberties—property and contract rights—the presumption was inexplicably turned on its head. While few Americans will discount the importance of the so-called civil liberties, the reality is that economic liberties are the lubricant of a market economy. It is important to know that one can speak one's mind without fear of government reprisal, and that due process will reign in the event of encounters with the judicial system, but property and contract are the stuff of day-to-day life.

Property rights have their own explicit protections in the 5th and 14th Amendments to the US Constitution and in every state constitution but, as explained in Chapter 6, that has done little to improve their second-class status. At least since Justice Oliver Wendell Holmes stated that regulations of private property are constitutional unless they go "too far,"[3] property rights have been subject to the will and whims of government officials, and the Supreme Court has struggled, with little success, to articulate a comprehensible and defensible takings doctrine.

Given the Court's ill-conceived deference to legislative and administrative judgment, even where individual liberties are at stake, and its predisposition to incremental change, even where precedent is barely defensible, property rights and economic liberties in general are likely to maintain their second-class standing for the foreseeable future. But as discussed in the concluding chapter, there is a better way.

Chapter 2

Police Power

In twenty-first-century American law, the police power is a catch-all for everything state governments actually do that does not fit within modern understandings of the taxation and eminent domain powers. Indeed one might conclude from modern commentary and case law that the police power encompasses everything state governments do, with taxation and eminent domain among the means available to pursue the ends of police power. In the case of *Hawaii Housing Authority v. Midkiff*, for example, the Supreme Court stated explicitly that the eminent domain power is coterminous with the police power.[1] The powers of local governments are viewed in much the same way, with the caveat that local government powers derive from state governments and are thus limited to whatever powers the state has chosen to delegate. Although seldom spoken of in police power terms, the powers of the federal government might be similarly categorized, with its police powers being limited to those delegated from the states in the Constitution. These limitations, implicit in the federal government being one of enumerated powers, have proven to be often illusory as a result of the Supreme Court's expansive interpretation of those enumerated powers and of the Necessary and Proper Clause. So the bottom line is that American governments at all levels have enormous powers, most of which are linked, in modern thinking, to the police power.

But it has not always been thus. There was a time, not that long ago, when the police power had a specific and limited scope. As will be demonstrated in this chapter, what came in the nineteenth century to be called the police power was, for centuries before, the power of the state to enforce private and public rights against private infringement.

The other things government did, relatively few as they were and however they were justified, were not construed as police functions. They were just things that government did, like building roads, protecting the public health, and providing for the poor, because government had the raw power and could acquire the means. If justification was needed, it was that, like the police power, these other powers are inherent in government. The fact of power was all the justification necessary until the ideas of the rule of law, popular sovereignty, and constitutional government took hold.

The American theory of popular sovereignty meant that government had no power, indeed government did not exist, except with the agreement of the people. Agreement came in the form of a social contract, though the contract was implied and every citizen was presumed to have consented. But in the United States there was more than presumptive consent. All of the states and the nation enacted constitutions that were approved by more or less democratic processes. The federal constitution enumerated the powers of the national government, thus providing a positive legal basis for determining the substantive limits of national power. State constitutions, however, were superimposed on preexisting colonial governments with powers long exercised. The drafters of the new state constitutions did not engage in the power definition equivalent of zero-base budgeting. State governments with their new constitutions picked up where the colonial governments left off. The new state constitutions were far more concerned with the allocation of government power among the three branches and with individual rights guarantees against the abuse of those powers, than with the nature and scope of those powers. Indeed the federal constitution provided more definition of state power than did state constitutions in the sense that some of the powers previously in the states were delegated to the national government or expressly prohibited to the states.

Neither the state nor federal constitutions, as originally enacted, gave definition of state powers. Those powers were presumed to exist as they always had in all governments. But this did not mean they were presumed to be unlimited. The theory of popular sovereignty from which government drew its legitimacy allowed government only those powers delegated by the people. The 10th Amendment to the US Constitution explicitly recognized that some powers might be reserved to the people[2]—powers that the national or state government would have only if the people chose to delegate them. So the states do not possess all possible government powers. Those delegated to the national government serve to define one set of powers not available to the states, at least to the extent they are not concurrent. Another set remains with the people. Both boundaries have proven to be illusive of definition, but more so the latter since no state constitution enumerates either the powers of state government or those reserved to the people.

Assume that the universe of things governments might do is encompassed by the circles in Figure 2.1. Prior to the establishment of the state or federal governments, all of those powers were rightfully in the people (Circle A), though many had been usurped by the Crown. With the Declaration of Independence and the adoption of state constitutions, the people delegated most of their power to the state governments (Circle B). In ratifying the Constitution of 1787, the people took some of the powers previously delegated to the states and granted them exclusively to the national government while other powers were delegated concurrently to the states and the national government (Circle C).

As a matter of historical interpretation, there is another way of describing the source of the powers illustrated in Figure 2.1. If one takes the view that the US government is a confederation rather than a

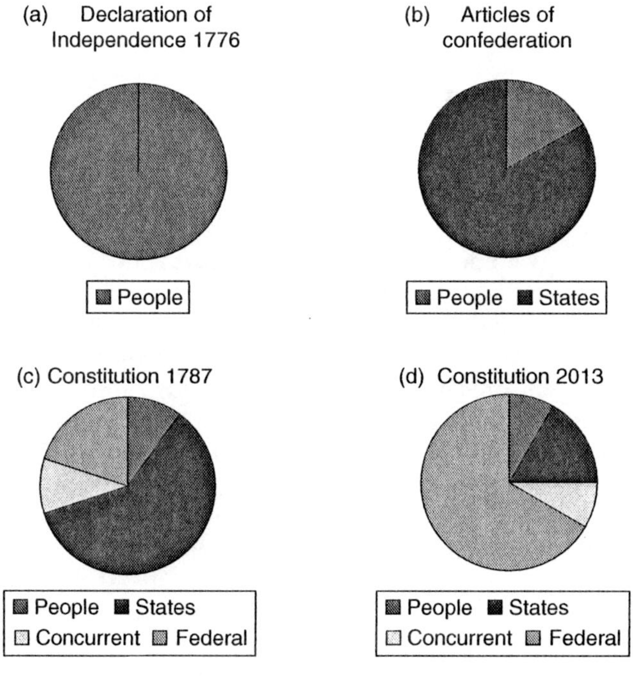

Figure 2.1 From Popular Sovereignty to Centralized Power

national republic, as most of the anti-federalists did, then the national government draws its powers from the states rather than directly from the people. In that case, the distribution of powers will look exactly the same, but the understanding will be that the states, not the people, agreed to carve off some state powers for delegation to the national government. While this alternative explanation may have implications for other constitutional questions, either explanation for how we got to the allocation of powers illustrated in Figure 2.1 leaves us with the same challenges when it comes to defining the nature and scope of state government powers. State powers are contained in the black and white wedges, though the state powers within the white wedge can be preempted by the national government pursuant to the Supremacy Clause of Article VI of the Constitution.[3]

Although the challenge of defining the boundary between federal and state power has generated hundreds of Supreme Court cases and many volumes of scholarly commentary, the more challenging problem is the definition of the boundary between state power (black and white) and those reserved to the people (dark gray). This boundary remains undetermined and largely unexamined, not for a lack of interest but for a lack of any basis to resolve the question. The best the courts and commentators have been able to do is defer to the democratic process. If the people or their representatives agree to a government action, it is presumed to be within the powers of the states. In the absence of other, more explicit, limits on state power, this is fair enough. But it does not mean that state powers are unlimited, even in the absence of express limitations.

It is rare that courts have occasion to address the scope of the police power in the abstract sense suggested above. Because few American courts render advisory opinions, courts do not have occasion to determine whether or not, for example, a state legislature has constitutional authority to mandate the preservation of wetlands or to subsidize the development of particular industries. Because citizens are generally precluded by standing and other justiciability rules from challenging the legitimacy of legislation absent a resulting personal injury, challenges to government action almost always involve a claim of individual right. Thus courts and those putting arguments to courts must address the boundary between individual right and government power, not the scope of government power in the abstract.

In the context of such claims of individual right, particularly of property or contract right, courts and defenders of government action often have found it useful to argue that particular regulations are legitimate exercises of the police power. To some extent this may reflect the still lingering influences of a legal taxonomy rooted in the English forms of action and in the legal science of Christopher Columbus Langdell, but it also serves the purpose, as it turns out, of easily disposing of the individual rights claim. There are various ways in which courts explain the conclusion that an individual right is not violated by exercises of the police power, but the general idea is that rights, particularly economic liberties, exist subject to the police power. In other words, if whatever the state has done can be said to be pursuant to the police power, it will not infringe rights of property or contract because those rights are held subject to the police power. The police power, not the right, is the trump.

From Enforcement of Rights to Pursuit of the Public Interest

So long as government is doing good, there is little political demand for justification. But doing good for some will often require doing harm to others, and the power to do good for the community is also the power to benefit the few at the expense of the community. The English Constitution emerged over several centuries in response to such perceived abuses of power. The American Constitution embraced and expanded on the rights of Englishmen as limits on government, but also sought to implement an entirely new approach to constraining power by insisting that government has only those powers that are granted by the people. These new ideas were more easily conceived and implemented in the context of creating a new national government, where none had existed before, than in the context of the ongoing governments of the states. Simple reality, supported by tradition, meant that state governments would exist with or without hard thinking about how to justify their powers. Certain powers were inherent in government—they existed of necessity. No more justification was required.

Among those necessary powers was that of internal police. It was concerned with the enforcement of rights and so, if fairly and properly exercised, could not be the source of government's infringement of rights. Consistent with this theory, the police power posed no threat to property rights, but that did not mean that a constitutional guarantee of private property rights was unnecessary. State and federal constitutional protections of property rights were needed to protect against the abuse of government powers other than the police power and to assure that the policing of rights was fair and just. As will be clear from Chapters 5 and 6, early case law recognized this distinction in assuming that exercises of the police power could not result in an unconstitutional taking. But as will be all too evident in this chapter, the modern view that the police power encompasses most of what government does leaves property largely unprotected so long as courts adhere to the view that the impacts of police power on property are largely exempt from takings challenges.

Over the course of American history, both state and federal courts have often been asked by property owners to limit the reach of the police power. As suggested above, these claims have generally been based on alleged violations of private rights protected by the 5th and 14th Amendment Due Process Clauses; the 5th Amendment Takings Clause; the Contracts Clause of Article I, Section 10; and in recent years the Privileges or Immunities Clause of the 14th Amendment. In the course of addressing these claims of constitutional right, the courts have sometimes taken the opportunity to discuss and opine on the nature and scope of the police power. Two judicial opinions were relied upon more than any others through the end of the nineteenth century and into the twentieth century to justify steadily expanding government regulation in the name of the police power. One was the decision of the Massachusetts Supreme Court in *Commonwealth v. Cyrus Alger*. The other was the US Supreme Court's decision in *Munn v. Illinois*.

Commonwealth v. Cyrus Alger—Police Power as Enforcement of Rights

Lemuel Shaw, who served from 1830 to 1860 as Chief Justice of the Massachusetts Supreme Judicial Court, was one of the most widely renowned state court judges of the nineteenth century. His opinion in *Commonwealth v. Cyrus Alger* was, until well into the twentieth century, the most frequently cited authority on the states' police powers.[4] Although the case was often cited as support for the view that an expansive police power allows state governments to impose all manner of limitations, without compensation, on private property rights in the name of the public interest, the facts and a careful reading of the case suggest that Shaw had a more constrained view of the police power.

Cyrus Alger was convicted for constructing, on his privately held tideland property, a wharf extending beyond a "harbor line" established for the Boston harbor by a law enacted by the Massachusetts Legislature. Alger acknowledged that the state had authority to establish a harbor line for the purpose of protecting public navigation and fishing in the harbor, but claimed that the law, as applied to him, was an unconstitutional impairment of contract and a taking of private property without just compensation. Chief Justice Shaw addressed two questions: (1) What are the rights of riparian landowners in the associated tidelands? (2) What authority does the state have to regulate and limit those rights?

On the first question, Shaw concluded that, at the founding of the colony, private riparian properties extended to the high water mark and ownership of submerged lands between the high and low watermarks was in the King as sovereign, held in trust for the ancient public uses of fishing and navigation. In 1628 all of the territory of the colony was granted by Charles I to Mr. Henry Roswell, along with the civil and political powers necessary for governance of the colony. Those powers of governance were subsequently transferred to the colonial government. Title to the submerged lands between the high and low water marks was granted to riparian landowners by legislative enactments of 1641 and 1647,

> subject to the restriction expressed in the proviso, "so as not to stop or hinder the passage of boats and vessels," &c., and subject to all such restraints and limitations of absolute dominion over it, in its use and appropriation, as other real estate is subject to, for the security and benefit of other proprietors, and of the public, in the enjoyment of their rights.[5]

Although there had been considerable controversy over the location of the high and low water marks, Shaw said there was never any question that "the grantees acquired a legal right and vested interest in the soil, and not a mere permissive indulgence, or gratuitous license, given without consideration, and to be revoked and annulled at the pleasure of those who gave it."[6]

If one read no further than Shaw's statement that private rights in tidelands are "subject to . . . restraints and limitations of [the state's] absolute dominion," it would be easy to conclude that the state's authority to regulate those rights was unlimited.[7] His description of the police power,

> the power vested in the legislature by the constitution, to make, ordain and establish all manner of wholesome and reasonable laws, statutes and ordinances, either with penalties or without, not repugnant to the constitution, as they shall judge to be for the good and welfare of the commonwealth, and of the subjects of the same,[8]

would seem to support that conclusion. Indeed Shaw's opinion in *Alger* has been relied upon to justify broad police power regulation free from the constraint of constitutional protections of property rights.

But Shaw's understanding of the police power was more limited. He was clear that the state and its predecessor sovereign authorities had power to make the grant of tidelands to private owners,[9] and he was equally clear, stating it twice, that the grant "could not be revoked by the power that gave it."[10] Shaw stated the common law maxim *sic utere tuo ut alienum non lædus* in these terms:

> We think it is a settled principle, growing out of the nature of well ordered civil society, that every holder of property, however absolute and unqualified may be his title, holds it under the implied liability that his use of it may be so regulated, that it shall not be injurious to the equal enjoyment of others having an equal right to the enjoyment of their property, nor injurious to the rights of the community.[11]

Thus, rights, not interests, define the boundaries of individual rights in property. Regulations to protect the property rights of others and the rights of the community are enacted pursuant to the police power, said Shaw, as distinguished from the power of eminent domain: "It is much easier to perceive and realize the existence and sources of this power than to mark its boundaries, or prescribe limits to its exercise."[12] But that does not mean that Shaw found the police power to be unlimited. Individuals may be restrained in the use of their property "not because the public have occasion to make the like use, or to make any use of the property, or to take any benefit or profit to themselves from it; but because it would be a noxious use contrary to the maxim, *sic utere tuo, ut alienum non lædas.*" Shaw wrote in the language of nuisance because most police power regulations of the time were intended to enforce by general legislation what would otherwise require a multitude of private lawsuits on behalf of those whose rights are violated by noxious, and therefore unauthorized, uses of property. But the protection of any individual or public right, whether or not founded in nuisance law, would justify exercise of the police power.

In theory, then, any constraint that might be imposed on the use of property by regulation might also be imposed by a common law court independent from any legislative rule. The challenge for a court is in determining the relative rights of affected individuals and the public. This challenge had been met for centuries on a case-by-case basis leaving property owners with less certainty in contexts not previously resolved by the courts. These uncertainties would have multiplied with the rapid industrial and economic development of the nineteenth century. Drawing on the ancient common law distinction between things *mala in se* and *mala prohibita,* and allowing that actions not punishable by common law may be made so by legislation "because they tend to injurious consequences," Shaw argued that legislation served "more especially for the sake of having a definite, known and authoritative rule which all can understand and obey."[13] He illustrated the point with the example of a powerhouse, which all would agree is a nuisance if within 200 feet but not if within 2,000 feet. Several courts might address the question and gradually settle on a rule to guide future conduct, but pursuant to its police power the legislature could simply announce a rule based on its best judgment. The legislature's purpose would be to clarify under what circumstances powerhouses, which all agree can be a nuisance, will be considered too close as a matter of law, not to declare previously legal activities to be unlawful nuisances.

The illustration was apt for the particular issue faced by the court in *Alger.* As Shaw demonstrated with a review of the law relating to tidelands, whether owned by the state or by a grantee or successor in title to a grantee, title is held subject to a public right of navigation and fishing in the overlying waters. Because the objective of the original grant was to allow use of the submerged lands for wharfs and other socially productive purposes, it was understood by all that Alger had a right to construct a wharf. But it was also understood that Alger's wharf could not extend so far as to obstruct navigation in Boston harbor. As in the powerhouse example, a series of court decisions might have established, over time, a rough guide to how far is too far. The legislative enactment claimed by Alger to be unconstitutional was, said Shaw, an appropriate way, in the interest of greater certainty, to resolve the question for all owners of Boston harbor tidelands. Although the lower court had concluded that Alger's wharf was not a nuisance at common law because it did not obstruct navigation, the effect of the harbor line statute was to displace the common law with a statutory definition of nuisance in the particular setting of Boston harbor. Thus, the statute did change Alger's rights in his tideland property. In recognition of this change, Shaw concluded that the law was "inoperative and void" as applied to that portion of Alger's wharf extending beyond the harbor line and constructed before the enactment of the law, but not with respect to that portion constructed after the law took effect.[14]

In reaching this seeming compromise, Shaw argued that applying the harbor line restriction to the preexisting portion of the wharf would be "*ex post facto,* contrary to the constitution and to the plainest principles of justice."[15] Presumably his thinking with respect to the portion of the dock constructed after the declaration of the harbor line was that Alger was on notice of the change, which is true, but nonetheless a change in his rights given that the lower court found Alger's wharf not to be a nuisance at common law. To this extent, it seems that Alger was correct in claiming that the state had taken a property right previously granted. But having explicitly stated that the grant "could not be revoked by the power that gave it," Shaw required a different explanation for the effect of the new harbor line on Alger's property rights.[16] That explanation lies in his recognition that prior to the lower court's finding that Alger's wharf was not a nuisance, Alger faced significant uncertainty on that question. The best he could do was guess how a court might rule. Shaw's view seems to have been that Alger and most other property owners would happily trade the uncertainty of predicting how a court might rule for the certainty of a legislatively mandated standard, particularly if that standard had only prospective application.

In the context of his powerhouse example—where to draw the line between 200 and 2,000 feet—Shaw argues that

> An authoritative rule, carrying with it the character of certainty and precision, is needed. The tradesman needs to know, before incurring expense, how near he may build his works without violating the law or committing a nuisance; builders of houses need to know, to what distance they must keep from the obnoxious works already erected, in order to be sure of the protection of the law for their habitations.[17]

Because Alger did not know, before the court declared that his wharf was not a nuisance, whether or not it would be found to be a nuisance, Shaw appears to take the position that the legislative enactment of the harbor line had the effect of clarifying, rather than taking, Alger's property rights. "[I]t seems to us highly important to have a more precise and definite law made and promulgated," said Shaw, "by which all persons may more certainly know their own and the public rights, and govern themselves accordingly."[18] The suggestion is that Alger more than offsets what he may lose in property right with the certainty he gains by the legislative enactment. Three-quarters of a century later Justice Holmes might describe this as an "average reciprocity of advantage," or yet another half a century later Richard Epstein might say that Alger's right has been taken but that implicit compensation has been paid in the form of greater certainty.

However it is described, it is clear that Shaw did not intend that his decision in *Alger* would contribute to ever more limitations on vested property rights in the name of the police power. To the contrary, Shaw's view that police power legislation served to clarify the vagaries of nuisance law and thus make property rights more certain was rooted in a genuine respect for private property as well as a concern for the public welfare. Shaw wrote:

> Having once come to the conclusion that a case exists, in which it is competent for the legislature to make a law on the subject, it is for them, under a high sense of duty to the public and to individuals, with a sacred regard to the rights of property and all other private rights, to make such reasonable regulations as they may judge necessary to protect public and private rights, and to impose no larger restraints upon the use and enjoyment of private property, than are in their judgment strictly necessary to preserve and protect the rights of others.[19]

Alger was a case about rights—private rights and public rights—and the appropriate role of the legislature in defining and enforcing those rights. It was not about the extent to which the state can alter or obliterate private rights in pursuit of the public interest. Alger had property rights originating in a 200-year-old grant from the King of England, as did his neighboring property owners on Boston harbor. The people of Massachusetts had very specific rights, deeply rooted in the common law and recognized in the original tideland grants, to navigate and fish in the waters overlying Alger's property. Shaw's task was to determine where Alger's rights ended and the rights of his neighbors and the public began. His conclusion was that the harbor line, prospectively applied, answered that question as a legitimate exercise of the state's police power to clarify and enforce vested rights.

Munn v. Illinois—Police Power as Pursuit of the Public Interest

The Illinois legislature established maximum permissible charges for the storage of grain in warehouses in cities of 100,000 or larger. The law was challenged as infringing the powers granted to Congress in Section 8, Article I; as exceeding state power as limited by Section 9, Article I; and as violating individual rights protected under the 14th Amendment of the US Constitution. The Supreme Court upheld the Illinois price regulations with two justices dissenting. In the course of his opinion for the Court, Chief Justice Waite expressed the view that the state legislatures had succeeded to all the powers of Parliament with the exception of those delegated to Congress and those reserved to the people as evidenced by express protections of individual liberties. Thus, the revolution resulted in a change in "the form, but not the substance, of their [the people's] government."[20]

According to the court, the provisions of the US Constitution on which those challenging the Illinois law relied spoke to the form of state government. But the substance was what it had been under Britain and what it must be in any government established by popular will or social contract.

> When one becomes a member of society, he necessarily parts with some rights or privileges which, as an individual not affected by his relations to others, he might retain. "A body politic," as aptly defined in the preamble of the Constitution of Massachusetts, "is a social compact by which the whole people covenants with each citizen, and each citizen with the whole people, that all shall be governed by certain laws for the common good."[21]

So whatever the federal and state constitutions might say about individual rights, some liberties individuals might have in a state of nature are necessarily compromised to government's pursuit of its mission. These inherent limits on individual liberty, and the implicit government powers they reflect, derive from two principles, said Chief Justice Waite. One, mentioned in Chief Justice Shaw's earlier opinion, is *sic utere tuo, ut alienum non lædas.* "[T]he very essence of government," said Waite, is "the establishment of laws requiring each citizen to so conduct himself, and so use his own property, as not unnecessarily to injure another."[22] "From this source come the police powers, which, as was said by Mr. Chief Justice Taney... 'are nothing more or less than the powers of government inherent in every sovereignty,... that is to say,... the power to govern men and things.' "[23] The second, stated by Lord Chief Justice Hale two centuries earlier, was that "when private property is 'affected with a public interest, it ceases to be *juris privati* only.' "[24]

> Property does become clothed with a public interest when used in a manner to make it of public consequence, and affect the community at large. When, therefore, one devotes his property to a use in which the public has an interest, he, in effect, grants to the public an interest in that use, and must submit to be controlled by the public for the common good, to the extent of the interest he has thus created. He may withdraw his grant by discontinuing the use; but, so long as he maintains the use, he must submit to the control.[25]

Taken alone, as Shaw had explained in *Alger*, the first principle was firmly rooted in government's traditional role as enforcer of individual liberties, a function familiar to courts. But the latter idea of property affected with a public interest, said Justice Field in dissent, "gives unrestrained license to legislative will.... The will of the legislature is made the condition upon which the owner shall receive the fruits of his property and the just reward of his labor, industry, and enterprise."[26] Justice Field did not disagree with Chief Justice Waite's reliance on Lord Hale's words "as if they had been found in Magna Charta," but he did insist that Waite had not understood what Hale had written.[27] In stating that property can be affected with a public interest, said Field, Hale had referred to franchises granted to private parties by the Crown. These were effectively monopolies, as were most of the examples cited by Waite in his opinion.

Although *Alger* and *Munn* were sometimes cited in the same case as authority for a virtually unlimited police power, the two cases offered very different explanations for the police power. In the view of Chief Judge Shaw, the police power encompassed the state's authority to enforce preexisting private and public rights. Historically this function was often performed by the courts in the context of individual lawsuits in both law and equity, but enforcement of rights also occurred through executive action pursuant to legislative enactments. In the view of Chief Justice Waite, the police power allowed government not only to enforce rights, but also to redefine those rights when in the judgment of the legislature it was in the public interest to do so. The only limit was that the exercise of any rights so altered had to be affected by a public interest, which was really no limit at all, as Justice Field made clear.

Because, as has been suggested in the introduction to this chapter, government actions pursuant to the police power generally have been understood to be exempt from the 5th and 14th Amendment property rights protections on the theory that property rights exist subject to the police power, the difference between the *Alger* and *Munn* explanations of the police power is very significant. Under *Alger* the police power exists to enforce and clarify existing rights. Under *Munn* the police power allows existing rights to be altered and even eliminated when it is perceived to be in the public interest to do so. An examination of the historical and intellectual foundations of the police power will demonstrate that the Supreme Court's decision in *Munn* constituted a serious break with the deeply rooted ideas of limited government and the rule of law.

ENGLISH COMMON LAW AND PREROGATIVES OF THE CROWN

Because the states "received" English common law as their own to the extent not modified by subsequent state legislation or judicial decision, pre-revolutionary English common law is important to understanding the rights of early Americans. But it would be a serious mistake to assume that the rights of Americans in relation to their governments were defined as well by English law. As New York Senator Gideon Hard observed in the 1845 case of *Russell v. City of New York*:

> The arbitrary exercise of . . . government [power] in derogation of the rights of the citizens, whereby private property was frequently taken without consent and without compensation, drew out from the patriots of the Revolution our declaration of rights. The burden of their complaints was that the rights of private property were trampled upon by public authority, that officers were sent among us "to harass our people and eat out their substance," and that soldiers were quartered among us without our consent. Hence originated that popular struggle.[28]

The American revolution, after all, was a rejection of the established relationship between English government and its American subjects. The American revolutionaries sought to establish a republic in which the long-claimed and often denied rights of Englishmen would be respected and protected.

Although Englishmen had a long tradition of individual liberty dating at least from the Magna Carta, the reality in England as well as America was one of a King and Parliament that often ignored formal declarations of rights. The English parliament was said to be supreme, meaning that no declaration of rights could limit its powers. In theory the Crown was limited by Magna Carta, the English Bill of Rights, and other such formal proclamations, but its many prerogatives put liberty at risk nonetheless. The 1606 decision in *Bate's Case*, for example, upheld a custom fee imposed by the King on top of one already enacted by Parliament. Bates, a merchant, refused to pay, objecting that the King had no authority to levy the fee. But the court of the exchequer ordered Bates to pay. "[T]he wisdom and providence of the King is not to be disputed by the subject;" wrote Chief Baron Fleming.

> The absolute power of the King . . . is only that which is applied to the general benefit of the people, and is *salus populi*; as the people is the body and the King the head; and this power is [not] guided by the rules which direct only at the common law, and is most properly named policy and government; and

> as the constitution of this body varieth with the time, so varieth this absolute law, according to the wisdom of the King, for the common good; and these being general rules, and true as they are, all things done within these rules are lawful. The matter in question is material matter of state, and ought to be ruled by the rules of policy, and if it be so, the King hath done well to execute his extraordinary power.[29]

This argument may have satisfied an English population that accepted the divine authority of the King. In his 1820 treatise on prerogatives of the crown, Joseph Chitty stated that "[T]he splendor, rights and power of the crown were attached to it for the benefit of the people and not for the private gratification of the sovereign."[30] But surely no one among the American revolutionaries would have agreed that the Crown could be so trusted, or would have argued that the new state governments inherited the prerogative powers of the English Crown. Whatever the powers of the state governments, they derived from the people and could be limited by the people. The prerogative powers of the King had no legitimacy within a theory of popular sovereignty, so whether or not the King purported to exercise his prerogative powers for the public good, the fact of their existence in English law provided no justification for their existence within the powers of the state governments.

Nor would the American revolutionaries have contended that their governments had the unconstrained powers of the English Parliament. Had Bates's challenge in the aforementioned case been to a Parliamentary assessment rather than a fee imposed solely by the King, Baron Fleming might have accurately stated that no objection can lie to the enactments of Parliament, which is supreme even in the face of constitutional objections. "Of the power and jurisdiction of the Parliament for making of laws in proceeding by Bill," wrote Sir Edward Coke, "it is so transcendent and absolute, as it cannot be confined either for causes or persons within any bounds."[31] Parliament, said Blackstone,

> hath sovereign and uncontrollable authority in making, confirming, enlarging, restraining, abrogating, repealing, reviving, and expounding of laws, concerning matters of all possible denominations, ecclesiastical, or temporal, civil, military, maritime, or criminal: this being the place where that absolute despotic power, which must in all governments reside somewhere, is entrusted by the constitution of these kingdoms.[32]

But in the new American republic the people, not their several legislatures, were understood to be supreme, hence the many constitutional limitations, in the form of individual rights, on the powers of both state and federal governments. And hence the general understanding that, as Chief Justice Marshall would later state, it is the "province and duty" of the courts to declare invalid laws enacted in contravention of constitutional limits including individual liberties.[33]

The fact that American governments found their legitimacy in popular sovereignty, rather than divine right or parliamentary supremacy, cautions against the simplistic conclusion that American state governments had the same powers as their English predecessors. But English precedent remains relevant both to understanding what governmental powers the former colonists were accustomed to, and how the use and abuse of those powers might have influenced the constitutional limits imposed on the new American governments. Most of those limits take the form of individual rights, rather than specific exceptions from the vast array of possible government powers illustrated in Figure 2.1 above. This is because, suggested The Federal Farmer in his 1788 pamphlet on the relative powers of the state and federal governments,

> the powers to be possessed by the government are often too numerous to be enumerated; [so] the people . . . often give general powers, indeed all powers, to the government . . . and then, by a particular enumeration, take back, or rather say they however reserve certain rights as sacred and which no laws shall be made to violate.[34]

Although this enumeration of rights as a means of limiting government power was common to state constitutions, and would be added to the federal constitution as a condition of its ratification, various such statements of rights dating from the Magna Carta had been part of the English tradition. But at least as important to the defining and limiting of government power as such formal declarations of rights was the common law itself. "It was the peculiar excellence of the common law that it recognized the worth, and sought specially to protect the rights and the privileges of the individual man," wrote Thomas Cooley in his 1868 treatise on constitutional limitations of state powers.[35] For this reason, as well, English legal history is important to the development of limited, constitutional government in the United States.

The term police power was not known to English law. But there was no doubt that the state, acting through both the Crown and Parliament, had authority to, in Blackstone's terms, regulate the "public police and oeconomy." The scope of this authority was narrow in practice but broad in concept. "By the public police and oeconomy," wrote Blackstone,

> I mean the due regulation and domestic order of the kingdom: whereby the individuals of the state, like members of a well-governed family, are bound to conform their general behavior to the rules of propriety, good neighbourhood, and good manners; and to be decent, industrious, and inoffensive in their respective stations.[36]

Offenses against public police included clandestine marriage, bigamy and polygamy, wandering soldiers and mariners, wandering "Egyptians, or gypsies" and, most significant to later American law, "common nusances." Offenses against public economy included idleness, excessive luxury and extravagant expenses, and gaming and various violations of wild game laws.

Separate from these categories Blackstone catalogued offenses against public health, public justice, public peace, and public trade, all of which, taken together, sound as if they might include the full panoply of modern police power functions. But the specific offenses, like those catalogued by Blackstone under public police and economy, were relatively few in number. Quarantine regulations to control spread of the plague and prohibitions of the selling of "unwholesome provisions" encompassed public health. Offenses against public justice included various interferences in criminal process, receiving of stolen goods and "common barretry," which was "the offence of frequently exciting and stirring up suits and quarrels between his majesty's subjects."[37] Offenses against the public peace included violations of the rights of the king (like shooting the King's game), rioting and "tumultuous petitioning," forcible entry onto the property of another, carrying dangerous or unusual weapons, spreading "false news" and "pretended prophecies," libel and defamation of others, and provoking breach of the peace. Finally, offences against public trade included smuggling, fraudulent bankruptcy, usurious lending, cheating in commercial transactions, monopolization of trade, and an assortment of actions thought to artificially increase prices in the market. Other offences against trade reflected what modern economists would call successful rent seeking and protectionism. For example, the "transporting and seducing [of home manufactures] to settle abroad"[38] and "owling"—which was the "transporting [of] wool or sheep out of this kingdom,"[39] usually at night—were prohibited, as was the "exercise [of] a trade in any town, without having previously served as an apprentice for seven years."[40]

There is nothing in Blackstone's account to suggest the police powers of the modern state, notwithstanding his seemingly open-ended general definition of government power to curtail offenses to the public police and economy. Indeed, much of the details of this particular category of authority would give most modern advocates of activist government a pause. In a day of moral relativism and behavioral license, government mandate of propriety, good neighborhood, industriousness, and acceptance of one's station in life is not the sort of activism they advocate. Even if Blackstone's other categories of public offense warranting government action are included, as they would be today, in the police power of the state, the English precedent provides little support for the all-encompassing police power of modern state government. Most offenses Blackstone describes under public justice, peace, and trade, though many are the subject of statutes, originated in the common law to guard against invasions of individual rights. The exceptions serve as good examples of rent seeking, including those benefitting the King who was the most successful rent seeker of all.

Early American Judicial Opinion

Not surprisingly, the language and substance of English law were adopted by the earliest American courts. In 1787 the South Carolina Court of Common Pleas described the powers of municipal corporations as "for the encouragement of their manufactures, trade and commerce, and for the regulation of their police and internal government."[41] In 1792 the US Supreme Court had reference to the "internal police" of a city.[42] Over the succeeding decades the term police power was gradually accepted as describing the powers recognized in these early decisions. But in both of these cases the issue was whether or not a particular aspect of the police power had been delegated by the state to a municipal corporation, not the general nature and scope of the police power. On the latter question, opinions ranged widely at the birth of the United States.

In a 1794 decision upholding a summary collection process requiring no notice or jury trial, the court embraced the argument of the Attorney General that the provision of the state constitution declaring "that the people of this state ought to have the sole and exclusive right of regulating the internal government and police thereof" was a declaration that common law rights operated as no limit on the lawmaking power of the legislature.[43] To accept that in a republican form of government the legislature is required to respect rights established by the common law, declared the Attorney General, would "leave us in the most miserable condition that can well be imagined."[44] "[It] would contradict the very spirit of the constitution, which in establishing a republican form of government, must have been inevitably led to foresee the great alteration which the new state of things would make necessary in the great fabric of the common law."[45] Nor, in the view of the North Carolina court, did constitutional guarantees of individual liberty pose any obstacle to legislative alteration of vested rights. Those provisions, like their predecessors in Magna Carta and the English Bill of Rights, were meant to guard against an "ambitious man [who] might usurp the power of dispensing with laws, or claim the right of exercising such a power,"[46] as had the kings of England and other tyrants of the past. There was no reason, said the North Carolina court, to worry of such usurpations in a democratic republic.

> Are these legislative bodies, charged and entrusted by their countrymen with their most important concerns, to be all regarded as men who either could not discover the unconstitutionality of a law, or were willing to countenance it? What interest have they in the continuance of an unconstitutional act more than the rest of their fellow citizens? Had the clauses been repugnant to the constitution, they would undoubtedly have repealed them.[47]

Although there was general agreement that democratic legislatures have wide-ranging powers, the North Carolina court's confidence in legislative respect for individual liberties was not widely shared, nor was it the view of most of the framers of the US Constitution. James Madison cautioned in Federalist #10 that "[i]t is in vain to say, that enlightened statesmen will be able to adjust . . . [the] clashing interests [of faction], and render them all subservient to the public good."[48] Based on their own experience since the revolution, the constitutional founders understood with Madison that a tyrannous majority can be every bit as abusive of rights as the English crown. Even the North Carolina court recognized that its confidence in majoritarian respect for rights might well be mistaken. While insisting that the summary collection statute was retrospective rather than ex post facto (and therefore not unconstitutional), a puzzling distinction agreed to four years later by the US Supreme Court,[49] the North Carolina court insisted that "[i]f the whole people should become prejudiced against a fellow citizen, he is not to fall a sacrifice to popular caprice or resentment."[50]

The unanswered question was how such popular caprice or resentment, or self-serving legislative acts at the expense of anonymous individuals, would be prevented if common law rights in property and contract could be abrogated in legislative promotion of the public good? Were such rights holders left to the goodwill of their elected representatives, notwithstanding that their immediate past experience had demonstrated the legitimacy of Madison's concern? Contrary to the divided opinion of the North Carolina court, most state courts agreed that both the common law and the new state and federal constitutions imposed limits on state legislatures—limits to be enforced by the courts. The problem remained, however, that the powers of the states, and particularly the police power, remained ill-defined. Absent constitutional definitions of the police power, courts and commentators were left to precedent and theory to establish whatever boundaries existed.

Because there was little or no precedent yet established under the new constitutions, the common law was the principal source of authority available to late eighteenth- and early nineteenth-century judges. Notwithstanding the North Carolina court's insistence that if the legislature must respect rights defined in the common law, "the common law is immutable and the Assembly cannot alter it by any legislative act,"[51] the reality in every state was one of property and contract rights defined largely by the common law. State legislatures had ample authority to alter and even invalidate the common law with an eye to local circumstances and future needs, but if the common law imposed no limits on such legislative power, as the North Carolina court found, than property and contract rights were not rights in any meaningful sense. Just as they had evolved over the decades and centuries to accommodate changing circumstances and social values, the common law rules of property and contract could change at the hands of the legislature. But according to the dominant view, change could come only in ways consistent with the common law principle of due process (*lex terrae*, or law of the land in English terminology). Otherwise the rule of law would be abandoned to majority tyranny.

Remarkably, the North Carolina court was fine with sacrificing the rule of law to the autonomy of the legislature. "Should the Assembly in any instance attempt to alter any rule of property, with respect to its transmission, descent, &c. so as to entitle any other person to it than is entitled by the common law," objected the Attorney General, "he that is entitled by the rule of the common law, may say, no man is to be deprived of his property or rights but according to the law of the land, or the common law."[52] Which, of course, is precisely what most lawyers and judges trained in the common law would have said then, or would say today. Indeed, in the very same year, a South Carolina court found a regulation of tallow chandler's shops "which constrains a citizen to submit his person and his property, to a tribunal that proceeds to give judgment on both, without the intervention of a jury" contrary to the constitution of the state and the law of the land. The South Carolina court did not deny that the city had authority to regulate offensive and dangerous trades, but it made clear that such regulation must not deprive those persons regulated of their property rights.[53]

The contrasting positions of the North Carolina and Massachusetts courts represented fundamentally different understandings of the police power. The North Carolina court, although evenly split, took the position that private rights must give way to legislative action even if the explicit purpose is to curtail or reassign those rights. The Massachusetts court recognized the legislature's power to regulate in the public interest, but insisted that such regulations must not violate private rights. Indeed, the regulation at issue in the Massachusetts case was best understood to be a flawed effort to enforce existing rights. It is unlikely that many in the Massachusetts legislature thought they were creating new rights in the public and thereby altering the rights of property owners. Rather it is safe to assume that most members of the legislature believed that the public and neighboring property owners had an existing right to be free from offensive and dangerous trades in populous locations, in which case property owners in those circumstances would be assumed to have no right to engage in such trades. The regulation would have been viewed as an effort to enforce those rights. The problem encountered by the court was the legislature's failure to respect the property owner's right to the established process for making the factual determination necessary to resolve a rights dispute. Neither that process nor the rights it was designed to secure could be compromised to a legislative determination that a different process or a different allocation of rights would better serve the public good.

THEORETICAL FOUNDATIONS

The distinct views of the police power reflected in these two cases were rooted in very different explanations for the source of that power. The Massachusetts court assumed that the rights of property owners in relation to their neighbors and to the general public were determined by the common law and the legislature was relying on its police powers to enforce those rights. As the term implies, the legislature sought to "police" private conduct to assure that rights were not being violated. The North Carolina court assumed that property rights were contingent on the discretion of the state to amend or eliminate them in the interest of achieving a higher public good. Both views were said to be rooted in the common law; the latter in the doctrine of necessity and the former in the maxim *sic utere tuo, ut alienum non lædas.*

Sic Utere Tuo ut Alienum Non Lædas

In its 1882 decision in *State v. Wheeler*, the New Jersey Supreme Court described the police power as "the mere application to the whole community of the maxim, '*sic utere tuo, ut alienum non lædas*' "—so use of your own as not to cause harm to others.[54] Freed of its Latin disguise, the principle was familiar to nineteenth-century Americans, as it had been to unnumbered countless generations before them. It was the Golden Rule—do unto others as you would have them do unto you—stated often in the context of private property and in the mysterious language of the law. But as a legal maxim, it was more than a moral guide post for social harmony. It served to define the boundary between one property right and another. *Sic utere tuo ut alienum non lædas* was meant to be a judicially enforceable standard for the resolution of disputes between neighbors. One's property right ends where his neighbors' rights begin, and vice versa. It could be no other way. It makes no sense to assert that one individual has a right to do that which other individuals' rights prohibit.

But saying that every right is limited by the rights of others does not resolve in any particular case where one right ends and the other begins. Recognizing this uncertainty in the general maxim *sic utere tuo, ut alienum non lædas,* Oliver Wendell Holmes described it as an "empty general proposition" expressing a "benevolent yearning,"[55] meaning that it was a noble idea but not a useful standard for resolving property disputes. A decade later Holmes would describe as a "shibboleth" the related but even more general maxim that each citizen has "[t]he liberty . . . to do as he likes so long as he does not interfere with the liberty of others."[56]

If Holmes meant to suggest that these legal formulations of the Golden Rule failed to establish formalistic, bright-line rules for the resolution of property and other interpersonal conflicts, he was surely correct. But the maxim *sic utere tuo ut alienum non lædas* had survived too many centuries in the law to be dismissed as an empty shibboleth. Its origins dated at least to Ulpian's and Justinian's accounts of Roman Law,[57] and it had been referenced often by the English commentators and courts over several centuries. Bracton, writing in the twelfth century, acknowledged the principle. In 1610 Lord Coke offered an expanded version—*prohibetur ne quis faciat in suo quod nocere possit alieno: et sic utere tuo ut alienum non lædas* (It is prohibited that anyone should do anything in his own land which might harm someone else; and you should so use your own as not to hurt others)[58]—in William Aldred's Case. Aldred objected to his neighbor Benton's converting of his orchard into a hog sty, and Coke found that Aldred had something like an easement to be free of the sights and smells of hogs "by prescription from time whereof."[59]

Citing William Aldred's Case as authority, Blackstone confirmed that in the law of "nusance," "the rule is, '*sic utere tuo, ut alienum non lædas*'."[60] Blackstone had noted earlier that the same maxim "is the only restriction our laws have given with regard to oeconomical prudence." His point, made in the context of a distinction between Roman and English law with respect to spendthrifts, was that English law recognized relatively few limits on the use of private property. Whereas under Roman law, "if a notorious prodigality was in danger of wasting his estate, he was looked upon as *non compos* and committed to the care of curators or tutors," under English law an "*unthrift*" was free to exhaust his estate without intervention. The Roman rule, wrote Blackstone, "hardly seems calculated for the genius of a free nation, who claim and exercise the liberty of using their own property as they please." Having undertaken to editorialize a bit, Blackstone went on to suggest that "the frequent circulation and transfer of lands and other property, which cannot be effected without extravagance somewhere, are perhaps not a little conducive towards keeping our mixed constitution in it's due health and vigour."[61]

Blackstone's claim that strong property rights serve the interests of a prosperous and free nation has been proven many times over in the succeeding centuries, but his suggestion that the maxim *sic utere tuo, ut alienum non lædas* is an exception to such a regime is misplaced, at least as the maxim was understood at the time. Lord Coke did not find that Benton's right to raise hogs must give way to Aldred's superior right to be free of hogs on neighboring lands. Rather he ruled that Benton did not have a right to maintain a hog sty on the property in question. Benton could not, or should not, have been surprised. That's the way it had been, said Coke, "for time out of mind." Consistent with the long tradition of the common law, Coke confirmed, in the language of the law, the custom of the time. He did not balance Benton's interests against those of Aldred. Nor did he balance Benton's interests against those of the community. He merely upheld Aldred's settled expectations that were based on established standards of reasonableness. In the words of George P. Smith, "the principle [*sic utere*] tests when a defendant's conduct is unreasonable or invasive of a plaintiff 's rights, not when it fails a test shaped and directed by social costs or benefits."[62] No doubt Coke understood that the public benefitted from his ruling, but that understanding was rooted in the fundamental, rule of law, premise of the common law, not in the particular facts of the case.

But this long history of reliance on the maxim *sic utere tuo ut alienum non lædas* was in the context of what came to be known in seventeenth-century England as nuisance. It was a private cause of action for a particular type of harm—"namely interference with an occupier's use and enjoyment of land, or his rights over or in connection with it."[63] How did the New Jersey court in 1882 conclude that the police power was the application of the maxim to the whole community? Public nuisance was the intervening step; that which connected the private cause of action rooted in *sic utere tuo ut alienum non lædas* with police power founded on the same principle. Writing in the thirteenth century, Bracton recognized that harm in the nature of a nuisance might befall everyone in a community as well as particular individuals.[64] At a time when common meant community, these harms were labeled common nuisances. Later they would be labeled public nuisances and generally related to obstructed rights of way and persistently loud occupations. Private nuisances were to be remedied by private cause of action in the King's courts, while public nuisances were to be remedied on the initiative of the sheriff in the criminal courts. Thus the state, acting through the sheriff and the criminal courts, became the enforcer of commonly held rights rooted in the maxim *sic utere tuo ut alienum non lædas.* Indeed for some time the common law courts had no jurisdiction to remedy a public nuisance, with the odd result that a defense to a private nuisance action was that the alleged harm was actually a public nuisance. But by the sixteenth century a private party could bring an action in the King's courts for public nuisance if the plaintiff suffered special damage not shared in common with others.

With or without the private action for public nuisance, state action to remedy a public nuisance became firmly rooted in both English and American law. Initially in England, the actual harms that could be remedied by an action in public nuisance were few. But over the decades and centuries the list expanded at the hands first of the courts and later of Parliament. In the 1660s "common nuisances" were reported to include

> matters affecting public highways and waterways; polluting the air "with houses of office, laying of garbage, carrion or the like, if it be near the

common high way"; victuallers, butchers, bakers, cooks, brewers, maltsters and apothecaries who sell products unfit for human consumption; running "lewd ale-houses"; and subdividing houses in good neighbourhoods "that become hurtful to the place by overpestring it with poor."[65]

Presumably this brief catalogue reflected the accepted customs of the day, as well as the desire and ability of the rich to exclude the poor. Writing in 1716 in what was the first comprehensive treatise on criminal law, William Hawkins included in "common nuisance" every offense that did not fit in other established categories of crime and defined it as "an offence against the publick, either by doing a thing which tends to the annoyance of all the King's subjects, or by neglecting to do a thing which the common good requires."[66] One might read Hawkins's open-ended definition of common nuisance as an invitation to special interest lobbying and unconstrained lawmaking by courts and legislatures alike. But the rule of law tradition of the common law served as a significant constraint in both England and America, as did America's commitment to constitutional government.

Thus, the ancient maxim *sic utere tuo ut alienum non lædas* was the basis first of private nuisance, then public nuisance, and finally the police power. This evolution suggested that the police power existed to enforce private and public rights. The sheriff could be called to prevent or halt violations of rights. The legislature could be called upon to enact regulations that would deter the violation of recognized rights and facilitate their prosecution. And the courts had the responsibility to resolve legal and factual disputes and to enjoin rights violations or remedy those that occurred. The courts also had the responsibility to enforce constitutional limits on the exercise of these various aspects of the police power.

Thus, a police power deriving from the maxim *sic utere tuo ut alienum non lædas* gave power to the state to regulate and remedy harms that might also be remedied in legal actions in private nuisance or prosecutions for public nuisance. By this view the police power allowed the state to enforce "social justice,"[67] and was, as well, "indispensably necessary to social intercourse, and the transaction of business."[68] It was not, as a New York court stated in 1815, a source of authority for the state to regulate "interior economy or management" of private property.[69] The link of public nuisance to the individual rights of private nuisance has had the effect of limiting the scope of the police power where it is justified on public nuisance. This explanation for the police power has persisted to the present day.

For example, in invalidating an ordinance prohibiting private operation of gas wells in residential zones, the Pennsylvania Supreme Court stated in 1994:

> We are mindful of the common law maxim *sic utere tuo ut alienum non lædas* (one should use his own property in such a manner as not to injure that of another). This maxim encompasses two principles. First, one must use his own property in such a manner as not to injure that of another. Second, one may use his own property in any manner which does not injure that of another.[70]

But, as noted above, there was another explanation for the police power.

Necessity

Thomas Cooley, in his 1868 Treatise on the Constitutional Limitations, wrote that "[a]ll contracts and all right . . . are subject to . . . [the police] power, and regulations which affect them may not only be established by the State, but must also be subject to changes, from time to time, with reference to the well-being of the community, as circumstances change, or as experience demonstrates the necessity."[71] At least two centuries of English and American case law provided support for Cooley's reliance on necessity as a foundation of the police power.

In a 1608 English case a fellow named Mouse objected that his personal property (a casket containing 113 pounds in coin[72], but no human body) was tossed overboard from a barge threatened by a large storm. Mouse sought to recover damages from the individual who had thrown his property from the barge, or from the ferryman to whom he had paid a fee for transport of himself and his merchandise. The court ruled against Mouse on the ground that necessity justified what would otherwise have been a trespass. The court cited in support the "plucking down of a house in time of fire," a commonly used example in later applications of the doctrine of necessity.[73]

Although there were a few high-profile cases in which necessity was argued in defense of the taking of one human life to save another,[74] the "plucking down of a house in time of fire" cases were far more common. Illustrative is an 1853 California case in which Pascal Surocco sought compensation for losses suffered when the mayor of San Francisco ordered the destruction of his property as part of an effort to forestall a fire then raging through the city. The California court held that no compensation was due because "[t]he right to destroy property, to prevent the spread of a conflagration, has been traced to the highest law of necessity, and the natural rights of man, independent of society or civil government." The maxim *necessitas inducit privilegium quod jura privata* (necessity induces a privilege because of a private right) was stated by the California court as the justification for Surroco having to bear his loss.

Like the maxim *sic utere tuo ut alienum non lædas*, the doctrine of necessity had both ancient and common law roots. The Roman jurist Ulpian stated that necessity justified "any act intended to avoid a threat to human life."[75] While later commentators argued that necessity did not justify the taking of life to avert a threat to another life, it was generally agreed through the Middle Ages that "[w]hen human life is under immediate threat, private property becomes public property for the public good."[76] This suggested that a destruction of property to protect human life was justified because there is in every property a public right to protect human life and therefore no private right to refuse to protect human life. Francis Bacon,[77] unlike Cicero before him,[78] had argued that the taking of life was justified even where, for example, one man lost at sea forced another from a plank that would support only one. But Blackstone, after identifying three categories of necessity under circumstances of compulsion, concluded that there was no general defense of necessity in the common law. Acknowledging that many "writers upon general law" including Grotius, Puffendorf, and "many other of the foreign jurists" have offered "ingenious, humane, and plausible reasons" that "a man in extreme want of food or clothing may justify stealing either, to relieve his present necessities," Blackstone concluded that "the law of England . . . [admits of] no such excuse at present."[79]

Blackstone's view was affirmed in two notable nineteenth-century cases, one English and one American,[80] involving shipwrecked mariners adrift at sea, but both involved the taking of human life to protect human life. Blackstone had concluded that necessity did not justify the taking or destruction of property, at least not where harm short of the loss of life was sought to be avoided. But many nineteenth-century American courts, like the California court in Surocco's case, disagreed. In numerous cases state courts ruled that necessity justified the destruction of private property.[81] "The instances usually given," said the Tennessee court in 1872, "are, to prevent the spread of a fire, the ravages of a pestilence, the advance of a hostile army, or any other great public calamity."[82]

But what has the law of necessity to do with the police power? In cases involving alleged murder or manslaughter, or where an individual was prosecuted for theft or criminal trespass, the state was performing what most would understand to be a police function. Necessity was argued in defense by the accused, not as a justification for the state's intervention. Necessity was also offered as a defense in purely private actions for trespass or other claimed private invasions of private property. On what basis could the state claim that necessity justified police power regulation of private property?

In all of the cases discussed above and in the analysis of the various commentators, the circumstances claimed to justify a defense of necessity were personal. An individual whose life was endangered could claim necessity as a defense, it was argued, because in a state of nature, or for reasons of humanity, every individual has a right of self-preservation. Bacon's point in the case of two men on a plank was not that one life was more valuable than another, rather it was that both lives held equal value under those circumstances, so each man had a right to eject the other. In the case of trespassing individuals whose circumstances were desperate but not immediately life threatening, there may have been an implicit conclusion that the benefit to the trespasser was greater than the loss to the property owner, but there was never any suggestion that the trespasser must first determine whether the property owner was in fact in less dire circumstances. The point is that in the line of cases following on *Mouse's Case* the defense of necessity did not involve a utilitarian calculus. The issue was one of relative rights between private parties, with necessity operating as a limitation on all property rights and, effectively, as a sort of contingent easement that all individuals possess in the property of all other individuals.

Viewed in this way, the state's role was twofold. First it was to enforce this particular allocation of rights in the adjudication of private disputes and to acknowledge the rights implicit in the defense of necessity in criminal prosecutions. In other words, the state had clear authority to police the established system of private rights and a duty to recognize the private right of necessity in the prosecution of crime. Because crime was understood to be an offense against the public or the state, recognition of the defense of necessity may have implied that the private interest outweighed the public interest. But there was nothing in the law of necessity to suggest that the defense depended on a balancing of interests favorable to the private defendant.

A second state role deriving from this private-rights meaning of necessity could be the creation of institutions for the relief of necessity before it led to alleged violations of private property rights. The state might reasonably conclude that the best way to protect the rights implicit in the defense of necessity is not to resolve disputes as they arise in court, but to provide relief and support to those in need. Blackstone's narrow view on the defense of necessity was based, in part, on the reality of such public relief. After citing Cicero and Jewish law "as certified by king Solomon himself" in support, Blackstone wrote:

> In this country especially, there would be a peculiar impropriety in admitting so dubious an excuse [as necessity]: for by our laws such sufficient provision is made for the poor by the power of the civil magistrate, that it is impossible that the most needy stranger should ever be reduced to the necessity of thieving to support nature.[83]

This proactive approach to recognizing rights implicit in the defense of necessity has the additional advantage of spreading the costs among taxpayers rather than being borne by randomly affected property owners.

To this point, necessity provides a foundation for the police power similar to that provided by nuisance. Indeed the maxim *sic utere tuo ut alienum non lædas* could be said to encompass the defense of necessity where it is understood to be an assertion of individual rights in particular circumstances (with corresponding limits on property rights). But the parallel to nuisance fails in at least two respects. First, nuisance law limits property owners from using their property in ways having particular external impacts, thus enforcing the rights of neighbors and others to exclude. The easements implicit in the defense of necessity allow for the use of one's property by others, thus limiting the right to exclude. Nuisance law says you can't invade the rights of others, the defense of necessity says you can.

Second, public nuisance encompasses those uses of property that would also constitute private nuisance if the impact was on one or a few rather than on the public in general. Except where there are injuries peculiar to the individual, an action in private nuisance does not lie for a public nuisance, not because the individual is not injured, but because the individual is equally injured along with everyone else. It is better for everyone, including the offending property owner, if there is one claim on behalf of everyone rather than endless claims by individuals. The claim on behalf of everyone can take the form of a preventative regulation as well as a legal action brought by the public prosecutor. Public necessity does not have the same tie to private wrongs. Inherent in the defense of private necessity is that circumstances have placed particular individuals in peril. Except, perhaps, as a justification for war, private necessities seldom aggregate to create a public necessity. Without a connection to private rights, the concept of public necessity justifies a very different police power than does the concept of public nuisance. Whereas both private and public nuisance give definition to property rights, the state can sometimes effectively enforce through regulation, and rights based on private necessity can sometimes be satisfied through public relief, the concept of public necessity has no foundation in individual rights or in rights held in common by everyone.

Most nineteenth-century American courts seemed to understand that a police power justified by necessity must be linked to the enforcement of rights, not to broad public purposes that might be conveniently described as necessary. Though the Tennessee court that identified necessitous circumstances as fire, pestilence, hostile armies, and other great public calamities used the term "public necessity" and insisted that "rights of property must be made subservient to public welfare" and that "private mischief is to be endured rather than a public inconvenience," it described "overruling necessity" as "the exercise of a natural right belonging to every individual, not conferred by law, but tacitly excepted from all human codes."[84] Does this mean that public welfare is nothing more than an aggregation of individual's welfare—that public necessity exists only when there is some critical mass of necessitous individuals? That may have been what the Tennessee court had in mind, but it is not what public necessity has come to mean as a modern justification of the police power.

The idea that there are public necessities independent from the private necessities that underlie the defense of necessity has similarly deep roots. An English case decided only three years before *Mouse's Case* has been cited often as authority for this public necessity in the common law; as recently as 1989 by the Idaho Supreme Court. In the *Saltpetre Case* the English court found that the Crown was justified in taking a property owner's saltpetre for munitions manufacture during a time of war. It was held to be valid because it was "for the defence of the whole realm, in which every subject hath benefit."[85] Although the *Saltpetre Case* and *Mouse's Case* often were cited together as authority for a police power rooted in necessity, the theories of the two cases were very different. *Mouse's Case*, as we have seen, had to do with the state acting to enforce private rights. The *Saltpetre Case* confirmed the state's power to act on behalf of the community. The distinction, as was pointed out by the New York court in 1840,[86] was not just a fine, technical, point for lawyers and judges. In *Mouse's Case* the state had no duty to compensate for Mouse's losses, because the benefits from destroying his property were experienced by individuals, not the state.

If compensation was due, it must come from those private parties benefitted. In the *Saltpetre Case*, on the other hand, "the ministers of the King who dig for saltpetre are bound to leave the inheritance of the subject in so good plight as they found it."[87] As the New York court explained the difference, government interventions justified on the theory of *Mouse's Case* are in the nature of police regulations. Interventions justified on the basis of the *Saltpetre Case* are exercises of the power of eminent domain.[88]

The reason that the theories of these two old English cases "are often confounded," as the New York court observed, should be evident. The state always seeks to avoid compensation when its actions take or damage private property. If the *Saltpetre case* as well as *Mouse's Case* is accepted as authority for a police power founded on necessity, there is potentially much the state can do without regard for the costs imposed on private property owners. Combined with an expansive view of nuisance as companion justifications for the police power, property rights are largely eliminated as restraints on the powers of government.

The fact that reliance on nuisance and necessity as justifications for the police power did not lead to unconstrained regulation of property rights in the nineteenth century, notwithstanding the expansive language of public rights and general welfare, is testimony to the strength of the entrepreneurial spirit, the dedication of government to facilitating that spirit (what Willard Hurst called the "release of energy"[89]), and to the judicial commitment to common law principles and the rule of law. But that did not mean that succeeding generations would not abandon the understanding of the police function as enforcement of rights and pick up on the invitation to expand government regulation of property in the name of the public good. Because public nuisance was always amorphous and would come to involve the balancing of public and private interests, it would serve to justify an expanding police power, as would the idea of public necessity, which has even more tenuous connections to the private interests that gave birth to the common law defense of necessity. Necessity also blended into an even less constraining theory of police power—namely the claim that it is inherent in sovereignty.

Police Power Is Necessary for Sovereignty

"The police power [is] inherent in every sovereignty," wrote W. E. Prentice in his 1894 treatise.[90] He also wrote that "[p]olice powers have their origin in the law of necessity."[91] But Prentice did not mean the necessity urged in defense of alleged trespass where life and limb are at risk. Rather he meant that police powers are a necessity of sovereignty, the "necessary guardianship of public interests and the public good." And pursuant to this necessity, said Prentice (with approval), "[c]itizens' rights or property, as they are frequently estimated by the public, are continually invaded anew by government."[92] That Prentice saw no connection between necessity and private rights he made clear in rejecting Blackstone's suggestion that necessity was analogous to self-defense. Self-defense has to do with the individual, said Prentice, while police powers have to do with society.[93] But the fact that the police power served public interests rather than private rights did not lead Prentice to conclude that compensation was due when exercises of the police power interfered with property rights. Indeed his argument in support of this conclusion contradicted his claim that the police power existed to provide for the public welfare. Compensation was due in eminent domain cases, said Prentice, because there is a public benefit that results. But no compensation is due from police power interventions because "there is no benefit to be recovered for by common law when property is necessarily destroyed."[94]

So, on the one hand Prentice argued that the police power necessarily exists in all sovereign governments to provide for the public welfare. Yet he also argues that compensation is not owing to negatively affected property owners because there is no public benefit warranting such compensation. This contradiction underscores the danger to private property in relying on necessity as an explanation for the police power. In its narrow, common law, sense, necessity is merely an aspect of *sic utere tuo ut alienum non lædas*.[95] As a justification for the police power it means that the state has authority to enforce the private right of necessity which exists as a limitation on all property rights. In the broad sense of powers inherent in all governments, necessity is a vague, open-ended explanation for government power. "The legislature becomes almost a dictator," acknowledged Prentice, "as under the old Roman formula to see to it that no part of the community has injury."[96] Together these very different arguments from necessity allow for almost unbounded interference with private property in the name of the public good, and no compensation to affected property owners on the contradictory argument that common law necessity is concerned only with private rights.

The arguments that the police power exists of necessity, that it is inherent in the sovereignty of all governments, and that it is really not amenable to abstract definition have been recurrent throughout

Anglo-American legal history. Despite efforts to supply theoretical explanations for the police power; explanations that might define boundaries, courts, and commentators have been unable to ignore the realities of political power. In England the Crown had its prerogatives and the Parliament its supremacy. In America the states picked up where the Crown and Parliament left off, building roads and canals, putting people in prison, regulating prices and the taking of wildlife, prohibiting hazardous and offensive activities, providing schools and, with all of that and more, keeping political supporters happy. Although the state and federal court reports are filled with cases claiming that state and local governments had overstepped their legitimate powers, rarely did a court conclude that a particular law was invalid for having exceeded the boundaries of the police power. Nor did legislatures decline to act in the view that they had no power to do so.

Thus, the only real limits on the police power were two: the voters, who could throw the rascals out if they did not like the laws the legislature enacted, and individual rights holders, who could claim that an otherwise legitimate exercise of the police power violated their constitutionally protected rights. More than a few rascals have been thrown out over the course of American history, imposing as least some limits on state and federal governments. Few would question that the constraints of democracy were an improvement on the pre-Revolutionary monarchy. But democratic majorities have their own ambitions and interests to be served by the police power. If democracy is the only limit on the police power, then the majority has license to do what it likes, even at the expense of minorities and of particular individuals. Rascals are replaced by other rascals.

So the only real limits on state governments are those few substantive exclusions enumerated in the US Constitution and in some state constitutions, and the constitutional liberties of their citizens. It is with respect to the latter, particularly rights in property, that all of the abstract discussion of the police power is important.

IS THE POLICE POWER UNBOUNDED?

The foregoing discussion suggests that, despite several centuries of court decisions and theoretical argument, we are no closer to a clear definition of the limits of the police power than when the discussion began. Despite the promise of rights reserved to the people and specific constitutional guarantees of property rights, the consequence has been a steady expansion of government powers with an inevitable and corresponding erosion of those rights. If there was a tipping point in American law, it was *Munn v. Illinois*.[97]

The *Munn* decision was repeatedly cited in subsequent cases in support of an expansive police power in the states. In *Mugler v. Kansas* Justice Harlan said, "[a] prohibition simply upon the use of property for purposes that are declared, by valid legislation, to be injurious to the health, morals, or safety of the community, cannot, in any just sense, be deemed a taking or an appropriation of property for the public benefit."[98] In *Budd v. People* Justice Blatchford said,

> there was little reason, under our system of government, for placing a close and narrow interpretation on the police power, or restricting its scope so as to hamper the legislative power in dealing with the varying necessities of society, and the new circumstances, as they arise, calling for legislative intervention in the public interest.[99]

Ignoring the often expressed concerns for the tyranny of the majority, Blatchford went on to suggest "that no serious invasion of constitutional guaranty by the legislature could withstand for a long time the searching influence of public opinion, which was sure to come sooner or later to the side of law, order, and justice."[100] In dissent, Justice Brewer stated the obvious, that "[t]here is scarcely any property in whose use the public has no interest."[101]

Through the twentieth century the Supreme Court did nothing to give a further or more precise definition to the states' police powers. Indeed the court stated in various ways at various times that the police power is not subject to definition. In *Holden v. Hardy*, just before the turn of the century, the court suggested that a significant expansion in police power regulations was appropriate in light of the rapid growth in dangerous occupations and hazardous activities.[102] The court thus linked the police power to the regulation of property uses causing harm to others, but a few years later in *Chicago, B. & Q. Ry. Co. v. Illinois* the court gave the police power a much broader meaning. "We hold that the police power of a state embraces regulations designed to promote the public convenience or the general prosperity," said the court, "as well as regulations designed to promote the public health, the public morals, or the public safety."[103] A dissenting Justice Brewer objected that the police power "has become the refuge of every grievous wrong upon private property. Whenever any unjust burden is cast upon the owner of private property which cannot be supported under the power of eminent domain or that of taxation, it is referred to the police power."[104]

Although Brewer foresaw clearly the court's future police power cases, the court continued to struggle with the definition problem because property owners refused to accept that the constitutional limits on state power were meaningless. In *Hudson County Water Co. v. McCarter*, Justice Holmes, a student of the common law, acknowledged: "It sometimes is difficult to fix boundary stones between the private right of property and the police power when, as in the case at bar, we know of few decisions that are very much in point."[105] A few years later in 1914, Holmes argued that regulation of oil transportation from a company's wells to its own refinery was invalid because the regulated activity was not a common carrier,[106] a sensible distinction consistent with many nineteenth-century cases, but another seven years later he would offer the unhelpful suggestion that the police power exceeds those boundary stones when it goes "too far,"[107] but that otherwise "property rights may be cut down, and to that extent taken, without pay."[108] Justice McKenna, along with three other members of the court, asked in dissent: "If such power exist what is its limit and what its consequences?" Among the consequences, argued McKenna, is the loss of "security of property [which] next to personal security against the exertions of government is of the essence of liberty."[109]

In *Eubank v. City of Richmond*, the court said that the police power "is not susceptible of circumstantial precision. It extends . . . not only to regulations which promote the public health, morals, and safety, but to those which promote the public convenience or the general prosperity."[110] It would be hard to imagine a broader definition for the regulatory powers of the states, and subsequent Supreme Court decisions confirmed that there was really no meaningful limit. In *Miller v. Schoene*, the court upheld as a mandate that property owners destroy ornamental cedar trees infected with cedar rust in order to protect neighboring apple orchards.[111] Although the court might have based its decision on the theory that the state was simply enforcing existing private rights under nuisance law, it explicitly rejected that approach, preferring to assert that "where the public interest is involved preferment of that interest over the property interest of the individual, to the extent even of its destruction, is one of the distinguishing characteristics of every exercise of the police power which affects property."[112] Four years later, perhaps in anticipation of the coming New Deal, the court invalidated a state requirement that ice dealers demonstrate a necessity for their business before being granted a license,[113] but Justice Brandeis made clear in dissent that such judicial obstacles to expanding regulation were fleeting. Brandeis argued that even the

Munn "affected with a public interest" test was too limiting of state power.

> [S]o far as concerns the power to regulate, there is no difference, in essence, between a business called private and one called a public utility or said to be "affected with a public interest." Whatever the nature of the business, whatever the scope or character of the regulation applied, the source of the power invoked is the same. And likewise is the constitutional limitation upon that power. The source is the police power. The limitation is that set by the due process clause, which, as construed, requires that the regulation shall be not unreasonable, arbitrary, or capricious; and that the means of regulation selected shall have a real or substantial relation to the object sought to be obtained.[114]

In effect, Brandeis's argument was that the substance of the police power encompasses every regulation the state might choose to impose subject only to the requirements of due process. "There must be power in the states and the nation to remold, through experimentation, our economic practices and institutions to meet changing social and economic needs."

The remolding of economic practices and institutions was a central objective of the New Deal, and was certain to have major consequences for property and contract rights. In 1934 the court upheld a Minnesota statute relieving mortgage debtors from foreclosure. Given the dire economic circumstances of the time, the court might have relied entirely on an analogy to the common law doctrine of necessity that justified, for example, the destruction of property in the face of a fire threatening to destroy the city. But it took the occasion of upholding a temporary interference with contract rights to expound a theory of a living constitution that would allow Brandeis's vision of a flexible, regulatory state to be fully realized. "It is no answer to say," wrote Chief Justice Hughes, "that this public need was not apprehended a century ago, or to insist that what the provision of the Constitution meant to the vision of that day it must mean to the vision of our time."[115] In a lengthy and impassioned dissent, Justice Sutherland wrote that one must "close . . . his eyes to the necessary implications of the decision, . . . [not] to see in it the potentiality of future gradual but ever-advancing encroachments upon the sanctity of private and public contracts."[116]

Sutherland's worst fears would be realized over the coming decades, particularly in the context of land use regulation, which had been given the green light in *Euclid v. Ambler Realty*[117] authored, ironically, by Justice Sutherland himself. Perhaps Sutherland had reformed his thinking in the years between 1926 and 1932, or maybe his eyes were closed to the potentialities inherent in his *Euclid* holding. Several decades later Justice Douglas seemed to be similarly conflicted, though his change of view was not so abrupt. In 1954 he described the police power, tellingly in an eminent domain case, in language similar to that in many present-day opinions:

> An attempt to define its reach or trace its outer limits is fruitless, for each case must turn on its own facts. The definition is essentially the product of legislative determinations addressed to the purposes of government, purposes neither abstractly nor historically capable of complete definition. Subject to specific constitutional limitations, when the legislature has spoken, the public interest has been declared in terms well-nigh conclusive.[118]

Nearly two decades later, dissenting to the court's refusal to review an Ohio court decision upholding the regulation of building heights near an airport, Justice Douglas suggested that the "police power comes to an end as a justification for public taking of private property . . . when the public at large is benefitted at the expense of an owner of private property who is refrained from using his land in a way that is not obnoxious to his neighbors."[119] The court's refusal to review the case evidenced, said Douglas quoting from Holmes in the Pennsylvania Coal case, "that '(w)e are in danger of forgetting that a strong public desire to improve the public condition is not enough to warrant achieving the desire by a shorter cut than the constitutional way of paying for the change.' "[120]

CONCLUSION

But the challenge of defining the police power remains. Judicial review for violations of constitutional rights identifies particular constraints on the police power, but it does not serve to define the scope of the police power, unless limitation of the right is the objective of legislative action. Seldom will a government's purpose be to limit individual rights, rather rights will be incidentally, although perhaps necessarily, limited in pursuit of many public purposes. For example, a government regulation prohibiting the filling of wetlands has the purpose of preserving wetlands for the public benefit, but has the incidental and unavoidable effect of limiting the use of affected private properties. Legal challenges to such a regulation will generally not assert that government has no authority to preserve wetlands, rather the objection will be that government cannot limit the use of private property in pursuit of that otherwise legitimate objective without providing compensation to the property owner. Whether preservation of wetlands or any other state objective is within a particular government's powers is likely to be addressed only where the government is, like the federal government, one of enumerated powers.

Chapter 3

Eminent Domain

Eminent domain, the power of government to acquire property from unwilling sellers, is nowhere mentioned in the US Constitution. But the power is presumed to exist. Otherwise, the final clause of the 5th Amendment is meaningless. The guarantee that "private property [shall not] be taken for public use without just compensation" makes sense only if government has the power of eminent domain.[1]

The 5th Amendment guarantee illustrates clearly the integral link between individual liberty and government power. The drafters of the Bill of Rights logically chose to use the language of rights in what is variously called the "Takings," the "Just Compensation," or the "Eminent Domain" Clause of the 5th Amendment. They could have as easily written it in the language of government power—e.g. "government shall have the power to take private property for public use upon payment of just compensation." Government power implies the absence of liberty. Liberty implies the absence of government power.

It is seldom disputed that government in the United States has the power of eminent domain. The questions that arise in relation to the exercise of the power are two: What constitutes public use? And what is just compensation? Before examining the law as it exists in the first decade of the twenty-first century, some reflection on the history of eminent domain will be instructive.

A Brief History of Eminent Domain

Roman Law

It has been often suggested that the concept of eminent domain existed as early as the ninth century BC when King Ahab is reported to have offered compensation to Naboth for his vineyard. But the passage from the Bible that reports King Ahab's offer also reports that Naboth refused and was stoned to death (under the influence of Ahab's evil wife Jezebel) and, because Ahab humbled himself before the Lord, he, but not his sons, suffered no consequence.[2] While some property owners subjected to the modern state's power of eminent domain may feel as much the victim of unjustified coercion as Naboth, there is really little to compare Ahab's approach on his personal behalf to the modern notion of eminent domain. As the counsel for plaintiff property owners in an 1856 Louisiana case observed to the Supreme Court of that state: "We may comfort ourselves that we are better off than our forefathers, in that a way has been devised, whereby governments can take the property of the citizen, without first taking his life; in that at least we show some progress in the science of government . . ."[3]

The Athenian Constitution of Aristotle contained, in Section 31, a requirement that in the settlement of a dispute between the cities of Athens and Eleusis, citizens of Eleusis whose property was desired by Athenians were to be compensated as determined by three valuers appointed on either side.[4] Absent any claim by Athens that the interests of the city were served by Athenian citizens taking property from Eleusian citizens, this example from ancient Greece is also not a case of eminent domain as we would understand it today (although some might say it is no different than what happened to Suzette Kelo in New London, Connecticut). But the Greek example is significant in evidencing that even at a time when territories were routinely conquered by one city state from another, there was a sense that justice required compensation, at least in the context of a political settlement of territorial disputes.

Although the term eminent domain had no parallel in Roman law, and there are reported cases of public works being stymied by refusals to sell or allow public use of private property as well as examples of uncompensated takings for asserted public purposes, we know in the later empire the Romans undertook sometimes massive public works projects (highways and aqueducts most notably) that surely would have required the use of private property. Because Roman law had significant influence on European law beginning after the Middle Ages, at which time the term eminent domain came into use, a brief mention of the Roman law precedents is relevant.

Roman law of property was every bit as complicated as modern property law, but an understanding of only a few basic concepts will be sufficient for purposes of a discussion of the law of eminent domain. Justinian classified private law as the law of persons, the law of things (*res*), and the law of actions. What we call property law was encompassed within the law of things, which was in turn divided between *res in patrimonio* (things belonging to someone, or private property) and *res extra patrimonium*. The latter took various forms including: *res communes*, or things open to everyone, including the air, running water, the sea, and the seashore to the high water mark; *res publicae* encompassing the property of the state such as highways, rivers, and harbors including the use of the banks for navigation and fishing; *res universitatis* including property of corporations like *civitas* (cities) or *collegia* (schools); and *res nullius*, the property of no one. All of these *res extra patrimonium* were in some sense public but, as we will see in the Chapter 4 on the public rights doctrines, at least some could become *res in patrimonio*, or private property, either by private initiative or public action.

Given the existence of private property and the possibility of existing public property becoming private, it must be assumed that the state plans for public projects like highways would sometimes confront private property in the planned route. Was there something in Roman law analogous to the eminent domain power, or did the state simply exert its superior force and take what property it wanted? Perhaps the Roman concept of *dominium*, with its linguistic relationship to the "domain" of eminent domain, will be instructive.

Dominium, in the words of W. W. Buckland, "is the ultimate right, that which has no right behind it."[5] Indeed *dominium* meant property in the sense of control over the thing in question. At the same time Roman law developed the concept *ius*, or right, and because *iura* (rights) were generally the product of agreements or promises made between specific and independent parties,they were fundamentally different from *dominium* that "was simply given by the fact, as it seemed to the Romans, of a man's total control over his physical world—his land, his slaves or his money."[6] As various rights of use were recognized it became possible for one to have *dominium* over a thing, but no right to use or benefit from it. Whether or not this was a puzzling arrangement to Romans, it is certainly so to modern practitioners of property law since that which gives any property right value is the authority to control use, or at a minimum to exclude others. Either because distinguishing it from rights made no sense or for other reasons, *dominium* came also to be viewed as a right on the extreme end of a continuum which included a wide variety of possible property rights.[7] This *dominium perfectum* might thus be similar to the modern concept of fee simple absolute from which other property rights have been carved, or it might be understood as the historic beginning of many different property interests that developed under Roman law.

In this latter historic sense, *dominium* would be helpful to our understanding of the foundations of eminent domain if ownership of all things rested originally with the state. But that was not how it was viewed by the Romans. *Dominium* existed as a reality of social life. It was in the nature of things—an aspect of the law of nature. Those who controlled land or other resources had dominion over them. The illogic of the distinction between *dominium* and *iura* (rights) was that *dominium* remained with the *domini* (owner) while control passed to others as rights of use were conveyed or otherwise created. As a matter of history it is useful to have a beginning point of ownership, *dominium,* from which other rights in property have arisen, but it is not a beginning from which the concept of eminent domain readily arises.

Had the Roman idea been that *dominium* was originally in the state, it would be theoretically straightforward, as we will see, to assert a retained right of reacquisition by the state. The term eminent domain (*dominium eminen*) might be understood to reflect the idea that control of property (*dominium)* was preeminent (*eminen)* or first with the state. That is not, however, the way the Romans saw it. With the Empire, Roman law did come to recognize *dominium* by the Emperor in conquered lands, of which there would be many. Although these lands might have been viewed as the personal *dominium* of the Emperor, rights of use identical in all but name to private *dominium* in Rome proper were granted to individuals in the conquered territories, leaving the Emperor with something very unlike property but very much like sovereign jurisdiction, as we might describe it today. So with respect to conquered lands subsequently granted to private individuals it was plausible to suggest that the Emperor retained, as part of his *dominium,* the power to reacquire lands even from unwilling sellers. There is not, however, any evidence that whatever powers of expropriation the Roman state claimed to have were justified on such a theory, and if there were it would not justify eminent domain powers with respect to non-conquered lands.

Notwithstanding the absence of anything resembling a theory of eminent domain, the Roman state did engage in expropriations of private property. Scholars of Roman law and history have provided us with a few concrete examples of such expropriations,[8] and there is presumably no other way the Romans could have constructed the highways and aqueducts that still mark the European and North African landscapes. While acknowledging "the paucity of surviving precedents for the expropriation of real estate," Nathan Matthews speculates that "this function must have been freely exercised . . . in aid of highways, municipal buildings and other public improvements."[9] But even those scholars who suggest that seventeenth- and eighteenth-century individualists distorted our understanding of Roman law for their own purposes fail to find a Roman theory that justifies expropriation by the state in the context of the elaborate system of Roman property law. J. Walter Jones suggests that the lack of such a theory was the result of "Roman jurists . . . being occupied almost solely with questions of private law, . . . [having] no occasion to enter upon a discussion of such deep and possibly dangerous matters." Had they addressed the question, said Jones, "they might have replied . . . that expropriation was an inevitable outcome of legislative omnicompetence working in the public interest but outside the sphere of private law."[10] Or they might have taken the view of nineteenth-century German scholar Rudolf von Ihering who argued that

> "there is no such thing as absolute ownership, *i.e.* ownership which is unaffected by social considerations." Only through the existence of expropriation as a legal institution "can property become a practical conception in touch with the needs of life . . . without it property reveals itself as the bane of society."[11]

But the fact of the matter, to the best of our knowledge, is that the Romans offered no theoretical justification for expropriations of private property, notwithstanding the considerable attention they paid to their elaborate system of property law. The power of the state to expropriate private property, like private property itself, was simply a reality of life and therefore part of the laws of nature.

Roman lawyers did pay considerable attention to the question of compensation when property was taken or damaged in some way. Because we have only scattered examples of expropriations by the state, most of our knowledge about compensation for property derives from other forms of legal process to recover for lost or damaged property. But it does appear that expropriations were thought to require compensation and that the measure of appropriate compensation for expropriation was not different from the measure in other types of cases.

The general rule under Roman law was that compensation for lost or damaged property should be based on ordinary or general value (*verum pretium*) rather than the value that a particular person might place on the property (*utilitas actoris*). Market value (*quanti venire potest*) would often be the same as ordinary value, but where it differed due to special value attached to individual properties by particular persons (*pretium ex affectu* or sentimental value), compensation was to be based on ordinary value. Thus the measure of value was not the price a particular individual would pay for a particular property, rather it was the price of comparable properties at the time of valuation. All of this will sound familiar to anyone with a knowledge of modern American approaches to assessing just compensation in an eminent domain proceeding. Then as now, the point was not to compensate the deprived owner for what he paid, or for what he might sell it for in the future, or for its sentimental value to particular individuals. The point was to compensate for the value of the property on the day of expropriation to ordinary purchasers in the market for properties like those the government sought to expropriate. No doubt the Romans avoided compensation based on special values for the same reasons we do today (generally relating to the impossibility of objectively assessing subjective values), but that does not alter the fact that such special values exist and go uncompensated whether we call it expropriation or eminent domain.

European Roots

European law dating from the sixteenth and seventeenth centuries has strong ties to Roman law, notwithstanding a thousand intervening years of human history on the continent. Before moral relativism and the studied avoidance of terms thought to be pejorative (even to people of bygone millennia) overtook the academy, the Middle Ages were often called the Dark Ages. Perhaps it is unfair to label the era from the fifth to the eleventh centuries as dark in the sense of being backward and unenlightened, but it is certainly dark in terms of written records. As a result we know little of the law of that long period and we can safely conclude that with virtually nothing in writing, the laws of the period had little influence on the later laws of Europe. Hence the revival of Roman law among the early European legal scholars who did commit their understanding of law to writing.

During the Middle Ages whatever notion of the modern state that may have developed in Roman law was lost to power struggles among competing princes and would-be kings. To the extent there was any theory of state power, it appears that the prince's sovereignty was thought to be unlimited (*Herrschersouveränetät*); at least that was, no doubt, the theory of the prince. Owners of private property might have held to a different theory (*Volkssouveränetät*), but it would be a few centuries before the idea of popular sovereignty would get a foothold in European thinking. And as we know from our own experience, the substitution of popular sovereignty for the unlimited power of the prince or dictator does not necessarily result in stronger protections for private property. Indeed, many have found it easier to justify limitations on property rights when such limits are said to be the will of the people as opposed to the command of the king.

The term eminent domain appears to have been first expressed in print (*dominium eminens*) by the great Dutch jurist Hugo Grotius in the early seventeenth century, but his use of the term does not suggest that it was his invention. Rather he refers to eminent domain without accompanying definition, suggesting that he expected it would be understood by his readers. In *On the Law of War and Peace*, Grotius includes "the right of eminent domain, which the state has over citizens and over the property of citizens for public use" among "the particular interests, with which he who governs concerns himself."[12] Eminent domain, said Grotius, is one of two ways (the other being penalty) "that through the agency of the king even a right gained by subjects can be taken from them.... But in order that this may be done by the power of eminent domain the first requisite is public advantage; then, that compensation from the public funds be made...."[13] The existence of these two limitations (public advantage and compensation) on the power of the state to take private property evidenced that eminent domain, as understood by Grotius, was not simply a reality reflecting the coercive powers of the state. It was rooted in the theory that all "property of subjects belongs to the state under the right of eminent domain."[14]

At the time Grotius was writing, most legal scholars embraced the Roman idea that there were two sources of property rights—natural law or the law of nations and municipal law. The former were the result of occupation or possession (*dominium* of Roman law), the latter the product of government grants. While Grotius accepted this distinction, he rejected the assertion that property owned under the law of nations could be taken "without cause and without compensation," insisting that ownership from either source originated in the law of nature and could not be taken "except as the result of causes which are inherent in ownership by its very nature, or arise from an act of the owner."

As we will see later in this chapter, some modern theories of eminent domain rely on the idea that all private property was originally the property of the state and that whenever and however it was transferred into private hands, the state reserved a right to reacquire title. In those contexts where land was conquered or purchased by the state and subsequently conveyed to private owners, it is plausible that the state might have reserved the right to reacquire the land. But in the ancient and medieval worlds where private ownership existed in the absence of anything resembling the modern state about which Grotius wrote, the idea of reserved rights or eminent domain in the state has no historical basis. Thus, Grotius's description of eminent domain as a sort of property interest held by the state in all property does not conform to a history in which private property was recognized in the absence of anything resembling the modern state. Somehow the state had to acquire that interest and history offers no explanation for how that might have happened. Of course the law has never been above reliance on occasional fictions to make its theories work, but if that is what we are doing in the case of eminent domain we should not claim history as our justification. Property rights, and the proof or lack of proof of their existence, are really all about history. Justifying eminent domain on a false claim that the state had original title from which it reserved the power is no better than individual A claiming a reserved interest in individual B's property where there is no evidence of individual A in the chain of title.

As suggested earlier in the context of the Roman law, the use of the term *dominium* to describe both private property and the Emperor's rights in relation to conquered territories was confusing to the extent it encompassed the Emperor's political control, or sovereignty, over such territories. Because the Emperor (and the monarchs that emerged after the Middle Ages) could possess land as personal property while also maintaining authority over lands even after they were granted to other individuals, there was a need for different terms to describe ownership of property and jurisdiction or sovereignty over that same property. It was for this reason that the late seventeenth-century jurist Samuel Pufendorf urged the use of the term *imperium eminens* as more appropriate. Grotius's fellow Dutchman Cornelis van Bynkershoek, writing in the early eighteenth century, also preferred *imperium eminens* to *dominium eminens*. But Grotius's terminology prevailed, at least in American law.

As we have seen from Roman times and perhaps earlier, not only was it generally agreed that the state or ruler could expropriate private property for public purposes, it was also widely accepted that compensation should be paid to the deprived property owner. While the requirement for compensation was often asserted without theoretical justification, Pufendorf offered an explanation that resonates as clearly today as one imagines it did in the seventeenth century.

> [W]hen public necessity demands it, the goods of any subject . . . may be seized and used for public purposes, although they may be more valuable than the

allotted share which he is supposed to give for the welfare of the republic. On this account, the excess value should ... be refunded to the citizen in question, either from the public funds, or from a contribution of the other citizens.[15]

Here Pufendorf was stating the principle that everyone is required to pay a fair share of the costs of government (generally in the form of taxes), but no one should be expected to pay more than their fair share.

Montesquieu, in *The Spirit of the Laws*, came to the same conclusion while drawing a distinction between the powers of the state with respect to persons and with respect to property. Drawing on the idea of a Golden Age in which all lived in harmony and shared the earth's abundance, Montesquieu argued that individuals acquired liberty by giving up their natural independence and agreeing to live under political laws and by giving up the natural community of goods to live under civil laws. It was therefore illogical in reference to property to say "that the good of the individual should give way to that of the public ... because the public good consists in everyone's having his property ... invariably preserved." Montesquieu was thus led to conclude that "when the public has occasion for the estate of an individual" it must have resort to the civil, and not the political, law. In other words, the state cannot simply take property pursuant to its power as the sovereign. Rather it must deal with the individual as would any other individual to the extent that compensation is required.[16]

The German philosopher Christian Wolff wrote in his eight volume treatise on natural law that "[i]f the public welfare requires that the Ruler of the State should dispose of the property of citizens in a certain manner, the law should give him power so to dispose of it." This power of eminent domain is a part of sovereignty, says Wolff, but is separable and can be reserved or limited by the people. Wolff also insisted, with Pufendorf, that when property is taken for a public purpose "there should be ... a satisfaction by the public, that the damage may be borne pro rata."[17] In other words it would be unfair to command the individual disproportionately to bear the costs of a public benefit. The eighteenth-century Swiss philosopher Emerich de Vattel agreed with Wolff that the power of eminent domain was inherent in sovereignty, but that it could be reserved by the people and that "justice requires that [the property owner] ... be indemnified at the public charge; and if the treasury is not able to bear the expense, all citizens are obliged to contribute to it; for, the burden of the State ought to be supported equally or in a just proportion."[18]

These principles were proclaimed in the French Declaration of Rights of 1789[19] and became manifest in the *Code Napoleon* in 1802, although there is evidence Napoleon paid little heed to the demonstration of public necessity (the language in the 1802 Code) or the requirement of compensation. With the restoration of the Bourbon Crown in France came the Charter of 1814 including the requirement that "[n]o one can be constrained to yield up his property, unless it be for the cause of 'Public Utility' and in consideration of a just and previous indemnity."[20] The theoretical underpinnings of this codification of eminent domain, explained the French jurist Bousquet, rest on "the maxim of every country, and of every epoch," that "[t]o the citizen belongs the ownership and to the sovereign sovereignty." Relying on the Roman philosopher Seneca as his ultimate authority, Bousquet rejected the idea that the power of eminent domain resulted from a reserved property interest of the state. Rather "[i]t consists solely in the power of governing" along with the power "of raising taxes on the same goods."[21] The significance of this insistence that the power of eminent domain arises from sovereignty, and not from the state having once been the owner of everything and having reserved a right to expropriate, is that the burdens associated with public takings of private land, like the burdens of taxation, must be distributed fairly among the citizens. And if the burdens are to be distributed fairly among the citizens, the taking must be for a public, not a private, use. That is, the citizens who are required to pay must benefit in some way from their contribution.

Because American lawyers and statesmen of the eighteenth century were very well familiar with both classical philosophy and with the writings of seventeenth- and eighteenth-century continental scholars, the developments in Europe influenced American thinking on eminent domain, as on many other legal subjects. Indeed it may be that early American law of eminent domain was influenced more by the European than the English experience, notwithstanding that the American states generally embraced the English common law as their own. As we will now see, English law never adopted the language of eminent domain, although it did embrace the concept under a different name.

English Law

Before the American Revolution, the law of England was the law of America. Even after American independence, most American states declared that they would "receive" the laws of England as their own to the extent they were relevant, and consistent with state law. The Northwest Ordinance of 1787 made similar provision for the application of the common law in American territories not yet encompassed within a state. Given this general acceptance of the English common law, including the law of property, one would expect that the early American law of eminent domain would reflect the comparable eighteenth-century laws of England. Although there were similarities, and no doubt lessons learned from the colonial experience, there were also striking differences. Most obvious is the difference that in England the term eminent domain never existed and is still not used today. We should not be surprised that the English common law with its roots in local custom should diverge in both substance and nomenclature from continental law with its roots in Roman law. If there is a puzzle in the terminology, it is that American states adopted the civil law term. As we will see, it is less puzzling that American law diverged from English law on the substance of the doctrine.

Modern English law uses the term "compulsory purchase"[22] to describe the taking of private property by government. Explicit in the name is that compensation will be paid, but this was not always the case nor is it required today in any constitutional sense. Early in the history of England, private property was sometimes taken without compensation and with no more justification than that the Crown had the physical power to do so. But to the extent that individuals considered that they owned property in any meaningful sense, they would have taken offense at any such unjustified and uncompensated taking. And they would have objected as the barons of the realm did at Runnymeade in 1215. Section 28 of the original Magna Carta provided that "[n]o constable or other royal official shall take corn or other movable goods from any man without immediate payment, unless the seller voluntarily offers postponement of this." This was clearly a concession in favor of the property rights of the barons and their tenants, but not one that precluded the king himself from taking land or other fixed property without compensation pursuant to the prerogative powers of the Crown.

Although the concept of prerogative powers in the Crown is deeply imbedded in the laws and Constitution of England, the origin and justification of these powers is something of a mystery to most Americans. Political realists might suggest that there is no mystery in a king's assertion of whatever powers he can get away with, but the prerogative powers of the English Crown were generally accepted, and not just because there was no other choice. Indeed the prerogative powers have been accepted even when they, and the king, might easily have been eliminated. The arguments offered in justification of a royal prerogative will be unpersuasive, for the most part, to those Americans who believe in the idea of popular sovereignty, but there has long been a pragmatic argument for the prerogative power that ties directly to an oft-repeated justification of the eminent domain power—government could not meet its responsibilities without it. Indeed, one explanation for the compulsory purchase power in England is that it derives from the royal prerogative, a view rejected by William Stoebuck in a good (and rare) effort to construct a theory of eminent domain.[23]

While most commentators on English law, both modern and historical, accept the existence of the royal prerogative with little explanation beyond its always having existed, William Blackstone did discuss the subject at some length in his *Commentaries on the Laws of England.* The term prerogative, says Blackstone, derives from the Latin *prae* and *rogo*, thus signifying "something that is required or demanded before, or in preference to, all others."[24] This is consistent with the earlier understanding expressed as "the king is prerogative," meaning the king had rights different from the rights of others only in degree, not in kind.[25] Blackstone identified two categories of prerogative power in the king: direct and incidental. Direct royal prerogatives regard "the king's royal *character*; . . . his royal *authority*; and . . . his royal *income.*" With respect to royal character Blackstone said that if the "mass of mankind" considered "their prince as a man of no greater perfection than themselves," they "will be apt to grow insolent and refractory." The royal prerogative countered this tendency by leading the people "to consider him [the king] in the light of a superior being, and to pay him that awful respect, which may enable him with greater ease to carry on the business of government." The concrete evidence of the king's superiority was, of course, the many powers encompassed within the royal prerogative. Specific prerogative powers were identified and discussed by Blackstone, but what he described was not an exhaustive list. In addition to the direct prerogatives there are incidental powers that are, one might say, necessary and proper to the exercise of the direct powers. Anyone familiar with American constitutional law will know that such incidental powers can make for a long list.[26]

Among the incidental prerogative powers was that "of entering upon private property for the purpose of erecting defenses against either the attacks of the public enemy or the inroad of the sea," and "erecting beacons or lighthouses . . . upon private property without compensation."[27] The king also had authority to take goods and produce for his own use, a prerogative limited, as we have seen, by the

Magna Carta requirement of compensation. Other prerogatives entitled the Crown to take private properties where wrongs against the Crown were committed, but at least by the time of Henry VIII something called an "inquest of office" could be instituted by the property owner, thus preventing the King from "enter[ing] upon and seiz[ing] any man's possession upon bare surmises, and without the intervention of a jury."[28] This "inquest of office" appears to be the earliest version of the modern English procedure for compulsory purchase, but for our purposes the English process for public takings of private property is of far less interest than the rationale.

To the extent that English governments or officials were operating under the authority of the Crown, they might claim to be taking property pursuant to the royal prerogative. But most government action at least since the seventeenth century has been authorized by Parliament or by governments whose legislative authority derives from Parliament. What was the English justification for a legislative power to expropriate private property? So long as the Crown survives, it could not be claimed that Parliament has somehow succeeded to the Crown's prerogatives. To the extent the Magna Carta and other declarations of rights imposed limits on the prerogative power to take private property, their purpose was to protect the rights of property owners, not to expand the powers of Parliament. But with the emergence of Parliamentary sovereignty came a justification of expropriation very similar to that offered in defense of the prerogative power—government could not function without something like the power of eminent domain. The seventeenth-century English, like many modern nineteenth- and twentieth-century American courts, embraced the view expressed by the Dutch jurist van Bynkershoek, that "all would readily acknowledge that if it [eminent domain] were destroyed, no state could survive . . . That the sovereign has this authority no man of sense questions."

It seems that few Englishmen of sense have questioned that the power exists. As Stoebuck wrote in 1972, "[t]he English to this day have not raised the subject of eminent domain to the imperative level at which it now exists in America."[29] It has been widely used in England for centuries and, although compensation is generally provided for, it is not required. Anything resembling a constitutional requirement of compensation would violate the fundamental concept of Parliamentary sovereignty. Politics, and presumably a sense of fairness or justice, lead to compulsory purchase rather than outright expropriation, but at the end of the day a truly sovereign Parliament is free to do as it chooses.

While acknowledging Parliamentary supremacy, Blackstone made it clear that private property was not to be lightly taken even for widely accepted public purposes. Magna Carta provided in Section 29 that "[n]o Freeman shall . . . be disseised of his Freehold, . . . but by lawful Judgment of his Peers, or by the Law of the Land." The law of the land, wrote Blackstone, placed a high value on private property. "So great moreover is the regard of the law for private property, that it will not authorize the least violation of it; no, not even for the general good of the whole community." This did not mean that property could not be taken for public purposes, but it did mean that it could not be done "by absolutely stripping the subject of his property in an arbitrary manner; but by giving him a full indemnification and equivalent for the injury thereby sustained."[30]

Notwithstanding the differences in both the theory and substance of English law relating to eminent domain as compared to European and American law, Blackstone confirmed that compensation was expected and it does appear that compensation is almost always paid, and for the same reasons compensation is generally thought to be the right thing to do. Writing in the seventeenth century on the subject of public sewers, the construction of which provided many opportunities for compulsory purchase, Robert Callis notes that while private property will be "prejudiced," "things that concern the commonwealth are of greater account in the law than the interest of private persons." But Callis does insist that "where any man's particular interest and inheritance is prejudiced for the commonwealth's cause, that that part of the country be ordered to recompense the same which have good thereby." In the same paragraph, Callis also spoke to the other limitation on eminent domain as it exists under the US Constitution, in writing if not in practice. "[U]nder the pretense of the commonweal," said Callis, "a private man's welfare [should] be not intended to the charge, trouble and burthen of the country." In other words, the power of the state to forcibly acquire private property is not to be employed for private benefit.

AMERICAN LAW OF EMINENT DOMAIN

Colonial American Law

There are important reasons why English precedent was not and is not very helpful to understanding the eminent domain law of the United States. To the extent the English doctrine can be said to derive from the royal prerogative, it is surely difficult for a nation that declared its independence on the basis of the king's "repeated Injuries and Usurpations" to then claim the royal powers for itself. Such a nation, claiming that the "just Powers [of government] derive from the Consent of the Governed," would better look to the powers of Parliament for a guide to its own authority. But the English Parliament, not the people of England, was said to be sovereign, so relying on the powers of Parliament also poses problems for American law. Thus it is not surprising that early American lawyers looked to natural law for guidance on the subject of eminent domain, as on many other matters of law. But before they got philosophical on the subject, the early American colonists were more concerned about getting by in a new and primitive land.

Because the land was largely unsettled, the earliest colonists had immediate needs for roadways to link their isolated homes and settlements. In laying out and building these roads, they could easily avoid developed private property and undeveloped private lands often had so little value as to not warrant private objections. Nevertheless, as early as 1639 in Plymouth Colony and 1656 in New Amsterdam, provision was made for compensating owners of developed private properties injured by road construction.[31] In 1691 authority was granted to lay out and construct streets in the City of New York, provided that damages were to be paid to owners of developed property who did not voluntarily cede their land. Two years later Massachusetts granted general authority for the construction of roads, again "provided, that if any person be thereby damaged in his property or improved grounds, the town shall make him reasonable satisfaction, . . ." The proprietors of Pennsylvania originally planned to lay out roadways before granting private lands but, upon realizing they had no idea where the roads should be, they, along with the proprietors of New Jersey, sought to avoid the need to compensate as roadways were developed by reserving 6 percent of all private grants for future road construction. However, both colonies did provide compensation where improved lands were affected by new roadways. Thus, it is clear that with respect to roads, something resembling eminent domain, including a requirement of compensation, existed from the beginning of the American colonies.

Over the first two centuries of American settlement there were few other government functions that required the acquisition of private property. However, there were private initiatives, thought to have important public benefits, that could and did impact on private property. Because public roadways were limited in number and did not reach every person's land, isolated property owners required authority to construct private roads across the property of others. Virtually everyone also required the services of a mill to grind their grains—in modern terminology, the mills may have been looked upon as privately operated public utilities. Mill operators could be expected to own the land on which their mill was located, but often their mill dam would intrude on the property of the landowner on the opposite side of the stream and the resultant millpond would flood neighboring properties.

No doubt most conflicts over the construction of both private roads and mills were settled between the affected parties, presumably with the purchase of something resembling an easement if not by outright transfer of the property. But most colonies made provision for private use of eminent domain where a private agreement could not be reached. The Plymouth Colony enacted the first such statute for the location of private roads in 1671.[32] At least seven colonies had mill acts,[33] the earliest being a 1667 Virginia law.[34] The Virginia statute stated that because the provision of mills "would conduce much to the convenience of this country" and because the construction of such mills was sometimes "obstructed by the perversenesse of some persons not permitting others, though not willing themselves to promote so publique a good," those willing to construct a mill could petition the county court to value the needed land and "put the same into the possession of the party building the said mill or mills, he paying the consideration the land is valued at." The act also allowed for the compensated taking of up to two acres for churches or courthouses, with the proviso that if such structures were deserted the land would revert to the original owner upon repayment of the compensation received.

Not until the time of the Revolution was the private use of eminent domain challenged as an inappropriate delegation of a government power. Proponents of an expansive interpretation of the public use language of the 5th Amendment (language also in most state constitutions) might be tempted to interpret this history of acceptance of private takings as evidence supporting their position. But such an argument is not as persuasive as it might seem. Aside from the private roadway and mill statutes, which generally were prefaced with an assertion of the public importance of such private takings (generally focused on commerce), eminent domain legislation was largely limited to the specific requirements of public road location and construction. Thus there was no general legislation authorizing the government's use of eminent domain. Because public roads are self-evidently for public use, there was no need to provide in the statutes that such takings must be for a public use. As a result there was little concern about possible abuses of the eminent domain power during the colonial period. But it is safe to conclude that there was an implicit understanding that the power could not be employed for purely private purposes. This conclusion derives from the fact that colonial legislatures felt compelled to articulate the public benefits of the private takings they authorized, and more importantly from the theory of eminent domain that developed through the colonial period as reflected in developments after the Revolution.

While colonial legislatures were focused on the practical challenges of building communities and they were constrained by the existing laws of mother England, opportunities to think in more theoretical terms would gradually arise. As indicated in the several references above to English, European, and Roman law, they also had the benefit of earlier thinking on the subject. But the new state constitutions adopted between 1776 and 1780, although most contained declarations of rights, had little to say on the subject of eminent domain. Only the constitutions of Vermont and Massachusetts required compensation when private property was taken for a public use.[35] Pennsylvania's constitution recognized the power of eminent domain but made no provision for compensation. Although the 5th Amendment to the US Constitution, requiring just compensation, took effect in 1791 and most of the states later admitted to the union required compensation in their first constitutions, five of the original states were still without such a provision when the 14th Amendment was enacted in 1868. But this did not mean that compensation was not generally required in all of the original states, except perhaps North Carolina. In practice, as we have seen under the earlier colonial governments, compensation was thought to be unnecessary only in the case of undeveloped and unimproved lands, but that exception reflected the reality that undeveloped lands were worth very little.

The best explanation for this lack of constitutional limits on the taking of private property in the original state constitutions is the same as the explanation for the absence of a bill of rights in the US Constitution of 1787—the framers of these various constitutions were firm believers in the concept of natural rights. Based upon their reading of Grotius, Locke, Pufendorf, Montesquieu, Coke, Blackstone, and other writers; and reflecting their understanding that as Englishmen they had many liberties notwithstanding the absence of a written constitution; and in reliance on their view that sovereignty rests with the people who delegate only those powers they choose to their government; Americans of the framing period saw no need to enact a constitutional list of rights they possessed in any event by virtue of being human beings. And there can be no doubt that among their natural rights was the right to acquire and possess private property and to hold that property against all who might take it including the government. That this was the almost universal understanding is best demonstrated by the fact that throughout the colonial period government takings were justified in relation to public purposes and were compensated whenever there was significant value in the property taken.

This reliance on natural rights rather than on constitutional guarantees was evidenced repeatedly in judicial decisions during the early years of independence. A South Carolina court held in 1792 that "it was against common right, as well as against *magna charta*, to take away the freehold of one man and vest it in another, and . . . without any compensation."[36] A Pennsylvania court held, in 1795, "the right of acquiring, possessing and protecting property is natural, inherent, and inalienable. It is a right not *ex gratia* from the legislature, but *ex debito* from the constitution."[37] But it was not necessary to rely on the opinions of just any judge on just any court. After 1816 Americans could look to the decision of the young nation's most prominent jurist, Chancellor James Kent of New York's high court. In the case of *Gardner v. Village of Newburgh* Chancellor Kent was faced with a statute providing for the taking of spring water from private land and the transporting of that water in pipes across the private land of others. The statute made provision to compensate these landowners, but did not allow for the compensation of downstream riparians affected by diminished stream flows. The absence of a bill of rights or any other guarantee of property rights in the New York constitution posed no obstacle to a ruling in favor of the injured water rights claimants. "In taking private property for public uses; the limitation [that compensation must be paid] is admitted by the soundest authorities, and is adopted by all temperate and civilized governments, from a deep and universal sense of its justice."[38] Six years later in a decision invalidating another uncompensated taking of property, New York Chief Justice Spencer stated:

> I do not rely on . . . [the 5th Amendment of the U.S. Constitution or the recently enacted similar provision of the New York constitution], as having a binding constitutional force upon the act under consideration . . . . But they are both declaratory of a great and fundamental principle of government; and any law violating that principle must be deemed a nullity, as it is against natural right and justice.[39]

In his *Gardner* opinion Chancellor Kent was deferential to the legislature, suggesting that it was surely an oversight that the water rights owners were not compensated. But in his more widely read *Commentaries on American Law*, Kent was explicit about the authority and responsibility of the courts to declare void legislative acts in violation of the natural rights of citizens. "We cannot but admire the intrepidity and powerful sense which led Lord Coke,... to declare... in *Doctor Bonham's Case* [7 Coke 118 (1610)] that the common law doth control acts of parliament, and adjudges them void when against the common right and reason."[40] Elsewhere in his *Commentaries* Kent stated, with respect to the power of eminent domain, that "a provision for compensation is a necessary attendant on the due and constitutional exercise of the power of the law-giver to deprive an individual of his property without his consent." The obligation to compensate clearly derived from natural law, but what was the source of the state's power to take property without the owner's consent? Did Kent mean to say that it derived from the constitution of the state? Or did he mean to say that it was inherent in the constitution of every state and nation?

Clearly he meant the latter, and therein lies an important, but little-noticed, link between the power of the state and the rights of property owners, at least as those matters were understood in the colonial and early national periods of American legal history. When the power of the state to take private property for public uses was not just assumed, it was almost always justified as inherent in sovereignty. Throughout the history recounted in this chapter, going back to ancient times, it was accepted that the power of the ruler or the state to take private property is a necessary attribute of sovereignty. We might conclude that this longstanding and unwavering principle was a simple reflection of the realities of physical power on the side of the state. But the inevitable private objections to such takings demanded justification of the power, and that justification was that the power was inherent in sovereignty.

The South Carolina case of *Lindsay v. Commissioners* upheld legislation providing for the taking of private property for construction of a road. Judges Grimke and Bay "considered the act in question as authorized by the fundamental principles of society..., one of the original rights of sovereignty, retained by the supreme power of every community at its formation."[41] In affirming the power of the state to take land for a canal, New York Chief Justice Spencer stated, "it does not admit of doubt, that the... [public officials] have a right to enter upon and occupy lands necessary to effectuate the objects of their appointment."[42]

Later in the nineteenth century the US Supreme Court reiterated the inherent nature of the eminent domain power. In the earliest case to confirm the eminent domain power in the federal government, Justice Strong wrote: "The right is the offspring of political necessity; and it is inseparable from sovereignty, unless denied to it by its fundamental law."[43] Three years later the court underscored that "[t]he right of eminent domain, that is, the right to take private property for public uses, appertains to every independent government. It requires no constitutional recognition; it is an attribute of sovereignty"[44] Chancellor Kent provided solid support for courts looking to justify the power of eminent domain as inherent in sovereignty. "The right of eminent domain, or inherent sovereign power, it is admitted by all publicists, gives to the legislature the control of private property for public uses, and for public uses only." As indicated previously, Kent goes on to emphasize that the power to take and the requirement of compensation are based on "an acknowledged principle of universal law."[45]

In other words, the power of eminent domain is in the nature of things. Like the private right to acquire and possess property, the public power to take it away is part of natural law. To make this work, it was necessary that the natural law also define how the private right can survive in the face of the public power. John Locke addressed this very problem in his *Second Treatise on Government.*

> For I have truly no *Property* in that, which another can by right take from me, when he pleases, against my consent. Hence it is a mistake to think, that the Supreme or *Legislative Power* of any Commonwealth, can do what it will, and dispose of the Estates of the Subject *arbitrarily*, or take any part to them at pleasure.[46]

The same point was made by a concurring judge in the South Carolina case of *Lindsay v. Commissioners* mentioned above:

> If the lex *terrae* [(law of the land)] . . . [supports] any law which the legislature might pass, then the legislature would be authorized by the constitution, to destroy the right, which the constitution had expressly declared, should for ever be inviolably preserved. This is too absurd a construction to the true one.[47]

This, of course, is the central challenge of eminent domain law to the present day. If we accept that government has, or even must have, the power to take property without the consent of the owner, yet we believe that private property warrants the protection of the state, we must determine the limit of state power, which will in turn define the limit of the private right. If the power of the state is without limits, there are no property rights. If property rights are absolute, the state can have no power of eminent domain. In the remainder of this chapter we will examine how that line has been drawn over the course of the nation's history. One thing we will see is that the power of eminent domain will continue to be justified in something resembling natural law terms—it's just the way it is, while natural rights arguments on behalf of property rights will fall into disfavor. If there is a weakness in the judicial analyses recounted below, it lies more with the adherence to natural law in defense of state power than in its abandonment in the justification of secure property rights.

American Law to the New Deal

From the colonial period through the middle of the nineteenth century, the law of eminent domain was reasonably settled and its underlying theories were generally accepted. The power was inherent in the sovereignty of the states, not as an inheritance from the English Crown but as an inherent power held by every sovereign government. With the exception of takings of unimproved lands with little or no value, it was generally agreed that compensation is due to those whose property is taken. It was also generally understood that government must have a public use for property taken. That is, it was accepted that government could not take the property of A and give or sell it to B for B's private use. Supreme Court Justice Patterson confirmed this understanding in 1795 while sitting as circuit judge in a Pennsylvania case. After stating that the "despotic power . . . of taking private property, when state necessity requires, exists in every government," Justice Patterson held void a Pennsylvania law granting title to land to which others had prior valid title. "It is . . . difficult to form a case, in which the necessity of the state can be of such a nature, as to authorize or excuse the seizing of landed property belonging to one citizen and giving it to another citizen."[48] But the issue of what constitutes a public use was seldom before the courts. Because the purposes for which property was taken were few, with rights of way for roads being the dominant need, there was little controversy over what constituted a public use.

As we have seen, eminent domain was widely used to acquire land for private roadways and mills. The theory was that both were important to the community. In the case of roads they were thought to facilitate commerce between the private owner and the rest of the community on the one hand, and the private owner's participation in community affairs on the other. In the case of mills, they provided a needed service to everyone in the community and could only be located where water power could be effectively harnessed. It is true that mills powering other forms of private enterprise benefitted from eminent domain, but even absent public access to the services of the mill, the scarcity of mill locations distinguished such mills from other forms of purely private business. Although there was little litigation on the question of public use, it is reasonable to assume that colonial and founding-era American jurists had an idea of what was required. We know they had the benefit of Blackstone who used the term "public good" and Grotius who used the term "public utility". The founding generation was familiar with the French Declaration of Rights, which used the term "public necessity" and, of course with their own 5th Amendment that used the term "public use." Were the authors of these various terms using different words to convey the same meaning, or did the varying terminology evidence differences of opinion about the limitations of the power of eminent domain?

By the middle of the nineteenth century, differences of opinion about the issue surfaced in American courts. At the same time, state legislatures started to weigh in on what purposes justified use of eminent domain. The construction of railroads raised the issue in a new context, although one similar to the public roads and highways for which eminent domain had long been employed. The difference was that railroads were generally constructed and operated by private corporations organized under state law. Generally, the articles of incorporation for a new railroad company granted eminent domain power for acquisition of right of way and other needed land. One such grant to the Tuscumbia, Courtland, and Decatur Rail Road Company was challenged before the Alabama Supreme Court in 1832 on the ground that it was not a public use. (The term "public use" was by then the norm among American courts because of its appearance in the 5th Amendment and, in this case, in the Alabama constitution.) Relying on Justice Patterson's opinion in *Vanhorne's Lessee v. Dorrance* and Chief Justice Spencer's decision in *Bradshaw v. Rogders*, the Alabama court took an expansive view of what constitutes a public use. In upholding the railroad's use of eminent domain, Chief Justice Lipscomb asked rhetorically:

> And is Alabama, alone, to be arrested from indulging the public spirit of her citizens, and marching hand in hand with her sister states, in the great work of internal improvement, by a conscientious jealousy of federal interference,

on the one hand, and an inability to give efficiency to the efforts of public spirited individuals in the cause, on the other?[49]

In the same year the Supreme Court of Massachusetts upheld the delegation of eminent domain power to a private corporation established to provide water power to various mills, stating that "[t]he ground of... [such legislation] is, that the legislature will not permit an individual, from caprice or obstinacy, to withstand the development of great natural advantages."[50] Also in the same year the New Jersey Court of Chancery was asked to invalidate a grant of eminent domain power to a water power company on the ground that "the public... [did not] have the privilege of participating in it directly and immediately."[51] While acknowledging that "[t]here must be a public use or benefit," the court refused to invalidate the private corporation's use of eminent domain, stating that "what... [the public benefit] shall consist of, or how extensive it shall be to authorize an appropriation of private property, is not easily reducible to general rule."[52] In this the New Jersey court anticipated cases to be decided more than a century later in the US Supreme Court.

The rapid development of canals, water power, and railroads made these and other courts cautious about placing limits on the private use of eminent domain. But it would not be long before many state courts began to take a narrower view of the meaning of public use, at least in the rhetoric of their opinions. An early and influential opinion on the meaning of public use was that of Senator Tracy in *Bloodgood v. Mohawk* in the Court for the Correction of Errors of New York. Tracy observed:

> Even Hobbes, the most ingenious of all advocates for the absolute powers of government, does not go further... than to say, that the property which a subject has in his goods, consists not in a right to exclude the sovereign from the use of them, but consists in a right to exclude all other subjects from the use of them."[53]

To Tracy, the power of eminent domain in a private corporation looked a lot like allowing one private party to take the property of another private party.

> When we depart from the natural import of the term "public use," and substitute for the simple idea of a public possession and occupation, that of public utility, public interest, common benefit, general advantage or convenience, or that still more indefinite term public improvement, is there any limitation which can be set to the exertion of legislative will in the appropriation of private property.... On what principle shall a law, transferring the title

from the owner to his more enterprising neighbor, on the payment of a just compensation, be pronounced unconstitutional, if using property beneficially to the public is to be deemed a public use of it?[54]

At the time, Tracy was disagreeing with the earlier opinion in *Beekman v. Saratoga* in which Chancellor Walworth stated:

If the public interest can be in any way promoted by the taking of private property, it must rest in the wisdom of the legislature to determine whether the benefit to the public will be of sufficient importance to render it expedient to exercise the right of eminent domain, and to authorize an interference with the private rights of individuals.[55]

Thus, between the Chancellor and Senator Tracy was stated the issue that has been revisited ever since, right up to and through the Supreme Court's 2004 decision in *Kelo v. New London*. While it was a loser in *Kelo*, Tracy's position gained some steam over the next few decades.

In the course of an 1861 opinion upholding an eminent domain taking on behalf of the federal government for a fort, the California Supreme Court discussed at length the public use requirement. While noting that "[i]t may be a use in which but a small portion of the public will be directly benefitted, as a street in a town, a bridge or a railroad," the court stated that "it must be of such a character as that the general public may, if they choose, avail themselves of it."[56] In 1868 the Iowa Supreme Court held invalid legislation authorizing acquisition by eminent domain of the property of a single landowner for a road that would provide access to a private coalmine. The case was significant in running counter to earlier cases upholding eminent domain for both private roads and for development of natural resources. The fact that the public had no right to use the road and was "not bound to work or keep such roads in repair" made it a private road, and therefore one that could not benefit from eminent domain.[57] In 1881 the Pennsylvania Supreme Court faced the interesting question of whether the taking of land, owned by a corporation and used as a public market, for the construction of a railroad depot by another corporation pursuant to a general grant of eminent domain power was invalid because the land in question was already in a "public use." In upholding the railroad corporation's use of eminent domain, the court concluded that the market was not a public use as that term was used in the Pennsylvania constitution. "To constitute a public use, the property must be under the control of the public, or of public agencies, or the public must have a right to the use."[58]

In these and many other cases, state courts sought to give meaning to the public use language without drawing a line that would make it impossible for the state to rely on private parties to provide the investment and management necessary to the provision of public infrastructure and services. Where the government would own taken property as in the case of a fort, school, or courthouse, all agreed it was a public use. But rather than insisting that the government must own and manage whatever property was taken by eminent domain, the courts sought to draw a line based on the public having a right to use or directly benefit from the services provided. It was not an easy line to draw, but courts in every state took a shot at giving meaning to what was generally viewed as the public use limitation on the otherwise unlimited sovereign power of eminent domain. Although there was no unanimity of view on where the line should be drawn, the majority view was best represented by the position of the Massachusetts Supreme Court rooted in the 1873 case of *Lowell v. Boston*, not, strictly speaking, an eminent domain case.[59] In *Lowell* the court held unconstitutional the expenditure of public funds for reconstruction of private residences and businesses after the great fire of 1872 on the ground that it was not a public use. The court considered that the expenditure of tax revenues or the commitment of public credit was limited to public uses in the same way as the exercise of the eminent domain power. Through numerous subsequent eminent domain cases, the Massachusetts court arrived at a rule summarized by Philip Nichols in the following terms: "To take property rights from *A* for transfer to *B* for *B*'s private enjoyment is not a public use, regardless of what ultimate public purpose the transaction is intended to further."[60] In other words, public use was understood by the Massachusetts court to mean available for use by the public, not merely promotive of the public interest or general welfare.

Though often described as a narrow view of the meaning of public use, it was not the narrowest view. Some courts had held that public use required public ownership, but that understanding would invalidate the well-established practice of using eminent domain for private roads and mills. So long as these private properties acquired by eminent domain were in some sense open to public use, they would satisfy the Massachusetts rule. In his widely used and respected treatise on eminent domain, John Lewis endorsed the Massachusetts rule as the better rule for these reasons:

> First, that it accords with the primary and more commonly understood meaning of the words; second, it accords with the general practice in regard to

> taking private property for public use in vogue when the phrase was first brought into use in the earlier constitutions; third, it is the only view which gives the words any force as a limitation or renders them capable of any definite and practical application.[61]

These efforts to limit the eminent domain power by giving definition to the public use term were aided by the "excess condemnation" cases in the first decades of the twentieth century. By taking more property than was physically necessary for the project in question, states were able to control subsequent development in the neighborhood and secure financing for the project. Once the state or its private agent had control of the property, it could sell what was not needed to whomever it chose, and often at a good profit since the value of the property usually would increase as a result of the project.

For example, in 1912 the Massachusetts legislature declared Salisbury Beach a public reservation and authorized the creation of the Salisbury Beach Reservation Commission with authority to acquire by eminent domain any or all of the lands on the beach, including those already developed with cottages and commercial enterprises. One section of the law provided that, subsequent to condemnation, the Commission could sell or lease any portion of the condemned lands not needed for the purposes of the reservation. The Massachusetts Supreme Court held that while "[t]he acquirement of beaches by eminent domain and at the public expense for bathing and other purposes of general utility has never been questioned in this commonwealth, "the seizure ostensibly for a public use and then diverted to a private use" was a clear violation of the public use requirement. To underscore its point the Court noted that under the challenged law "[i]t would be possible for the commissioners . . . to take this entire summer colony with its numerous houses and other buildings and substitute themselves for the petitioner as landlord, and lease all the cottages and buildings indefinitely, or ultimately to sell them."[62]

Other state courts took a similarly dim view of condemnations in excess of that necessary for a legitimate public use. The Pennsylvania court invalidated the taking of land around a public square where the plan was to resell or lease the lands with an eye to controlling the nature of the private uses.[63] In New Jersey it was held that a taking of fee simple title for highway purposes, where an easement would do, is not a public use.[64] In Indiana a condemnation to create a Chatauqua grounds was ruled a private use. In invalidating the condemnation, the Indiana court summarized three lines of decision found among the various state courts: "First: Cases which hold that 'public use' means 'use by the public' . . . Second: Cases which hold that 'public use' means public benefit, advantage, or utility . . . [and] Third: Cases which hold that the true definition lies somewhere between these two contending doctrines."[65] In settling on the first as the better approach, and thus agreeing with the rule in Massachusetts, the Indiana court said:

> However the courts may decide on this matter throughout the Union, it seems to be well settled in Indiana that it is essential to constitute a public use that the general public have the right to a definite and fixed use of the property appropriated, not as a mere matter of favor or by permission of the owner, but as a matter of right; and if the special benefit to be derived from the lands sought to be appropriated is wholly for private persons, the use is a private one, and is not made a public use by the fact that the public has a theoretical right to use it, or that the public will receive an incidental or prospective benefit therefrom.[66]

The Indiana and Massachusetts rules represented the majority view, but the minority view was well represented in state court decisions. The drawing of lines suggested by the Indiana court was more easily done in theory than in practice. Although a focus on the nature of a property's intended use after condemnation appropriately emphasized the actual constitutional language in question, a combination of real-world politics and real-life complexities made it difficult to fit particular cases into general categories. Thus, notwithstanding nineteenth- and early twentieth-century efforts to define a meaningful public use boundary for the power of eminent domain, the result was "a massive body of case law, irreconcilable in its inconsistency, confusing in its detail and defiant of all attempts at classification."[67]

The New Deal, Urban Renewal, and Activist Governments

Not surprisingly, this effort to give definition to the public use requirement gradually gave way to New Deal enthusiasm for activist and interventionist government. Even before the New Deal, the US Supreme Court upheld a federal taking of property subsequently transferred to private corporations for use in what were considered essential defense industries, although not public utilities.[68] The decision might have been thought of as an exception, given the extreme public necessities in a time of war, but the Court was able to rely on earlier decisions that questioned the line state courts had sought to draw between public use and public purpose. Although writing (in 1916) in the context of a condemnation by a private electric power company, and thus within the context of a generally accepted exception for public utilities, Justice Holmes offered this:

> In the organic relations of modern society it may sometimes be hard to draw the line that is supposed to limit the authority of the legislature to exercise or delegate the power of eminent domain. But to gather the streams from waste and to draw from them energy, labor without brains, and so to save mankind from toil that it can be spared, is to supply what, next to intellect, is the very foundation of all our achievements and all our welfare. If that purpose is not public, we should be at a loss to say what is. The inadequacy of use by the general public as a universal test is established.[69]

Few would have found the words that Holmes used, but his argument flows naturally from the generally accepted idea that the eminent domain power is inherent in all governments. That is, if the eminent domain power is necessary to government, then it must surely be available in aid of government's promotion of the general welfare. By this view, the eminent domain power, like the powers to regulate, tax, and spend, is a means to be used in pursuit of government's legitimate ends. Because the states retain all sovereign powers except those delegated to the US government or limited by the state or US constitutions, the eminent domain power is thus subject only to those same limits. It is coextensive with the police power. Of course this is precisely the concern Senator Tracy expressed eight decades earlier in *Bloodgood v. Mohawk*. If the eminent domain power is coextensive with the police power, then the public use language in the United States and state constitutions is surplusage—it adds nothing to the requirement that the state compensate when it takes private property. Where Holmes was at a loss to explain what purpose is public if private harnessing of the energy of a river is not, still some found themselves at a loss to explain what purposes are not public if private enterprise providing goods and services to others warrants use of the eminent domain power.

In the case of the US government's use of eminent domain, the parallel to the regulatory, taxing, and spending powers was more than apt in the wake of the New Deal. Having had some of its New Deal legislation invalidated as not within its power to regulate interstate commerce,[70] Congress turned to the general welfare or Spending Clause as constitutional authorization for regulation of the economy. The so-called Spending Clause of Article I, Section 8, provides that "Congress shall have Power . . . to pay the debts and provide for the common Defense and general Welfare of the United States." The question of what constitutes general welfare is very much like the question of what constitutes a public use in the context of eminent domain. Although the Supreme Court had held in *United States v. Butler*[71] that Congress's power to tax and spend was not unlimited and that the Agricultural Adjustment Act of 1933 was unconstitutional as it was an attempt to do that through the Spending Clause what Congress could not do pursuant to the Commerce Clause, a year later it abandoned any effort to define the limits of the spending power in upholding federally mandated unemployment compensation in *Charles C. Steward Machine Co. v. Davis*[72] and old age benefits in *Helvering v. Davis.*[73]

The Supreme Court's view with respect to the authority of state governments was the same. Indeed, even before the apparent transformation of the Court's position on the scope of Congress's constitutional authority to determine public purposes, the Court had exercised significant deference to state legislative definition of public purposes. Among the most radical government interventions in traditionally private economic affairs in American history was the Progressive program enacted in the state of North Dakota in 1919. It provided for, among other things, an Industrial Commission to operate various utilities and businesses, a state bank and agricultural marketing entities to be operated by the Industrial Commission, a Home Building Association also under the authority of the Industrial Commission, and expansive bonding and eminent domain authority to facilitate the transition to and creation of these expansive state enterprises. The entire program had withstood challenge in the North Dakota Supreme Court,[74] before coming to the US Supreme Court. To the extent the various programs resulted in the taking of private property and the expenditure of taxpayer revenues, it was challenged as a violation of the 14th Amendment Due Process Clause, which by that time had been found to incorporate the 5th Amendment Takings Clause as a limitation on state governments. In *Green v. Frazier* a unanimous Supreme Court upheld the North Dakota program.[75] Noting that "many . . . states and municipalities have in late years seen fit to enter upon projects to promote the public welfare which in the past have been considered entirely within the domain of private enterprise,"[76] Justice Day stated that "[c]ourts, as a rule, have attempted no judicial definition of a public as distinguished from a private purpose, but have left each case to be determined by its own peculiar circumstances."[77] In the case of state legislation, it was not for the Supreme Court of the United States to second guess the conclusions of the people, legislature, and courts of North Dakota. While Justice Day's deference may have been rooted in federalism more than in a conclusion that the term public use is beyond judicial definition, the case certainly anticipated the New Deal abandonment of any effort to limit either the spending or eminent domain powers via a distinction between public and private activities.

This New Deal era abandonment of a constraining concept of public use occurred in the context of many social welfare programs, significantly among them the various state and federal urban renewal and slum clearance programs. The earliest such program enacted by Congress did not get a friendly judicial reception. In *United States v. Certain Lands in City of Louisville*[78] Federal District Judge Dawson held that the low-cost housing and slum-clearance provision of the National Industrial Recovery Act was invalid to the extent it relied upon the federal eminent domain power. Dawson held that "public use means a use by the government for legitimate governmental purposes, or a use open to all the public, even though practically available to only a part of the public, whether the property condemned is held by the government or by some private agency."[79] To accept the broader notion that public use means any public purpose within the authority of government to pursue would, said Dawson, make "the property of every citizen in this country . . . subject to the whims and theories of any temporary majority represented in the legislative branch of the government."[80] Dawson acknowledged that there was an ongoing emergency in the country, but, citing the Civil War habeas corpus case of *ex parte Milligan*,[81] insisted that emergencies do not create powers not already provided for in the Constitution.

Dawson's decision in the Louisville case was upheld by the Sixth Circuit Court of Appeals,[82] but the Tenth Circuit would conclude three years later that the construction of low-cost housing in Oklahoma City was a public use under the US Constitution.[83] The Supreme Court might have resolved the issue in the government's appeal of the Sixth Circuit's decision, but on the government's petition the appeal was dropped after the court had granted certiorari. In the meantime Congress passed new legislation providing for federal funding of slum clearance and low-cost housing construction by state governments, in an effort to sidestep Judge Dawson's holding. As a result the legal battles shifted to the state courts where the Tenth Circuit view of public use prevailed.

In fact the Tenth Circuit had been preempted in embracing an expansive definition of public use a year earlier by the New York Court of Appeals, a successor court to the one from which Senator

Tracy had led the early charge for a narrow understanding of public use. Pursuant to the New York State Housing Law, the New York City Housing Authority sought to condemn various properties for the purpose of slum clearance and housing reconstruction in the borough of Manhattan. Affected property owners challenged the law as not satisfying the public use requirements of the US and New York constitutions. The New York high court held that "[u]se of a proposed structure, facility, or service by everybody and anybody is . . . a public benefit and, therefore, . . . a public use."[84] "[T]he court stated that the fundamental purpose of government is to protect the health, safety and general welfare of the public . . . [and] it seems constitutionally immaterial whether . . . [the power of taxation, the police power or the power of eminent domain] is employed."[85] The New York court's indifference as to the state's claimed source of authority was reflected two years later in a Pennsylvania Supreme Court decision also holding that slum clearance and low-income housing development are public uses. "When the power of eminent domain is called into play as a handmaiden to the police power and in order to make its proper exercise effective," said the court, "it is necessarily for a public use."[86] By 1948 the high courts of at least 22 states had rejected the narrow public use requirement in favor of total judicial deference to legislative judgments of public purpose.[87] Even the Massachusetts Supreme Court came around to the view that the eminent domain power is coextensive with the police power, but without bothering to overrule its prior decisions to the contrary.[88] Writing in 1940, Philip Nichols, author of a leading treatise on eminent domain, concluded that, in light of these judicial decisions, "the requirement of public use . . . is [no longer] . . . part of the law of eminent domain, and will become of minor importance in eminent domain cases."[89]

Nichols's prediction proved to be remarkably accurate for the remainder of the twentieth century. Although property owners continued to object that their property was being taken for non-public uses, they seldom found any support in the state or federal courts. The reason was that the intended use of condemned property was no longer relevant under the expanded public use doctrine. The question was now whether or not the condemning government had the constitutional authority to pursue whatever purpose the taking of private property was intended to support. For state governments this meant that only the scope of the police power defined any limits of the eminent domain power. For the federal government the eminent domain power was limited to that government's enumerated powers, but with the New Deal those powers began expanding by leaps and bounds.

Unlike the state courts, federal courts were hesitant to take a firm position on the public use debate, although the trend against the narrow rule was evident by the turn of the nineteenth century. Most eminent domain cases in the federal courts involved challenges under the 14th Amendment to takings by state governments. In these cases the federal courts tended to defer to state court determinations of state power and to state lawmakers' assessments of justifying local circumstances. While the Court insisted it was not taking a position on the public use versus public purpose distinction, Justice Moody observed in 1908 that "[n]o case can be recalled where this court has condemned . . . a taking upheld by a state court as a taking for public uses in conformity with its laws."[90] By 1916 Justice Holmes, writing on behalf of a unanimous court, made explicit that court's rejection of the narrow, "use by the public" rule.[91] With the New Deal came a much more activist federal government and thus many more cases involving the federal government's reliance on eminent domain. Notwithstanding Justice Holmes's 1916 opinion and other federal cases taking an expansive view of the public use language, property owners continued to press in the federal courts for a more constraining understanding of public use, while also urging that even the broader idea of public purpose was limited by the constitutional enumeration of federal power.

In some federal cases the link to an enumerated power was reasonably direct. The condemnation of private lands for a railway right of way is plainly within the government's power under the Commerce Clause.[92] The constitutional powers to declare war and to raise armies justify the condemnation of private lands to create a national war memorial at Gettysburg.[93] Condemnation of private forest lands for the purpose of controlling soil erosion harmful to navigable waterways is authorized by the long-accepted federal powers under the Commerce Clause.[94] The acquisition by eminent domain of lands for a public park in the District of Columbia is within Congress's authority to legislate for the federal district.[95] These cases and many more may have been justified on the theory that the power of eminent domain is inherent in government and available in pursuit of any legitimate government purpose, but they all could have satisfied the narrow test of public use. New Deal legislation would require the federal courts to confront the public use issue head on.

As we have seen, urban redevelopment and slum clearance had, for a brief period in the early 1930s, made the US government a defendant in federal courts. Congress's quick detour into state managed housing programs shifted those challenges to state courts, but the

District of Columbia Redevelopment Act of 1945 put the US government back in the crosshairs of property rights defenders. In *Berman v. Parker*[96] the owner of a successful department store in Washington, DC, challenged the condemnation of his store on the ground that it was not a public use to take his land and transfer it to other private owners. Many of the earlier state court decisions upholding the use of eminent domain in slum clearance programs had emphasized that slums and blighted properties pose health and safety risks for the public. No one doubted that the states have police power authority to regulate such health and safety risks and, pursuant to the idea that eminent domain can be used in support of any legitimate state purpose, condemnation of blighted properties is, therefore, a public use. Congress, which exercises the police power for the District of Columbia, had embraced this theory in the 1945 Act:

> [O]wing to technological and sociological changes, obsolete lay-out, and other factors, conditions existing in the District of Columbia with respect to substandard housing and blighted areas, . . . are injurious to the public health, safety, morals, and welfare, and it is hereby declared to be the policy of the United States to protect and promote the welfare of the inhabitants of the seat of the Government by eliminating all such injurious conditions by employing all means necessary and appropriate for the purpose.[97]

But the department store owner objected that his property was not blighted and could not be taken under this theory of eminent domain in support of the police power. Justice Douglas disagreed. The public welfare represents values that "are spiritual as well as physical, aesthetic as well as monetary," wrote Douglas for a unanimous court. "It is within the power of the legislature to determine that the community should be beautiful as well as healthy, spacious as well as clean, well-balanced as well as carefully patrolled."[98] The fact that particular affected properties are not blighted does not exempt them. "Once the question of the public purpose has been decided," said Douglas, "the amount and character of land to be taken for the project and the need for a particular tract to complete the integrated plan rests in the discretion of the legislative branch."[99]

Nothing more Justice Douglas might have said could have given the public use requirement less significance. A public use is anything that will or may promote the welfare of the public, in the judgment of the legislature. It is not for the courts to second guess or impose constraints. Although Douglas's opinion in *Berman* may have greatly expanded the scope of public purposes satisfying the public use requirement in eminent domain law, it should not have come as a surprise to those familiar with the Supreme Court's land use regulation decisions. In *Village of Euclid v. Ambler Realty* the Court had held that "before the ordinance [establishing exclusive use zones] can be declared unconstitutional, [it must be demonstrated] that such provisions are clearly arbitrary and unreasonable, having no substantial relation to the public health, safety, morals, or general welfare."[100] If eminent domain is the handmaiden of police power and police power extends from health and safety to morality and anything affecting the general welfare, as *Village of Euclid* had confirmed, there can be no meaningful public use limit on the power to condemn private property.

After *Berman* there was some split among state courts, but a significant majority were in agreement with the expansive view of the Supreme Court. On the restrictive side were a few cases like *Hogue v. Port of Seattle*[101] in which the Washington Supreme Court invalidated the condemnation of well-developed agricultural and residential lands for resale as industrial property adjacent to a public port. "No matter how desirable from an operating standpoint the Port's exclusive control of land use in a given area may appear to be," said the court, "it is the duty of the courts to uphold the rights of private property against the inroads of public bodies who seek to acquire it for private purposes which they honestly believe to be essential for the public good."[102] But taking the expansive view of *Berman* were far more cases like *Courtesy Sandwich Shop, Inc. v. Port of New York Authority*[103] in which the New York Court of Appeals upheld the condemnation of private property to make way for and raise revenue for the World Trade Center. In overruling the decision of the appellate division invalidating as not a public use the condemnation of properties for the sole purpose of raising revenue to support the larger public purpose of promoting world trade through New York City, the Court of Appeals held that any condemnation contributing to that important end would satisfy the public use requirement. Said the court, "[t]he history of western civilization demonstrates the cause and effect relationship between a great port and a great city." [104] Apparently, part of that cause-and-effect relationship was the authority of the state to condemn properties that could be resold at a profit to the financial benefit of the port authority's ambitious project.

In addition to slum clearance and urban redevelopment, post–New Deal governments became ever more involved in providing a growing national infrastructure for commerce and communication. Many of these projects required acquisition of large amounts of land. To the extent condemnation was necessary, and with the future of Western civilization in the balance, there was little chance courts would be persuaded to revive a more limiting concept of public use. But, as in the World Trade Center case, there was often a question about how much property needed to be taken to accomplish the public purpose.

One such controversy that made its way to the US Supreme Court involved the construction by the Tennessee Valley Authority of the Fontana Dam on the Little Tennessee River in North Carolina. It was not doubted that Congress had authority to authorize the dam, nor that the lands that would be flooded by the resulting reservoir could be acquired by eminent domain from unwilling sellers. A hitch was that the reservoir would cut off access to a rural settlement. The obvious solution was the construction of a new road around the reservoir, but the state and county did not have the resources to build the road. The TVA proposed to pay damages, but the amount offered was insufficient to allow the state and county to provide necessary police, school, and health services to the cutoff community. So the TVA decided to acquire all of the land from the isolated property owners and transfer it to the bordering Smoky Mountains National Park. A few landowners refused to sell and claimed that the TVA could not condemn the land because it was not for a public use.

The trial judge agreed with the landowners and the court of appeals unanimously affirmed. Judge Parker, writing for the appellate court, seemed to rely on the "use by the public" test.[105] The difficulty was that the public would, in fact, have use of the lands in their ultimate home in Smoky Mountains National Park. But for Parker, not just any public use would do. The public use for which the TVA could condemn property was, he said, limited to the public purposes of the authorizing law, and those did not include the expansion of a national park. The case was, therefore, like the excess condemnation cases. It did not make any difference that the excess lands were transferred to another government department rather than being sold to other private owners. Although it is likely that the National Park Service could have used eminent domain to take the same properties, Judge Parker was surely correct, at least to the extent that the case for condemnation for national park purposes was never actually made by the government. In taking people's private property, the government should be expected, at a minimum, to make its case for the public use to which the land will actually be put.

The Supreme Court, on which Judge Parker would have served but for a single vote in the Senate,[106] took a unanimously different view. In an opinion written by Justice Black, the court upheld the condemnation as part of "a single integrated effort on the part of T.V.A. to carry on its Congressionally authorized functions."[107] To affirm the lower courts would allow for the judiciary to interfere in essentially legislative functions. In Black's view, the courts must defer to Congress unless "it is shown to involve an impossibility."[108] Whether that language was understood to mean that it must be impossible for a court to imagine that Congress would have intended a particular purpose or that a purpose intended by Congress was impossible to achieve by condemning the property in question, it was about as deferential as it could possibly be. In the case of the TVA, Congress sought to produce electricity, control floods, provide for recreation, and promote commerce. Justice Black's decision seemed to hold that the federal power of eminent domain could be used for any property acquisition that might serve those broad objectives, and it is not for the courts to second guess Congress or an implementing agency on that cause-and-effect connection.

On the question of the judicial role in determining public uses under the 5th Amendment, there was some disagreement among the justices in the TVA case, at least in principle. Justice Reed, with concurrence from the Chief Justice, declined to sign on to the majority opinion because, in his view, Justice Black seemed to conclude that "a good faith determination by [the TVA]...that property is necessary for the purposes of the Act bars judicial review."[109] Justice Frankfurter also concurred with the holding in the case, but disagreed with Justice Reed's interpretation of Justice Black's opinion. Although "[i]t is...true that in the numerous cases in which the issue was adjudicated, this Court never found that the legislative determination that the use was public exceeded Constitutional bound," said Frankfurter, "[t]his Court has never deviated from the view that under the Constitution a claim that a taking is not for public use is open for judicial consideration,..."[110]

From the perspective of property owners who did not wish to sell and sought protection under the Public Use Clause of the 5th Amendment, whatever disagreement was there on the Supreme Court was of little consequence. Of course the courts would not acknowledge having no power to review legislative or executive determinations of what constitutes a public use. That language is, after all, part of the constitution, and it is "emphatically, the province and duty of the judicial department, to say what the law is."[111] But the growing reality for property owners in both the federal and state courts was that the public use limitation was no limitation at all. Public use had come to mean public purpose, and eminent domain had come to be nothing more than a tool available to government in pursuit of any legitimate governmental purpose. It was unseemly for judges to be overruling the choices made by the elected branches of the government, and they seldom did. Judge Alex Kozinski, now Chief Judge of the Ninth Circuit Court of Appeals, used to give an illustrated lecture in which he demonstrated what had happened to the public use language. Kozinski had an electronic board on which many constitutional provisions appeared. Some were in very large blinking letters. Others, including "public use" were in dim, small, very nearly invisible letters.

But because the courts continued to insist that the meaning of public use is finally a judicial question, condemnations of private property continued to be challenged. The prospects for success in the now well established urban renewal and social infrastructure initiatives by government had become almost nil. But sometimes governments have new ideas about what might serve the public interest. Such was the case with a land reform program enacted by the Hawaii legislature and discussed in Chapter 2 of the companion volume, *Private Property and State Power*. For historic reasons, most of the land in Hawaii was owned by relatively few large landholders. The result was that most private homes sat on land leased from these few landowners. In an effort to create a more competitive real estate market and thereby promote home ownership and reduce the cost of homes, the Hawaii legislature enacted a program by which the state would acquire land by eminent domain, if necessary, and resell it to the owners of the overlying homes. This nearly direct transfer of land ownership from one private party to another was challenged as not constituting a public use.

As in the earlier TVA case, the Court of Appeals had ruled for the property owner. The appellate court stated that "[i]t is not a public purpose to take the property of one person in order that it may become the private property of another," and concluded that such a transfer of title was the sole substantive outcome of the Hawaii land reform law.[112] A dissenting opinion argued that the federal courts should not overturn a law approved by the legislature and courts of Hawaii, that as a small island Hawaii posed a special case, that the land reform program in Puerto Rico provided ample precedent and that in much of the world, including Hawaii, land reform is necessary to democratic government. The latter factor (on which there was no evidence in the record), said the judge, "may be considered by the Court, if only subconsciously."[113] At least for this Ninth Circuit judge there are, evidently, factors to be discussed openly and other considerations for private contemplation before rendering a judicial decision on a constitutional claim. Of course the reality of such ad hoc and unbounded considerations is what drove the pursuit for a brighter line rule on public use over the prior century.

But from the US Supreme Court there again would be no bright-line rule. Writing for a unanimous court, Justice O'Connor said the starting point in the analysis is *Berman v. Parker*. That dispensed with a couple 100 years of precedent and allowed O'Connor to accept without question that the eminent domain power is available in support of all other government powers—"merely a means to the end,"[114] including the police power in the case of the states. "Subject to specific constitutional limitations," wrote O'Connor (quoting from *Berman*), "when the legislature has spoken, the public interest has been declared in terms well-nigh conclusive."[115] That very small gap between well-nigh conclusive and conclusive presents the only occasion where the courts might exercise the power of constitutional interpretation, which O'Connor, like her predecessors in *Berman*, insists the courts retain. The very limited role this leaves for the courts, and therefore the almost nonexistent protection the public use language provides for property owners, is made crystal clear by Justice O'Connor. "[W]here the exercise of the eminent domain power is rationally related to a conceivable public purpose, the Court has never held a compensated taking to be proscribed by the Public Use Clause."[116]

The Hawaii case was widely understood to close the door for good on claims that the Public Use Clause limited the eminent domain power. But then the Supreme Court agreed to hear the *Kelo* case. At least four members of the Court must vote to grant a writ of certiorari, so perhaps there was hope the justices would reconsider their ruling in *Midkiff*. Or maybe they would, at least, draw a line in the sand distinguishing the two cases. Although eminent domain was employed in both cases to transfer property from one private owner to another, Hawaii's law transferred land ownership to private home owners while New London's law transferred much of the land to a for-profit corporation.

But it was not to be for Suzette Kelo and her fellow homeowners in New London. The Public Use Clause merely confirms that legislatures have plenary power to determine the public good and the eminent domain power is available as a means to whatever ends are so proclaimed. On Judge Kozinski's electronic display of the Constitution, the bulbs on the Public Use Clause were not just small and dim, they were out.

Chapter 4

Public Rights

A common argument in support of limitations on the use of private property is that particular uses infringe upon public rights. In making the argument, it is generally implied, if not expressly stated, that public rights take precedence over any conflicting private rights. It is sometimes also claimed that public rights both limit otherwise legitimate governmental actions and mandate untaken governmental action. Thus the concept of public rights is at once complex and potent. Public rights are said to trump both private rights and public acts while also requiring particular public actions. Indeed, it is sometimes claimed that public rights mandate particular private actions.

If public rights do trump private rights, or if public rights warrant special consideration when private rights and public purposes conflict, it is critical to the maintenance of private rights as a meaningful tool in defining the relationship between the individual and the state that public rights be justified and clearly defined and delimited. If public rights claims are merely a justification for any and all public actions or limits on private actions thought to serve the public interest, private rights will have been reduced to irrelevance outside the context of purely private relations.

Regrettably, the term "public rights" is seldom defined with any precision. It is one of those terms often used, including by courts, to settle the question or to gain the moral high ground. What individual or group could possibly claim that their private interests, even their individual rights, override the rights of the public?

Because public rights claims tend to have rhetorical appeal in relation to claims of private right, it is commonplace for advocates of just about any policy to appeal to public rights in much the same way they might appeal to the public interest. It is not a coincidence that those claiming to promote the public interest or to protect public rights usually have a personal preference for the end sought. But rarely if ever will they urge public action on the grounds of personal preferences or private benefits. Almost always they will claim to be promoting the public interest or protecting the public's rights. Indeed, as we will see, many claims of public right rest on nothing more than a claim that the public interest will be served thereby.

What are public rights? Where do they come from? Who can assert them, and who enforces them?

The term "public right" is frequently used to describe three very different concepts with legal relevance. One, rooted in the principle of popular sovereignty, might be stated as the public right of every citizen to participate in and share the benefits and burdens of democratic government—what the American framers called public liberty. Second is the view that there is a public right in property owned by the state. And third, founded in the common law, are public rights in particular uses of land and other resources. After a review of the historic antecedents of the concept of public rights, this chapter will examine these distinct conceptions.

Historic Antecedents

Roman Law

Though the term "public rights" is of relatively recent origin, the concept of commonly held rights has deep roots. Two distinct Roman law concepts are often cited today as predecessors to modern concepts of public right.

The *jus publicum* is frequently said to encompass public rights, but there is little evidence that it was so understood by the Romans. Just as modern lawyers distinguish between public law and private law, the Romans distinguished between *jus publicum* and *jus privatum*. Most modern authorities on Roman law make very little reference to *jus publicum* beyond noting that it was the law relating to the functions and procedures of the state. While the Romans may have understood the *jus publicum* to guarantee to citizens regularity in the actions of the state, a modern tendency to interpret *jus publicum* as "public right" (usually in relation to navigable waters) has no basis in Roman law.

Roman law also described three categories of resources that are encompassed in some modern notions of public rights. *Res publicae* included things belonging to the state, like highways, rivers, and harbors. *Res communes* applied to things belonging to everyone, like the air, running water, the sea, and seashore. *Res nullius* included things belonging to no one, but accessible to everyone, like wild animals.[1]

These concepts have been relied upon and often misunderstood by modern proponents of public rights. Today, things belonging to the state, *res publicae*, include vast real estate holdings and improvements, natural resources, business enterprises like the US Postal Service and Amtrak, housing, and services like garbage collection and water supply, to name a few. The state is the proprietor as a matter of public policy, not because state title is necessary or inevitable. The usual case for public ownership is that the benefits provided are public goods in the economic sense of the term, but whether or not state ownership of these things is good or bad policy depends on what is sought to be accomplished and how public ownership compares to private ownership in the achievement of those goals. In any event, it is indisputable that private proprietorship, *res privata*, is an alternative with respect to all of these things and functions. Public rights in this sense are merely proprietary interests that can be acquired and disposed of at the discretion of the state.

Things belonging to everyone, *res communes*, have often been described as things incapable of ownership because of their physical characteristics, or as things that should be available to everyone as fundamental necessities of life. Neither rationale is fully accurate, particularly given the capacities of modern technology. Even in Rome, private parties and the state could own running waters and the seashore. Today, exclusive permits to pollute the air and fish the oceans have most of the characteristics of private ownership. So the case for common ownership by everyone is increasingly founded on moral claims, to which there are counter-moral claims. Claims of public rights in this sense are really policy arguments rooted in moral claims that must compete with other policy arguments that may also lay claim to the moral high ground.

The final Roman category, *res nullius*, applied to many things in addition to wild animals. It was really a simple recognition of the fact that many things, particularly things distant from population centers, were not owned by anyone. According to second-century Roman jurist Gaius, the first occupier of such unowned things becomes the just owner.[2] While unowned things are rare in today's densely populated world, the modern American norm with respect to wild animals is consistent with Gaius. Although the states are said to own wildlife, individuals can acquire title by capture. The US Supreme Court has held that the principle of state ownership of wildlife is really just a way of asserting that the public has a strong interest in wildlife conservation, thus justifying state regulation of the private right of capture.[3]

Persistent appeal to these concepts of ancient Roman law, even if often misinformed, is not surprising given the common law origins of the US legal system. Respect for precedent is essential if the rule of law is to prevail. That does not mean the law is frozen in time, but it does mean public authorities cannot willy-nilly change the law and ignore precedents on which people have relied in assessing the legality of their actions. Proponents of expansive public rights as trumps on private rights or on legislative and executive action are thus drawn to the precedent of Roman law with its ancient pedigree.

Magna Carta

Magna Carta also has been referenced as a source of public rights with ancient pedigree. Two provisions of Magna Carta are often cited as precursors to modern claims of public rights in natural resources, although neither was intended to serve the ends now attributed to it. Beginning in the nineteenth century, Chapter 16 was said to be a prohibition on the King's granting of exclusive fisheries, though its original purpose was to forbid the King from exercising preferential access to privately owned riverbanks and requiring riparian owners to prepare the roads and bridges for his visits. Chapter 23 is said to confirm a public right to unobstructed navigation of waterways, although its purpose was to preclude the King from placing weirs in rivers and streams to restrict fish passage to downstream property owners.[4]

Two other chapters of Magna Carta were actually intended to protect what would be thought of as public rights today. Chapter 9 affirmed the shared rights of citizens and a public right of self-governance in its guarantee of "all the old Liberties and Customs" of the City of London and of "all other Cities, Boroughs [and] Towns."[5] It is clear, however, from Magna Carta's many other guarantees of individual liberty (though not for everyone) that the public right of self-governance was not understood to be a blank check for public impositions on shared or individual private rights.

Chapter 30 affirmed that "[a]ll [foreign] merchants... shall have safety and security in going out of England, and in coming into England, and in staying and in travelling through England, as well by land as by water, to buy and sell, without any unjust exactions, according to ancient and right customs."[6] In conjunction with the

"Liberties and Customs" of Chapter 9, understood to include a comparable right of domestic merchants to engage in commercial intercourse, this guarantee served not just the merchants but the general public. A modern parallel, though not often thought of as protecting a public right, is the US Constitution's Commerce Clause of Article I, Section 8, which guarantees commercial freedom unobstructed by state interventions.

Magna Carta has been frequently referenced (though usually as Magna Charta in the nineteenth century) by the US Supreme Court. Generally these references have been in the context of the private rights not to be deprived without due process of law,[7] or consistent with the "law of the land" ("*legem terre*") in the language of Magna Carta.[8] Other than an oft-cited statement in the nineteenth-century case of *Hurtado v. California* that Magna Carta "rightly construed ... [is] a broad charter of public right and law,"[9] the Supreme Court's reliance on Magna Carta as a source of public rights has been exclusively in the context of rights to navigable waterways and their associated submerged lands.

The statement in *Hurtado*, penned by Justice Matthews, is striking for its purpose of justifying public interference with and alteration of the very private rights sought to be protected by Magna Carta. After stating that "[t]he concessions of Magna Charta were wrung from the King as guaranties against the oppressions and usurpations of his prerogative" and noting that "bills of attainder, ex post facto laws, laws declaring forfeitures of estates, and other arbitrary acts of legislation ... occur ... frequently in English history," Matthews went on to argue that "rightly construed as a broad charter of public right and law," Magna Carta, like the common law, should be adapted to "the new and various experiences of our own situation and system."[10] "[F]lexibility and capacity for growth and adaptation is the peculiar boast and excellence of the common law," wrote Matthews, as it should be, he argued, for Magna Carta.

It is not surprising that Progressive era justices would look to Matthews's "public rights" argument in *Hurtado* as precedent for upholding later legislative and executive intrusions upon long-established private rights. The irony, of course, is that both the private rights and the public rights relied upon to limit those private rights were said to be rooted in Magna Carta. As a dissenting Justice Harlan said in challenging Matthews's argument,

> due process of law ... must be so interpreted as not to deny to the law the capacity of progress and improvement.... It is difficult ... to perceive anything in the [challenged state procedures] suggest[ing] that the state ... has

entered upon an era of progress and improvement in the law of criminal procedure.[11]

"[D]ue process of law," said Harlan, "[is] broad enough to cover every right of life, liberty, or property secured by the settled usages and modes of proceedings existing under the common and statute law of England at the time our government was founded."[12]

Contrary to Matthews's suggestion in *Hurtado*, Magna Carta provides little support for modern claims of public right. The agreement struck in 1215 at Runnymede between King John and the feudal barons, and reaffirmed by King Henry III in 1225, is overwhelmingly a recognition by the King of the rights and liberties of individuals and the Church. It is rightly celebrated as a foundational document of English and American liberty, though its frequent characterization as a grant from the King runs contrary to the deep natural rights tradition of American constitutionalism and to the seventeenth-century writings of Sir Edward Coke who viewed Magna Carta along with his own 1628 Petition of Right as reaffirmations of the ancient liberties of Englishmen.

But Magna Carta offers little to those seeking authority for modern claims of public right. Chapter 16 and 23 represent the King's acceptance that he must respect the private rights of other large land holders, and chapters 9 and 30 are far more about individual rights held in common (again, not by everyone) than about public rights in the modern sense of the term.

Early American Understandings

Magna Carta, subsequent developments in English constitutional law including the Petition of Right (1628) and the English Bill of Rights (1689), and seventeenth- and eighteenth-century political theory—all influenced American colonial thinking related to the modern concept of public rights. Although the colonies were a part of Great Britain and thus subject to the Crown's prerogatives and parliamentary sovereignty, distance gave them opportunity and reason to question both.

Thomas Hobbes (*Leviathan*, 1651), John Locke (*Two Treatises of Government*, 1698), and Jean-Jacques Rousseau (*The Social Contract*, 1762) all contributed to the idea that government draws its authority from the consent of the governed—that sovereignty rests with the people rather than with parliament or a divinely endowed monarch. Relying heavily on these and other political theorists, the men who convened in Philadelphia in the summer of 1787 to consummate the revolution in an enduring constitution understood that the legitimacy of the state governments they represented was rooted in a social contract among the people of each state.

But they did not purport to have authority among themselves as delegates from the states to enact a new constitution. Rather they provided in Article VII that to have legal effect the proposed constitution must be ratified by a minimum of nine state conventions elected for the purpose. Thus, the constitution would become the law of the land only after a majority of the people in at least nine states agreed to delegate a portion of their popular sovereignty to a new national government, thereby transferring to the national government some of the authority they had previously delegated to their state governments.

What this most significant event in the political history of the United States meant for the concept of public rights is surely open to debate. But there can be no doubt that a generally accepted view at the time of the national founding was that governments at all levels had only those powers granted by at least a majority of those subject to each government's authority. Of course this presumption raised several thorny questions: (1) If legitimate government is formed by a contract among those governed, why are those in the minority, who have not agreed, bound? (2) Why are those too young to vote or later born bound by the authority of a government to which they have had no opportunity to give consent? (3) What about the many people—women, slaves, non-property owners—not allowed to vote? All good and challenging questions, but none cast doubt on the principle that government has no authority or rights independent of or superior to those of the people.

The idea that the states, or governments in general, possess rights was not foreign to the founders of the American nation. In agreeing to the Articles of Confederation as the constitution of their new confederation, the state legislatures were careful to preserve their rights as sovereign states. Much of the Anti-Federalist objection to the proposed constitution was rooted in a fear that states' rights were being compromised to a powerful central government. Although Thomas Paine properly objected that government "has of itself no rights; they are altogether duties,"[13] it was generally understood that the term "states' rights" had reference to the powers of the states relative to each other and relative to the national government. Few if any of the founding generation seriously contended that states have rights in relation to individuals. Making such a claim would have contradicted their underlying claim to the legitimacy of their governments rooted in popular sovereignty. In America, as James Madison pointed out, a constitution had become a grant of power made by the people to the government, not, as in Europe, a charter of liberty granted by power.[14]

Appeal to states' rights has persisted throughout American history, but always in the context of the constitutional allocation of power between the states and the national government. Thomas Jefferson wrote of "states' rights" to Albert Gallatin in 1822 in objecting to proposed internal improvements to be constructed by the federal government. He later wrote of "rights retained by the states" in an 1825 Declaration and Protest of Virginia objecting to federal "usurpations of powers" rightfully belonging to the states. South Carolinian John Calhoun appealed to states' rights in pressing his view that states had the authority to nullify acts of Congress, and the next generation of southern leaders proclaimed states' rights in declaring their secession from the Union. Nearly a century later "states' rights" was the battle cry of those resisting federal civil rights legislation, and the idea remains commonplace in disputes over the relative powers of the state and federal governments. But the term "states' rights" as it has been used for nearly two centuries of US history has little relation to the concept of public rights as a trump on private rights or on the executive and legislative powers of government.

However, there was, in the founding generation, a profound belief in the idea of public liberty understood as a right of self-governance inherent in the concept of popular sovereignty. Public liberty was thus the natural companion of private liberty. Among the natural rights of all citizens is participation in the governance of the state in which they reside. When the state is governed by authorities to whom the people's sovereignty has not been delegated, the public liberty, which consists in the aggregated private liberties of all citizens, is violated. "Public liberty," explained historian Gordon Wood, " was thus the combining of each man's individual liberty into a collective governmental authority, the institutionalization of the people's personal liberty, making public or political liberty equivalent to democracy or government by the people themselves."[15]

Viewed as the expression of every individual's right to participate in the exercise of popular sovereignty, public rights are rights held equally by all. The early nineteenth-century Italian federalist Pellegrino Rossi divided rights into three categories: private, public, and political. While political rights might be recognized on the basis of the varying capacities of different groups—i.e. women and children may be unqualified to vote—everyone is equally entitled by public rights. The French jurist Denis Serrigny held similarly that public rights reflect social equality, though he too allowed for distinctions based on perceived natural competences. Of course neither of these nineteenth-century theorists would gain the approval of modern egalitarians, but their failing was not in the conception of public rights as rights held equally by all, but in their acceptance of contemporary notions of political competence. Rossi and Serrigny were on the same intellectual path as William Blackstone before them. Blackstone viewed public rights as the "broad interest of the public at large in being protected against criminal acts." In his *Commentaries on the Laws of England*, Blackstone differentiated private from public wrongs thus:

> [T]he former are an infringement or privation of the private or civil rights belonging to individuals, considered as individuals; and are thereupon frequently termed civil injuries: the latter are a breach and violation of public rights and duties, which affect the whole community, considered as a community; and are distinguished by the harsher appellation of crimes and misdemeanors.[16]

That public rights were remedied by criminal prosecution meant that the individual's only remedy for infringement of public rights was participation in the political process.

This public liberty of self-governance did translate into one particular claim of state right under the constitution. In the words of James Madison it is the "right to insist that the forms of government under which the compact was entered into, should be *substantially* maintained."[17] That single state right flows from the national government's duty to "guarantee to every state . . . a republican form of government".[18] And what is a republican form of government but one of representatives elected by the people as an exercise of their popular sovereignty. In a constitutional system founded on the principle of popular sovereignty, there can be no "states' rights," "public liberties," or "public rights" not derived from an exercise of that popular sovereignty.

Those who fought in the revolutionary war, wrote the new state constitutions, and endorsed the Articles of Confederation were confident in the view that because public liberty is founded on popular sovereignty, its exercise could never threaten private liberty. The people would never approve the infringement of their liberties. In the words of John Adams, "a democratical despotism is a contradiction in terms."[19] But ten short years of state legislative impositions on private liberties in the name of the public good taught the lesson that founding government on public liberty does not guarantee private liberty. There are many ways in which the majority and its elected and appointed representatives can exercise tyranny beyond the obvious method of persuading a majority that it is in their personal interests or the public's interest to burden the rights of others. Particularly effective among those methods is the assertion of public rights as trumps on private rights.

THE LAW OF PUBLIC RIGHTS

For rights claims to have legal effect—to function as trumps on otherwise legitimate private or public actions—they must be recognized by courts. While it is not practical to review the whole range of judicial opinions for the purpose of this chapter, a summary glance at US Supreme Court opinions is instructive. What we find are three distinct understandings of the concept of public rights.

The Public Right as Popular Sovereignty

The most common usage of the term public rights in Supreme Court decisions is as a surrogate for the public interest or public good and derives directly from the foundational principle of popular sovereignty. In the 1837 *Charles River Bridge* case the court declined to invalidate a state charter for the construction of a private toll bridge over the Charles River, rejecting the argument made by the proprietors of the existing Charles River Bridge that they held an exclusive franchise based on an earlier charter from the state.[20] As concurring justice McLean explained, the original grant should be narrowly construed against the grantee (meaning the earlier grant was non-exclusive absent express language to the contrary) because later actions by the state are presumed to be in the public interest. This is so, said McLean, because there is a public right that the legislature act in the public interest.[21]

While modern public choice theory would suggest it naive, the presumption that the state legislature acts to protect public rights, rather than to serve private interests in contravention of public rights, was rooted in a no doubt idealistic American belief that popular sovereignty is the antidote to tyranny and the abuse of power. As under English law, said McLean, where the power to grant charters was part of the king's prerogative, the exercise of that power by the representatives of the sovereign people is required to be, and is presumed to be, in conformance with the public right.

Despite the not too distant revolution, reference to the king's prerogative is not so surprising as it may seem, given the "reception" of English law by the American states and the aspiration of the framing generation to restore the rights of Englishmen. The antidote of popular sovereignty would assure that prerogative powers sometimes abused by the king would be exercised for the public good in the democratic republic of the United States. But even accepting that power is sometimes abused in democratic republics, what had been the prerogative powers of the king were inherent to any government capable of providing for the public good. In explaining why a state statute of limitations did not bar a US government suit to recover damages, Justice Story, writing in an earlier Circuit Court case, observed that, though the king's exemption from such limitations is

> sometimes asserted to be, because the king is always busied for the public good, and, therefore, has not leisure to assert his right within the times limited to subjects, [the true reason] is to be found in the great public policy of preserving the public rights, revenues, and property from injury and loss, by the negligence of public officers. And though this is sometimes called a prerogative right, it is in fact nothing more than a reservation, or exception, introduced for the public benefit, and equally applicable to all governments.[22]

The idea that government authority derives from and is constrained by a public right inherent in popular sovereignty has been a common theme over two centuries of Supreme Court history. The court has held that public rights come with sovereignty and cannot, therefore be alienated;[23] that regulation pursuant to the police power serves to protect and preserve public rights;[24] that there is a public right that the laws be enforced and that legislative and executive officials perform their responsibilities.[25] The court has also concluded that public rights can be created[26] and extinguished[27] by legislation. The latter necessarily flows from the principle of popular sovereignty, for if one legislature can create public rights that a subsequent legislature cannot repeal, there is no popular sovereignty. As used in these and many other judicial rulings, the concept of public rights serves to underscore that all government authority exists with the consent of the governed. Because the governed share a right in common to govern themselves, properly elected and appointed officials are both required and presumed to act for the public good. That is the public's right.

As a theoretical matter, the foregoing cases suggest that the public right inherent in popular sovereignty gives birth to regulation for the public good, also framed as the public welfare, the common welfare, the common good, the commonweal, and the public interest. The public right in this sense is simply the right of the people to govern themselves subject to rights they have reserved to themselves. But this logic was turned on its head in a series of cases dating from 1876 in which the Supreme Court held that there are public rights in private activities affected with a public interest.[28] While this principle had deep common law roots in the context of common carriers, highways, and water-powered mills (serving not only to justify regulation but to extend to the regulated the power of eminent domain),[29] the court would later apply the principle to justify regulation of all manner of private activity having some effect on others. [30] Thus, the legislative power to regulate private activity was found to stem not from a delegation of that power by the people, but from the legislators' or judges' conclusion that private activities are affected with a public interest, without regard to whether the people, in consenting to be governed, reserved the right to engage in the newly regulated activity.

Any distinction between the concept of public right and the concept of public interest or public good has been further blurred by the Court's growing reliance on balancing tests over the past several decades. The idea of rights as trumps has given way to the balancing of rights and government interests conflicting with those rights. It is an approach to constitutional rights interpretation assured to diminish rights and expand government power. When can the claim of a single individual, whether framed as a personal interest or a right, counterbalance the claims of the public? Never; which is why rights, if they are to be more than private interests among a sea of competing interests, must function as trumps.

Despite the proliferation of balancing tests in the judicial enforcement of constitutional liberties, the idea of rights as trumps still carries weight in legal argument. More so, as we have seen, when personal and civil liberties, as opposed to economic liberties, are at stake. But even in the context of economic liberties, any discomfort with balancing private rights against the public interest is no doubt alleviated by substituting public rights for the public interest in the balance. Or better yet, substituting private interests for private rights, as at least four members of the court did in describing the issue in the prosecution of an individual who refused to testify before the House Committee on Un-American Activities as "the balancing of public rights and private interests."[31]

Because popular sovereignty is ultimately rooted in the sovereignty of the individual, public rights in the pursuit of the public good might be viewed as private rights held in common by all citizens. But the Supreme Court has made clear that public rights in this sense are different from private rights in several respects. For one, citizens have a duty to comply with duly enacted laws, including a duty to pay taxes incurred in promotion of public right.[32] At the same time citizens have an equal right to the benefits of government action undertaken for the general public good, but their remedies for the vindication of these shared public rights, or if they object to duties imposed, are different from those available to assert private rights. The Supreme Court explained in a 1953 opinion that public rights are granted by statute and generally available to all or are asserted by the state in criminal and civil proceedings. "[T]he most usual differentiation," said the court, "is between the [public] legal rights or duties enforced through the administrative process and those left to enforcement on private initiative in the law courts."[33]

American courts have never accepted that public rights, in the sense of a shared right to have a government that serves the public good, might be relied upon to trump legislative or administrative actions. In 1867 the Supreme Court stated that "[t]his court does not sit as conservators over public rights, and as such to guard them in the very beginning against the execution of an obnoxious law."[34] It is a characteristic of American law observed by Alexis de Tocqueville a generation earlier. "It will be seen," wrote Tocqueville, "that by leaving it to private interest to censure the law,... legislation is protected from wanton assaults and from the daily aggressions of party spirit."[35] Although the Court began wavering on the principle a century later in the context of lawsuits claiming failed or inadequate enforcement of federal laws, the logic of judicial deference to administrative and legislative determination of the public interest was reaffirmed in a 1968 dissent by Justice Harlan. In the context of a taxpayer challenge to federal expenditures for the purchase of textbooks for parochial schools, Harlan relied upon the legal theorist W. N. Hohfled[36] to draw the following distinction:

> [T]he rights and interests of taxpayers who contest the constitutionality of public expenditures are markedly different from those of "Hohfeldian" plaintiffs, including those taxpayer-plaintiffs who challenge the validity of their own tax liabilities. We must recognize that these non-Hohfeldian plaintiffs complain, just as the petitioner in Frothingham sought to complain, not as taxpayers, but as "private attorneys-general." The interests they represent, and the rights they espouse, are bereft of any personal or proprietary coloration. They are, as litigants, indistinguishable from any group selected at random from among the general population, taxpayers and nontaxpayers alike. These

are and must be, to adopt Professor Jaffe's useful phrase, "public actions" brought to vindicate public rights.[37]

Whether or not one agrees with Harlan's conclusion that the federal courts are not constitutionally empowered to consider generalized grievances against democratically enacted legislation, it cannot be doubted that the judicial role in such cases would be fundamentally different from its role in considering individualized private rights claims of the types contemplated by Hohfeld. Once courts assume the position of assessing the validity of legislative and executive actions on the basis of public rights claims founded on differing opinions of the public good, the courts have unavoidably become policy makers rather than enforcers of the rule of law.

Justice Reed made this point on behalf of the court in a 1944 case brought by individuals seeking to enjoin an order issued by the Secretary of Agriculture. In overturning a lower court dismissal of the claim, Justice Reed stated:

> When Congress passes an Act empowering administrative agencies to carry on governmental activities, the power of those agencies is circumscribed by the authority granted. This permits the courts to participate in law enforcement entrusted to administrative bodies only to the extent necessary to protect justiciable individual rights against administrative action fairly beyond the granted powers.... This is very far from assuming that the courts are charged more than administrators or legislators with protection of the rights of the people.[38]

Half a century later, Justice Scalia reminded "public interest" claimants in an environmental case that " '[i]ndividual rights,' within the meaning of [Reed's] passage, do not mean public rights that have been legislatively pronounced to belong to each individual who forms part of the public."[39]

Since Harlan's 1968 dissent in *Flast v. Cohen* the court has wavered at times from the principle that generalized grievances are for the give and take of the political process, not the courts, by allowing "public interest" challenges on the basis of highly attenuated injury claims. For example, in *United States v. SCRAP*, the court allowed a student group to challenge federal approval of a railroad surcharge on shipment of recycled materials on the basis of alleged personal injuries resulting from higher consumer prices and increased utilization of non-recycled materials taken from lands and forests frequented by the students.[40] But as a general rule the court has adhered to the quite proper understanding that when policy preferences are expressed as public rights claims, they are of a different character than private rights claims. The latter can function as trumps on legislative and executive processes without involving the courts in those policy decisions. Not so the former. When political losers are allowed to assert their policy preferences as public rights claims in the courts, popular sovereignty is sacrificed to judicially assisted minority tyranny.

Thus the idea of public rights as trumps on properly enacted legislation and administrative rules runs directly counter to the foundational premise of popular sovereignty. Either the people are sovereign or they are not. If elected representatives, and executives employed to do their bidding, are limited by public rights, then the people are not sovereign—someone other than the people is deciding what the state can do. That is why the Supreme Court has consistently interpreted public rights to be the equal right of every citizen to exercise their liberty to participate in governance and to be responsible to comply with the will of the people. The 14th Amendment's Equal Protection Clause and its later application to the federal government as inherent to due process are best understood as needed reaffirmations of these principles.

The conclusion that public rights cannot trump legislation without denying popular sovereignty does not mean that private rights cannot trump legislation and regulation. Popular sovereignty finds its legitimacy in personal liberty. The private right to enter into the social contract of governance is the same as the private right to enter into a private contract. In both cases, benefits and responsibilities are conditioned on consent. The powers of government delegated by the social contract of the US Constitution are explicitly limited by some private liberties (the bill of rights) and impliedly limited by others (see the 9th Amendment).

Public Rights in State Property

A second category of what might be called "public rights" relates to actual proprietary ownership by government. Federal and state governments combined own 40 percent of the total land area of the nation, ranging from 1.5 percent in Rhode Island and less than 2 percent in Kansas to over 95 percent in Alaska. Local governments also own land, although a recent Reason Foundation study found that only 17 of the 50 states have a reliable way of knowing how much.[41]

While most smaller parcels of government land used for office buildings and other government facilities are generally viewed, like private parcels, as properties to be bought and sold in the real estate market, larger government holdings are often thought of as having special status as the property of the people. It is commonplace in policy debates relating to management and use of lands owned by the federal and state governments for advocates to contend that their policy preferences will serve the public good, and that there is a public right that it be so.

The legal reality is that the vast majority of the lands owned by the federal and state governments can be sold, leased, traded, or even gifted at the sole discretion of legislators or administrators authorized by legislators to engage in such transactions. Although government proprietors have advantages relative to private property owners—exemption from property taxes and many regulations, for example—they are much like private proprietors when it comes to authority to change uses and alienate title. Given this similarity between public and private proprietors, the claim of a public right in government lands sounds more of political than of legal relevance.

Original, non-Indian, title to land in colonial North America was acquired in various ways. Some was simply occupied by settlers or claimed by the Crown pursuant to the doctrine of discovery, while other lands were acquired by purchase from Indian tribes. Whatever the legitimacy of the original European claims to ownership, the reality was that the various colonies came by various means to hold title to significant amounts of land. In many cases the land was granted by the Crown to individual proprietors with the understanding and expectation that it would be sold, in turn, to other private owners as the colonies were settled.

Because there were no established governments in most of the granted territories, the proprietary grants generally included a delegation of the sovereign powers of the Crown. In other words, the proprietors were both owners of the land and governors of the territory. But these two functions were understood by everyone to be separate and distinct. When land owned by the proprietors was sold to another private party, sovereign authority over the conveyed land remained with the proprietor. This fundamental distinction between state sovereignty and state proprietorship was confirmed unequivocally by the US Supreme Court long after the original proprietors gave way to colonial governments that later gave way to state governments. Although referring to both sovereignty and propriety as "public rights," the court stated that "[a] grant of the proprietary title will never operate as a release or extinguishment of a sovereign right not necessarily included within the scope of the grant."[42]

The framers of the Constitution anticipated that the federal government also would own property, but they could never have imagined that the federal government would one day own one-third of the nation's land on a permanent basis. In empowering Congress to "dispose of and make all needful Rules and Regulations respecting the Territory and other Property belonging to the United States,"[43] the framers had in mind properties necessary for government offices, forts, and other facilities as well as territories that had and would come to the government as a result of cessions of western land claims by seven of the original 13 states. No doubt those of an expansionist mind also contemplated federal acquisition of lands then held or claimed by other nations, but no one envisaged massive federal land holdings decades, let alone centuries, later.

What was contemplated was government ownership of lands necessary to performance of the government's functions, and disposal of land in western territories to the private citizens of future states. That is the way it happened in the ceded lands that would come to constitute the states from Wisconsin and Michigan in the north to Mississippi and Alabama in the south where federal ownership today is relatively insignificant. What the framers did not anticipate was the late nineteenth-century interest in retaining in federal ownership vast swaths of land acquired by the federal government from France (Louisiana, 1803), Britain (Oregon Territory, 1846), Mexico (the modern American southwest, 1848), and Russia (Alaska, 1867).

For most of the century the longstanding policy of land disposal led to land grants to new states for the support of schools and colleges, grants to railroads to subsidize railroad construction and facilitate economic development of the west, and transfer to individuals pursuant to the Homestead Act and other Congressional enactments. Until the last decades of the century no one imagined that the federal government would retain significant amounts of these territories in perpetuity.

The combination of a conservation movement inspired by unsustainable harvesting of eastern and midwestern forests (and associated flooding) and some powerful private interests realizing that they might benefit from federal retention of western lands led to a movement to withdraw significant expanses of federal land from availability for private acquisition. While continuing to receive increasingly generous land grants, the railroads were quick to support the setting aside of 2.2 million acres for what would later become Yellowstone National Park, and for preservation of other natural and scenic wonders to which they could transport visitors. Although there was significant state and local resistance to forest land reservations created by Presidents Harrison, Cleveland, McKinley, and T. R. Roosevelt, by the end of the Roosevelt administration over 190 million acres had been set aside (an area nearly the size of the original 13 states).

For the first half of the twentieth century, the reserved federal timberlands were managed (some would say unmanaged or mismanaged) largely as timber farms for the benefit of a thriving timber industry and local governments that received payments based on the volume of timber harvested. Mining and grazing were also widespread, the former generally unregulated under the terms of the 1876 General Mining Law,[44] and the latter unregulated until enactment of the Taylor Grazing Act in 1934.[45] Because the timberlands were vast and populations relatively sparse, there was little conflict between the timber, mining, and grazing interests and the one hand and those looking to use the federal public lands for other purposes like recreation on the other.

That all changed with the modern environmental movement and growing demand for outdoor recreation. Although the idea of a public right to use the public lands was not foreign to timber, mineral, and grassland users, it took on a new significance with environmentalists. They claimed, and were successful in pressing Congress for legislation to support their claim, that the public right in the natural preservation of the federal lands was a trump on consumptive uses. The refrain that the "public lands are our lands" resonated with Congress and led to enactment of numerous laws giving ordinary citizens and special interests the ability to influence and, more importantly, delay public lands decision making.

Lands transferred by the federal government to new states at the time of their admission to the union were granted in trust to be sold or leased for the benefit of the public schools or, in the case of the Morrill Act,[46] for the support of colleges. Some states sold all or most of their school lands, others retain them still today. It is sometimes suggested that the lands retained by the federal government are similarly held in trust for the people of the nation, but unlike with school trust lands, that claim has no real legal significance. We might hope that we can trust in Congress and federal land agencies to manage these federally owned lands and resources in the best interest of the public, but there is no legally enforceable trust analogous to that limiting state management of school trust lands. The states do have a trust responsibility. The federal government has nothing more than a political responsibility.

The same can be said of the idea of a public right in lands to which the federal government or any government holds legal title. Governments' legal interest is no different from that of any other proprietor. It can sell, lease, gift, manage, and mismanage its properties subject to the same property laws (absent special exemption or legal restraint) as any other property owner. Elected and appointed officials have full discretion within their legal authority. The public right with respect to public property is only the political right held by citizens in any democratic republic to demand different policies of their elected representatives or to replace those representatives with different people.

But there is one notable exception.

Public Rights in the Common Law

Writing for the majority in the case of *Lucas v. South Carolina Coastal Commission*, Justice Scalia referred to "restrictions that background principles of the State's law of property and nuisance already place upon land ownership."[47] The context was a private property owner's claim that regulatory limits on his use of his property constituted an unconstitutional taking in violation of the 5th and 14th Amendments. Scalia's pedestrian and obvious point was that there can be no taking when a property owner does not own the right claimed to be taken. Under the common law, all property is acquired and held subject to certain conditions on use. Those conditions reflect the preexisting rights of others and exist whether or not mentioned in the deed or the instrument of conveyance by which a property is acquired. Although not the point of Scalia's reference in *Lucas*, background principles also help define rights inherent in all property, absent express provision to the contrary.

The most obvious right inherent in all private property is the right to exclude others. Unauthorized physical invasion of a person's property by a neighboring property owner or anyone else is trespass. But harm can result from acts that do not involve physical invasion or occupation of another's property. The law of private nuisance precludes all property owners from the unreasonable, unwarranted or unlawful use of their property in a manner that substantially interferes with the enjoyment or use of another individual's property. Thus the background principle of private nuisance helps to define both the extent and limits of rights in property.

Public Nuisance

In addition, there are preexisting rights shared by all members of the public that condition the use of private property. The law of public nuisance encompasses a grab bag of harms to the public in general, some of which can result from the use of private property. Private property rights never include a right to use one's property in a way that poses unreasonable and substantial risks of harm to the general public. The remedies for such invasions of the public right are regulation and criminal prosecution by the state. Although they share in the public right, like the non-Hohfeldian objectors to properly enacted legislation, individuals have no personal right to object unless they also suffer distinct personal harm in the nature of a private nuisance.

In its earliest formulation, public nuisance was an infringement of the rights of the Crown. By the fourteenth century, the concept had broadened to include invasion of public rights represented by the Crown and remedied by criminal prosecution. Harms that could be remedied by an action in public nuisance encompassed interference with the public health, safety, morals, peace, and comfort—thus truly a grab bag of offenses allowing much discretion in the courts to regulate private activities that caused widespread harm. The only constraint on creative judges was that the offending activity had to be so unreasonable as to constitute a criminal offense. Thus, activities that caused incidental harm to others but that were widely practiced or generally accepted as important to the employment and economy of the community were not considered public nuisances because they were not unreasonable. There were *damnum absque injuria*—loss without injury.

Because the difference between private and public nuisance is that a private right is infringed in the former and a public right is violated in the latter, the concept of public rights has been ubiquitous in the law of public nuisance. But neither in the cases nor the legal commentary is the concept of public rights defined. The presumption seems to be that whatever makes an action sufficiently antisocial to constitute a crime also defines a violation of public right sufficient to constitute a public nuisance. This understanding is confirmed by the gradual replacement of public nuisance by statutory criminal regulation. In some states that transition is complete and actions for public nuisance no longer lie, but in others the common law action survives, and everywhere the concept of public nuisance lives on.

The Restatement of Torts defines a public nuisance as "an unreasonable interference with a right common to the general public." Three factors are said to determine whether there has been such an unreasonable interference: (1) whether there has been a "significant interference" with the public health, safety, peace, comfort or convenience, (2) whether the conduct is prohibited by statute, ordinance or regulation, and (3) whether the conduct is continuing or has had a permanent or long-lasting effect on the public right.[48] This provision seeks to establish boundaries on the scope of this amorphous tort, but does nothing to define the concept of public right.

It is not surprising, therefore, that particular interests unsuccessful in achieving all that they seek from legislative and regulatory authorities have appealed to the courts for intervention in the name of public nuisance. The most recent and audacious such appeals have come from environmental interests in the form of a national barrage of lawsuits asserting that everything from the filling of wetlands to carbon emissions are public nuisances (as well as violations of the public trust, see below) that should be curtailed by judicial decree.

To the extent that courts agree to apply historic public nuisance principles to the complex interrelationships of modern life, they will unavoidably upset the vested rights systems upon which the economy depends. Indeed a major reason public nuisance law has been widely displaced by statute and regulation is that judges have little competence, and most lack the inclination, to be lawmakers. As the protection of public rights has come to be understood as little different from pursuit of the public interest, it has become increasingly clear that definition and enforcement of public rights is the business of legislators rather than judges.

Justice Scalia understood that in *Lucas*. His reference to background principles was not meant to create an opening for judicial lawmaking. Rather it was to make the simple point that regulations prohibiting what the common law already prohibits cannot result in the taking of private property because there is nothing taken.

Public Trust

A second category of common law constraints on the use of private and public properties is also among Justice Scalia's background principles. Since the earliest colonial period, a public right of access to coastal and tidal waters for the purposes of navigation and fishing has been recognized, generally under the rubric of the public trust doctrine. Present-day proponents of expansive public rights in environmental protection and preservation look to this public trust doctrine as a broad background constraint on the use of land and other resources. To give their argument added heft, they claim that the doctrine has ancient provenance in Magna Carta and, before that, in Roman law.

While Roman and early English law actually provide very little precedent for American public trust law, even in its well-established sense of a public right of commercial navigation and fishing in navigable waters,[49] the doctrine did emerge in the seventeenth century in England and was adopted in the colonies. In England this public right of access for fishing and navigation extended to coastal waters and those affected by the tides. These hydrologic characteristics effectively encompassed all navigable waters. In America, with its many large interior rivers, the geographic scope of the doctrine was extended to include waters navigable-in-fact.

The practical effect of this public trust doctrine is that owners of riparian and submerged lands cannot obstruct navigation and fishing (and sometimes bathing) in the waters adjacent to or overlying their lands. Thus, while a riparian landowner has a right to "wharf out" for purposes of creating functional access to a navigable waterway, that right is limited by the condition that a dock or other associated structure may not obstruct public use of the waterway for navigation. Similarly, owners of submerged lands have a right to fill those lands (witness the large areas of many American cities built on fill), again subject to the public trust limits (and today subject to very restrictive state and federal regulations designed to preserve wetlands).

The public trust doctrine also limits government's use and disposition of lands adjacent to and beneath waters that are navigable in fact or affected by the tides. The classic Supreme Court case on the subject is *Illinois Central Railroad v Illinois.*[50] In 1869 the Illinois legislature granted most of the waterfront of the City of Chicago to the Illinois Central Railroad for the purposes of laying tracks and constructing docks and other facilities to link the railroad to commercial navigation on Lake Michigan. Four years later the legislature revoked the grant. The Railroad claimed that the revocation violated its contract and due process rights under the constitution. The Supreme Court ruled that, under Illinois law, the public trust doctrine precluded the State from making the grant in the first place because it infringed upon the public's right of access to Lake Michigan.

The *Illinois Central* case was infrequently cited by the Supreme Court over the ensuing decades, but the Court's understanding of the traditional public trust doctrine was embraced by most states as a background principle of their law of property as it applied to riparian and submerged lands. Coastal lands affected by the tides and lands riparian to navigable-in-fact rivers and lakes were held subject to the public trust, other riparian and submerged lands were not.

A related, but distinct, legal issue was title to riparian and submerged lands. Because lands affected by the tides and riparian to navigable waters were subject to the public trust, it made sense that the default ownership rule was that the states held original title to the submerged lands. This left open the determination of what lands are submerged, a question resolved differently by different states based on vegetation line, high or low water line or, or some other physical indicator. The default rule with respect to lands submerged beneath non-navigable waterways was that riparian landowners held title to the center (thread) of the stream or lake or to the entire bed if both sides were owned in a single parcel.

Modern advocates for expansive public rights based on the public trust doctrine have sought to link the public right of navigation and fishing to the bed ownership question as a means of limiting the state's power to alienate title to submerged lands. *Illinois Central*, they contend, is precedent for this position. But the Supreme Court held no such thing, nor could it have without overturning numerous precedents and explaining how it was that vast areas of submerged lands once owned by the states from the time of statehood were then in private ownership. *Illinois Central* does not stand for the principle that state lands subject to the public trust cannot be alienated. Rather it stands for the narrow principle that such lands cannot be alienated so as to interfere with the public right, which was the result in that case because almost the entire waterfront had been granted to the railroad. The 1869 Illinois grant to Illinois Central was invalid, not because the public trust doctrine precluded that state from alienating its submerged lands, but because the particular massive alienation in question interfered with public rights of navigation. The reality is that state-owned submerged lands were often alienated for the purpose of promoting navigation.

The public trust doctrine has been misunderstood or distorted in a second and more significant way by modern public rights advocates. Inspired by a 1970 law review article by Professor Joe Sax,[51] environmentalists have pressed to, in Sax's words, break the "historical shackles" of the public trust doctrine.[52] The historic doctrine is limited by two fairly precise parameters: it recognizes public rights in commercial navigation and fishing; and it applies, quite logically, only to waters that are navigable in fact. Obviously there can be no right to navigate on waters that are not navigable. Thus, to expand the doctrine's reach as a constraint on the use of public and private properties, both the uses guaranteed to the public and the geographic scope of the doctrine must be extended.

Innovative public trust theories range from protection of additional public uses (i.e. recreation and wildlife habitat preservation) on a much broadened geography (i.e. all waters tributary to navigable waterways), to court-ordered regulation of carbon emissions as a protection of a public right to be free from the effects of climate change. Once the historic shackles of the doctrine are broken, and there have been several courts willing to do the breaking, there is no limit to the possible scope of public rights that can be held to function as background principle limitations on the use of both public and private property.

The power of these public rights claims should not be underestimated. If public rights are understood to function as trumps on legislation and regulation and on the use of both public and private property because they are presumed to have existed from time immemorial, private rights and popular sovereignty are severely curtailed. Hence, the appeal of the public trust doctrine to self-described public interest groups. Rather than compete in the political process or in the market for property, they claim a trump on the former and an exemption from the latter. And no longer will friendly legislators and regulators hesitate for fear that their actions supporting special interests might be overturned in the courts as an unconstitutional taking. As Scalia made clear in *Lucas*, there can be no taking if nothing is taken.

Creative extension of public rights does not come without theoretical difficulty. It might be asked, for example, by what authority state courts can extend the reach of and the rights protected by the public trust doctrine. The standard response is that common law courts have always had the power to adapt the law to changing circumstances and public needs. While the need for continuing adaptation of the law is obvious, and common law courts have certainly made changes to the law over time, it is also obvious that without clear limits on this power of judicial law reform the rule of law is sacrificed to the rule of the judges. Just as the common law originated as judicial interpretations of existing customs and practices, judge-made changes in the law have generally reflected evolving customs and practices in the pursuit of established ends rather than mandate new directions thought by judges to serve the public interest.

Furthermore, any need for judicial initiative in the adaptation of law to changing circumstances is much reduced in a democratic republic where elected representatives are the constitutionally prescribed lawmakers and law reformers. Numerous foundational principles of American constitutional law—namely the prohibitions on uncompensated takings of property and impairment of contracts, the due process requirement and the proscription on ex post facto laws—stand as clear bars to the invention of new rights at the expense of existing rights.

Judicial pronouncement of new public rights as the natural evolutionary offspring of long-recognized and narrowly defined public trust rights is as much a violation of these constitutional principles as is any legislative act accomplishing the same illegitimate end.

CONCLUSION

Public rights claims come in three flavors, only one of which, properly understood, constitutes a legitimate limit on private property rights.

Public right, in the framers sense of public liberty, is the right shared by all people to be governed only by a government to which they have consented. There is a public right to popular sovereignty. It is a guarantee of equality in participation, not outcome, and of equal protection with respect both to the benefits and burdens of government. There is a public right to expect that the government to which they have consented will act to promote the public good and not the private interests of a few.

To be fully respectful of the private liberty from which public liberty arises, the rule of governance would be unanimity—an uncompromising approach that may work in traditional New England town meetings but is not practical in an extended republic. So we settle on rule by simple majority, except in the amendment of our constitutions. But recognizing the risks of majoritarian tyranny our constitutions restrain the majority through structure (like separation of powers) and trumps on the majority in the form of individual rights. The public right in this sense provides no justification for majority impositions on vested private rights.

Public right in the property of the state is the same. The public has a right to expect that the government to which they have consented will acquire, manage, and alienate land and other resources for the public good. The mere fact of state ownership does not imply particular constraints on legislative or executive authority different from whatever constraints apply to other government actions. To imply such constraints contradicts the principle of popular sovereignty.

Public rights founded in the common law are different, at least with respect to their relationship to private rights. Public nuisance and public trust do limit private property rights because they, by definition, predate all acquisitions of private property—they are background principles in Justice Scalia's formulation. All private rights in land are acquired subject to the public right that the land not be used to create a nuisance. All private rights in land submerged under or riparian to navigable waters are acquired subject to the public right of navigation and fishing. Thus, there is no basis for legal objection when the use of private property is prohibited as a public nuisance or a violation of the public trust.

Just as the public rights guaranteed in these background principles cannot be compromised for the benefit of private property owners without denying the existence of public right, so too the public rights of public nuisance law and the public trust doctrine cannot expanded without denying private right. It is true that the balancing aspect of public nuisance creates a vague boundary between the public and private rights. But there is a categorical difference between boundaries made less vague by decades of precedent and boundaries moved freely by well-intentioned, policy-making judges. Given its narrowly defined historic parameters and despite a recent spate of judicial creativity, the public trust doctrine is likely more resistant to change than public nuisance. But both doctrines will continue to be aggressively pressed as vehicles for judicial rewriting of the law of private property.

Efforts to expand public rights will persist because public rights promise to trump private rights, and even government policies. Why not take the more obvious and direct path of seeking legislation or constitutional amendments declaring new public rights? Because neither approach will overcome the obstacle of vested private property rights guaranteed by the self-same constitution. It is not plausible to contend that legislation or constitutional provisions enacted today establish public rights that have always existed. That is the wonder of these two common law doctrines, if only their historical shackles can be broken.

Chapter 5

Economic Liberties and the Presumption of Constitutionality

Protecting Property Rights—A Central Governmental Function

The framers of the American Constitution believed that a core function of government is the protection of private property rights. Early in the deliberations of the Philadelphia convention, James Madison urged that "[t]he primary objects of civil society are the security of property and public safety."[1] Alexander Hamilton said that "one great objt. Of Govt. Is personal protection and the security of Property."[2] Everyone else who spoke on the subject concurred, with the exception of James Wilson who "could not agree that property was the sole or the primary object of Governt. & Society," rather it was "[t]he cultivation & improvement of the human mind was the most noble object."[3] But even Wilson did not disagree that protection of property was an important governmental function.[4]

Perhaps some of the framers were concerned primarily with their own property rights and economic interests as Charles Beard argued a century ago,[5] and as Woody Holton argues in his recent book *Unruly Americans*.[6] But even if their motivations were not pure, they understood that property rights are meaningless without enforcement and that government is the only effective mechanism for protecting the rights of citizens in their relations with other citizens. At the same time, the framers understood, as the English had since Magna Carta, that government also poses a threat to private property. Ironically,

"Americans were not as secure in their property rights between 1776 and 1787 as they had been during the colonial period."[7] Because the new state legislatures were "less squeamish about invading private property rights" than their British forebears,[8] the framers learned first-hand of governmental threats to property rights. Corrupt public officials can use the substantial powers of government to deprive others of their property rights. Even well-intentioned government officials face strong political incentives to limit property rights in pursuit of their conception of the public interest and in service to the demands of their political supporters.

Notwithstanding this early American history of concern for property rights and the inclusion of explicit constitutional prohibitions on government interference with property and contract rights, economic liberties have not fared well over the last century of constitutional interpretation. Economic liberties have acquired a second-class status in the pantheon of American constitutional rights. They have been compromised and sacrificed to legislative and executive declarations of higher public needs. Though they would be disappointed in this turn in constitutional understanding, the framers of the Constitution would not be surprised and would likely have two explanations. One would be the early nineteenth-century abandonment of republican principles in favor of Jacksonian democracy, precisely the sort of unconstrained populism that dominated the state governments after the Revolution. The other would be the failure of the post–New Deal courts to enforce the clear mandates of the constitution.

Many who defend the modern court's indifference to economic liberties take the view that the framers were less concerned with property rights than with the creation of a strong central government able to rein in the states and provide for the national welfare. They point out that the original Constitution contained but two protections of economic liberties, only one of which related explicitly to property. Article I, Section 10 prohibits state legislatures from passing any "law impairing the obligation of contracts." Article IV, Section 2 required the return of fugitive slaves. By modern standards, the latter provision was a morally objectionable but perhaps necessary political compromise to allow for adoption of the constitution. By contemporary standards, although some objected on moral grounds, the fugitive slave provision was both politically pragmatic and a protection for widely held property rights in slaves.[9] Although the 13th Amendment effectively repealed Article IV, Section 2, by banning slavery throughout the United States, only two years earlier in 1863 President Lincoln gave serious consideration to compensation for slave owners whose slaves were freed under the Emancipation Proclamation.[10] While slavery and the idea of compensation for government-mandated emancipation are universally condemned today, the fact that compensation was seriously contemplated by a president engaged in a civil war resulting in part from disagreement over slavery evidences a strong commitment to property rights,[11] which had long been protected against federal confiscation by the 5th Amendment.

It should also be remembered that property rights were not the only individual liberty interest apparently neglected in the original constitution. There is very little in the document drafted in Philadelphia over the summer of 1787 relating to individual liberty, not because the framers were unconcerned with liberty, but because they all understood and agreed that the government they were forming had the protection of liberty as one of its central purposes. "Interferences with ... [the security of private rights, and the steady dispensation of Justice]," James Madison reminded his fellow delegates, "more perhaps than anything else, produced this convention."[12] Indeed, those delegates were so confident in the shared view that their proposal for a national government of limited powers protected rather than threatened liberty that, according to James Wilson of Pennsylvania, the lack of a bill of rights "never struck the mind of any member in the late convention till, I believe, within three days of the dissolution of that body, and even then of so little account was the idea that it passed off in a short conversation."[13] When the absence of a bill of rights later became an obstacle to ratification, Wilson asked of the Pennsylvania ratifying convention: "[W]ho will be bold enough to undertake to enumerate all the rights of the people?—and when the attempt to enumerate them is made, it must be remembered that if the enumeration is not complete, everything not expressly mentioned will be presumed to be purposely omitted."[14]

When it became clear that the Constitution would not be ratified by all 13 states without a bill of rights, it was agreed, in a remarkable act of faith, that the first business of the new Congress would be the enactment of a bill of rights to be submitted to the states for subsequent ratification. In the resulting document numerous liberties were guaranteed in ten provisions, the ninth of which made it clear that those rights enumerated in the prior eight "shall not be construed to deny or disparage others retained by the people." The ten amendments constituting the Bill of Rights, ratified by the states effective December 15, 1791, include three specific protections of private property. The 3rd Amendment prohibits the quartering of soldiers in private homes without the consent of the owner. The 4th Amendment prohibits unreasonable searches and seizures. The 5th Amendment provides: "nor shall any person . . . be deprived of life, liberty or property, without due process of law, nor shall private property be taken for public use, without just compensation." After the Civil War a fourth protection of private property was added to the Constitution in the 14th Amendment, which prohibits state governments to deprive individuals "of life, liberty or property, without due process of law." Although seemingly redundant with the 5th Amendment, the 14th Amendment guarantees were made necessary by the Supreme Court's earlier holding, in *Barron v. Baltimore*,[15] that the Bill of Rights was intended to apply only to the federal government.

This did not mean that prior to the 14th Amendment property rights were unprotected against intrusions by state governments. While only two states (Vermont and Massachusetts) had constitutional prohibitions on uncompensated takings at the time of the Philadelphia convention, the practice in every state, consistent with the common law, was to compensate when private land was taken for public use. The only widespread exception was in the case of undeveloped or "waste" lands that were often neglected by their owners and, in any event, had little economic value. By the time of the enactment of the 14th Amendment, every state, by constitutional provision or statute, required compensation when property was taken by the state, and many state courts had embraced the vested rights doctrine serving the same end.[16] Justice Joseph Story wrote in 1829 that he knew of no case in any state "in which a legislative act to transfer the property from A. to B. without his consent, has ever been held . . . constitutional."[17] Of course regulatory constraints on the use of property are not the same as government-mandated transfers from one person to another, but at a time when the regulation of private property mirrored common law constraints on the use of property, the idea of a regulatory taking would have made little sense. Justice Story and the state court judges on which he reported could not have imagined the regulatory ambitions of twentieth-century lawmakers.

CONSTITUTIONAL PROTECTIONS OF PROPERTY RIGHTS

In the 1897 case of *Chicago, Burlington & Quincy Railway Co. v. Chicago* the Supreme Court held that the Takings Clause of the 5th Amendment was "incorporated" in the due process guarantee of the 14th Amendment and is thereby applicable to the states.[18] Thus, both federal and state (including local) government limitations on property rights could be challenged in both state and federal courts under the 5th Amendment as applied to the states by the 14th Amendment. Another consequence of the incorporation of 5th Amendment property protections into the 14th Amendment Due Process Clause is that state courts must provide private property with at least as much protection as the US Supreme Court holds is required by the 5th Amendment. While the Supremacy Clause of Article VI, Clause 2 requires state compliance with Supreme Court interpretations of the US Constitution, states are free to provide more protection for property under their state constitutions. As will be evidenced in this and the next chapter, the Supreme Court has not developed a coherent approach to property rights claims and, in general, property owners have not fared well in their federal constitutional claims.

Most present-day debates over the nature and scope of constitutional protection for private property focus on the 5th Amendment language stating: "nor shall private property be taken for public use without just compensation." But the constitutional protection of property rights is more fulsome than a simple requirement that government pay for what it takes. The 3rd Amendment's ban on quartering soldiers and the 4th Amendment's constraint on searches and seizures evidence that property involves more than investment and expected financial return. Personal privacy, the right to be left alone and the right to exclude others, including the state, are essential to individual autonomy, freedom, and self-fulfillment. The due process guarantee of the 5th and 14th Amendments references property as well as life and liberty because, as Justice Stewart wrote in *Lynch v. Household Finance Co.*, a property right is "no less than the right to speak or the right to travel, . . . in truth a 'personal' right." "Property does not have rights," said Justice Stewart, "[p]eople have rights."[19]

The attributes of constitutionally guaranteed property rights are also what give property economic value. But as critics of market resource allocation invariably point out, not all values can be measured in dollars and cents. No one begins to imagine that compensation for lives lost or liberty denied fully repairs the harm done. Even when compensation is paid for pain and suffering, we know it is a rough approximation, at best, for harms that are really immeasurable in economic terms. When damages are paid in a wrongful death action or compensation is paid to an individual wrongfully imprisoned by the state, no one doubts that irreparable harm remains. The constitution's several guarantees of property rights make clear that compensation for property taken often leaves personal injury without remedy. There is no better demonstration of this deeply personal nature of property rights than the popular reaction to the *Kelo* case discussed in Chapter 2 of the companion volume, *Property Rights and State Power*. The City of New London could pay Susette Kelo the market value of her land, or much more than the market value, but by forcing her to sell the City nonetheless intruded upon her personal freedom in a way that a large majority of Americans found deeply offensive. Where the interests of the community warrant the taking of life and liberty, insistence on due process is the best we can do. Where community interests warrant the taking of private property, we have the good fortune to be able to mitigate the loss by financial compensation. But we deceive ourselves, particularly where homes and family businesses are involved, if we proceed as if nothing else is lost when property is taken.

WHAT THE TAKINGS CLAUSE SAYS

Various theories for interpreting the 5th and 14th Amendment property protections have been propounded by both academics and the courts. Many have attempted in vain to make sense of the Supreme Court's case law. Others have sought to develop a theory against which both federal and state case law can be evaluated. The most coherent such theory is that offered by Professor Richard Epstein who starts from the premise that property rights are fundamental and therefore can only be abridged under those conditions and processes set forth in the Constitution. The Due Process Clauses of the 5th and 14th Amendments forbid governmental deprivation of property unless done in compliance with the minimum process required by the Constitution and whatever process the government has chosen to impose on itself. Among the constitutionally prescribed processes is that set forth in the final clause of the 5th Amendment, a provision variously referred to as the "Takings," the "Compensation," or the "Eminent Domain" Clause.

Having reference to the literal language of the constitutional provision, Epstein says there are really four distinct issues to be addressed reflecting these different descriptions of the clause, which provides: "nor shall private property be taken for public use, without just compensation." According to Epstein, "nor shall private property be taken" poses two questions: has private property been taken? And, if so, is the taking justified by the police power of the state? As Justice Scalia made clear in the 1992 *Lucas* case,[20] these two questions are really one. To say that the police power justifies a taking of property is really to say there is no property right to the extent of that justification. As will be explained in the next chapter, this restatement of Epstein's four-step analysis does not alter its coherence, but it is important to correcting the Supreme Court's misguided reliance on a balancing test in most takings cases. The second phrase of the clause, "for public use," poses the question of whether a taking is for a public use, which requires the court to define what constitutes a public use. Finally, "without just compensation" poses the question of what compensation is just, a question that arises only where there has been a taking for a public use. In other words, private property can be taken by government *if* it is taken for a public use and *if* just compensation is provided. It seems straightforward enough, but the Supreme Court case law has been anything but straightforward in interpreting this language in particular cases.

THE ROOTS OF CONSTITUTIONAL BALANCING

The ambiguities of modern takings jurisprudence are rooted in the Supreme Court's longstanding fascination with balancing tests and the associated failure to provide bright-line rules based on the language of the Constitution. Early on the courts drew a broad distinction between exercises of the police power that constrain the use of private property and exercises of the eminent domain power that take private property for a public use. Compensation was required in eminent domain takings, but not for police power regulations, even where most or all use of private property was prohibited, because such regulations were designed to prevent harm to private and public interests. For example, in *Mugler v. Kansas*[21] the Court found no taking where the government's ban on liquor manufacture left the plaintiff's plant with little remaining value because the liquor ban served to protect public health and welfare. In *Hadacheck v. Sebastian*,[22] the Supreme Court found no unconstitutional taking where an ordinance forbade brick-making at an established factory after residential growth surrounding the factory made brick-making a noxious use, even though the value of the brick-maker's property decreased by more than 90 percent. As will be explained in greater depth in the next chapter, this distinction made sense so long as the police power was understood as the power of the state to enforce preexisting limits on rights of private action. Consistent with traditional understanding, police power regulations could not be takings because there never was a right to engage in the prohibited use or action.

But in 1922 the Supreme Court held that a particular police power regulation resulted in an unconstitutional taking. In *Pennsylvania Coal v. Mahon*, Justice Holmes wrote that "[g]overnment hardly could go on if to some extent values incident to property could not be diminished without paying for every such change in the general law."[23] But Holmes found that the Constitution does require compensation in some circumstances, including the instant case in which the state of Pennsylvania had required coal miners to leave sufficient underground support (generally in the form of unmined coal) for inhabited surface structures. In the words of Justice Holmes, "if regulation goes too far it will be recognized as a taking." Of course, there is nothing obvious about what is "too far", so the Holmes opinion in *Mahon* left the Court with little guidance in future cases. Indeed, more than a half century later, the Court found no taking under very similar facts and an almost identical Pennsylvania statute. The difference, wrote Justice Stevens for a 5–4 majority in *Keystone Bituminous Coal Ass'n v. DeBenedictis*,[24] was that the state had articulated several important public purposes promoted by the later statute, which together outweighed the harm to the property owner and thus did not go "too far."

The outcome in *Keystone* was not surprising to those who had followed takings jurisprudence since *Mahon*, but it was not consistent with Holmes's holding in that case. As will be explained in greater detail in the next chapter, Holmes meant to convey that regulations that go "too far" are only valid, and must be understood, as exercises of the eminent domain power for which compensation is due. But modern courts and commentators generally interpret Holmes's "too far" language to mean that some police power regulations result in unconstitutional takings while others do not. In terms of the outcome of any particular case, it makes no difference whether a taking is described as a police power regulation that has gone too far or as an exercise of the eminent domain power because it goes too far to be a legitimate exercise of the police power. In either case the property owner is compensated. But from an abstract property rights perspective, the difference is critical. Allowing that some police power regulations result in takings and others do not makes property rights contingent and the police power a source of government authority to do good as well as prevent harm. Insisting that legitimate exercise of the police power can never result in a taking, as Holmes did, makes the police power a source of government authority to prevent illegal harm by enforcing the defined limits of property rights. Consistent with this understanding of the police power is the conclusion that any legitimate governmental authority to limit or alter vested property rights derives from the eminent domain power. Holmes's "too far" test was, thus, intended to define the boundary between police power and eminent domain, not the boundary between police power regulations that are takings and those that are not. If the difference between *Mahon* and *Keystone* is, as Justice Stevens argued, that the state had more weighty interests in protecting surface estates in 1982 than in 1922, it is not a difference that would have mattered to Holmes. In both cases the subsurface owners had clear, vested rights to mine the coal. The fact that the public's interest in restricting those rights was greater later in the century was relevant only to the policy choice of whether or not to condemn the rights and bear the costs of compensation.

Property rights do not vary with the magnitude of the interests of others who covet but are excluded from the property. Had the property rights, including as defined by the police power, been different in the two cases it is possible, consistent with Holmes's view, that an identical statute would result in a taking in *Mahon* but not in *Keystone*. But that was not the basis of the *Keystone* Court's distinction. Rather the difference was that under the circumstances of *Mahon*, the state went "too far" in its exercise of the police power, while under the circumstances of *Keystone* it had not. But too far did not mean the state had exceeded its police power. It meant only that the state had to pay just compensation. *Keystone* thus confirmed that, contrary to *Mahon*, police power regulations were no longer limited to the enforcement of preexisting constraints on private rights. Police power had become the source of the state's authority to pursue all manner of public purposes with compensation to be paid to affected property owners not on the basis of their vested rights, but on a judicial determination of whether the state has gone too far in affecting those rights. Although this view of the police power is consistent with late nineteenth- and twentieth-century understandings of the sources of state government powers (as explained in Chapter 2), it led to the abandonment of the clear, previous, distinction between police power regulations and eminent domain takings in favor of a balancing of public and private interests.

This balancing understanding of the *Mahon* opinion continues still today as the prevailing approach to takings claims, and Holmes earned some of the blame given that the "too far" test invited balancing whether distinguishing one police power regulation from another or distinguishing the police power from the eminent domain power. But Holmes did suggest a useful approach for connecting the takings and compensation questions and thus salvaging something of the 5th Amendment's property rights guarantee. Some regulations, said Holmes, offer an "average reciprocity of advantage"[25]—meaning that those suffering the burdens of regulation also experience roughly proportionate benefits from the regulation—and therefore present no takings problem. As Professor Epstein would explain the matter, those regulated have suffered a taking, but the benefits they experience constitute implicit compensation and therefore satisfy the constitutional requirement. Thus, it is not the case that an interpretation of the Takings Clause favorable to property owners will make regulation impossible or too costly. Many regulations provide relatively equal benefits to those regulated—average reciprocity of advantage as Justice Holmes described it, thus allowing much of what government does to "go on" unimpeded by the rights of property owners. What should be forbidden by the Takings Clause is, as Holmes said in *Mahon*, uncompensated regulation that benefits many while imposing the costs on one or a few.

In the decade following the *Mahon* decision, the Supreme Court decided a handful of property cases under both the Due Process and Takings Clauses. The outcome under due process was a rational basis test with the burden on the property owner to prove that no reasonable legislator would find a plausible connection between the public purpose sought and the regulatory means employed. Under takings, a property owner had the burden of demonstrating that regulation had gone too far. Although the Court provided no standards for determining how far is too far, the facts of the cases made clear that the regulatory destruction of most of the value of a property was not too far. In *Miller v. Schoene*[26] the Court held that compensation was not owed to property owners whose cedar trees were destroyed to protect neighboring apple orchards from cedar rust. The public interest in preserving the apple orchards, concluded the Court, was sufficient to justify the burden on cedar tree owners. In *Village of Euclid v. Ambler Realty Co.*[27] the Court upheld a zoning ordinance against a due process challenge, finding it rational for the legislature to conclude that the public interest in segregating land uses justified limits on property use that diminished property values by as much as 75 percent.

Two years later in *Nectow v. City of Cambridge*[28] the Court found that a zoning ordinance that reduced a property value to almost nothing violated the Due Process Clause, not because the property value was almost totally lost but because the restrictions placed on the plaintiff's property had no substantial impact on the public interest promoted by the regulation. This requirement that the chosen means somehow promote the claimed public purpose flowed logically from the utilitarian calculus inherent in asking whether a regulation has gone too far. Too far in relation to what? The clear implication since *Mahon* had been that a regulation might go too far and result in a taking if the public benefits realized were slight in relation to the resulting private costs. Under those circumstances government could pursue the regulation but it might have to pay for the harm done. But if there was no public benefit at all, government was precluded by the Due Process Clause from enforcing the regulation. Although the property owners prevailed under the too far test of *Mahon* and the means–ends test of *Nectow*, neither case provided a strong foundation for protecting property rights in general. It is a simple matter for legislatures to assert that their regulatory means serve legitimate ends and to claim public benefits that outweigh the interests of the private claimant. Seldom will the one prevail against the many absent the trump of individual liberty.

ACTIVIST GOVERNMENT AND THE DECLINE OF ECONOMIC LIBERTIES

With the onset of the New Deal and more activist government at both the federal and state levels, the Supreme Court's property rights jurisprudence was founded on two basic propositions: (1) to comply with due process, a regulation limiting property rights must have some rational relation to achieving the purpose of the regulation, and (2) regulations of property satisfying this due process requirement are valid unless they go "too far." Not surprisingly, the dramatic, mid-1930s, shift in the Supreme Court's views on the constitutional scope of federal powers was accompanied by nearly four decades of near-silence on the 5th Amendment Takings Clause. Activist government was on the ascendency leaving little room for claims of economic liberty that might stand in the way of expanding regulation.

In the spirit of the New Deal, and absent judicial intervention in the name of constitutionally protected property rights, legislators and administrators imposed ever greater restraints on private property in pursuit of the public good (and in service to future success at the ballot box). Property rights scholar Jan Laitos writes that this extended period of judicial deference to steadily more restrictive regulation of property was rooted in two basic assumptions deriving from what he calls "republicanism ideology": (1) "[p]rivate property is an inferior right" and (2) "[t]he judiciary is less capable than the legislature in matters involving economics and property."[29] Although Laitos suggests, optimistically, that beginning in the 1980s both of these assumptions "have been challenged by property owners, commentators, and ultimately, the courts," a few moments' reflection is warranted for two reasons. First, both ideas identified by Laitos have influenced Supreme Court jurisprudence well beyond the realm of property rights. Second, as we will see in this and the next chapter, notwithstanding the challenges beginning in the 1980s, property rights claims continue to struggle for respect even in a Court with a sometimes conservative majority.

The idea that economic (including property) rights are inferior to other constitutionally protected rights is part and parcel of the modern Supreme Court's methodology in individual rights cases. Seventy years ago in the case of *United States v. Carolene Products*, Justice Stone stated for the majority that it "is to be presumed, for regulatory legislation affecting ordinary commercial transactions . . . that it rests upon some rational basis within the knowledge and experience of the legislators."[30] This brief statement reflected both assumptions noted by Laitos and placed property rights in a constitutional hole from which they have yet to, and may never, fully emerge. Two often restated principles of modern constitutional doctrine have derived from Stone's brief statement. One is a presumption that legislation is constitutionally valid, on which the rational basis test is grounded. The other is a secondary status for economic liberties, deriving from Stone's reference to commercial transactions.

Levels of Scrutiny Analysis

In perhaps the most famous footnote in American judicial history, Justice Stone elaborated, in an almost off-handed manner, on what might limit the presumption of constitutionality. He suggested that "[t]here may be narrower scope for operation of the presumption . . . when legislation appears on its face to be within a specific prohibition of the Constitution, such as those of the first ten Amendments."[31] One might reasonably conclude from this suggestion that a 5th Amendment takings claimant would prevail or at least warrant greater than rational basis review, but that was not Stone's conclusion. Rather he effectively confirmed that economic liberties, even if express in the Bill of Rights, are inferior to civil and political liberties. Stone also suggested that "legislation which restricts those political processes which can ordinarily be expected to bring about repeal of undesirable legislation" might . . . "be subjected to more exacting judicial scrutiny . . . than are most other types of legislation."[32] In this regard he had in mind legislation discriminating against "discrete and insular minorities," but that certainly was not intended to include property owners or those engaged in ordinary commercial transactions.

At the time, *Carolene Products* seemed a rather innocent and insignificant decision. Carolene Products objected that a federal prohibition on the interstate shipment of filled milk, a product containing coconut oil as well as natural milk products, exceeded Congress's power under the Commerce Clause and violated their property rights under the 5th Amendment. Even if the law was really designed to benefit dairy farmers at the expense of the competition rather than to protect health, it was not the sort of issue likely to agitate the public. But the *Carolene Products* opinion has had far-reaching impacts. It provided the foundation for varying levels of judicial scrutiny in constitutional cases and for the prioritization of constitutional rights and plaintiffs. If you can allege the violation of a fundamental right or that you are a member of a suspect class, you will earn strict scrutiny, which generally means you win and the government loses. However, if you are claiming the violation of a non-fundamental right and/or you lack any special minority status, the legislation you object to will be presumed constitutional, the rational basis test will be applied, and you will lose.

Although there have been some refinements of this either–or approach in recent years in the form of intermediate levels of scrutiny, economic liberty claims have not benefitted. The effect of a sliding scale of judicial scrutiny is to raise or lower the burden on those challenging government action. Economic liberty claims continue to bear an almost insurmountable burden in the face of the presumption of constitutional validity granted to economic and social legislation.

Although the property owner prevailed in the 1922 *Mahon* case, Holmes's opinion in that case and Stone's opinion in *Carolene Products* are two peas in the pod of present-day judicial balancing in constitutional jurisprudence. In the world of constitutional balancing, rights are no longer trumps, as Ronald Dworkin described them.[33] They are just some of the many values that must compete for political favor, with judges in the peculiar position of deciding which are more important. But where in the language or history of the Constitution is it even suggested that individual rights are to be ranked in order of importance or that the courts have authority to effectively waive those rights when, in the view of the court, individual liberty is outweighed by a public purpose? Where in the Constitution does it provide or imply that courts are to scrutinize some constitutional claims more carefully than others on the basis of the nature or source of those claims? Levels of scrutiny analysis is just balancing under cover of seeming judicial principle—a license for judicial lawmaking. In the absence of constitutional rankings of liberties or rights claimants, levels of scrutiny analysis has no better grounding than the policy and personal preferences of the judges who establish what level of deference to allow the legislature.

It has been argued, perhaps most persuasively by John Hart Ely,[34] that strict judicial scrutiny is appropriate where the rights of what Justice Stone labeled "discrete and insular minorities" are claimed to be infringed. The argument is rooted in the assumption that individuals who have a minority status (particularly one that has been the basis of historic discrimination) that prevents them from assembling a majority of individuals sharing that status are more likely to have their rights violated by majority action. Of course the parallel assumption is that democratically enacted laws are unlikely to violate the rights of ordinary individuals because a majority of those individuals will not agree to having their constitutional rights infringed. Special judicial care to guard against majoritarian discrimination against individuals of minority racial and ethnic backgrounds is certainly warranted in a society with a history of such state-sponsored denial of rights. But the general proposition that similar judicial care is not otherwise required is flawed in at least two respects. First, there is no evidence that political majorities in a totally homogeneous society are disinclined to use the power of the state for the benefit of those in the majority, even when the rights of people like themselves are compromised. To the contrary, as evidenced by the recent success of Oregon's Measure 49 revoking rights previously recognized by Measure 37, the tyranny of the majority is what should be presumed. Second, the assumption that people of a minority race or ethnicity will be of a single mind that destines them for minority status in the political process denies the very individuality that makes both rights and participation in democracy meaningful. The reality is that political majorities, whatever their defining characteristics, have strong incentives to employ the powers of the state for partisan and personal advantage. When that advantage comes at the expense of the rights of others, strict judicial scrutiny should always be the rule.

A Presumption of Constitutionality

Under current Supreme Court doctrine, however, rational basis review is the default approach. This means that the question for a court faced with a claim of unconstitutionality is whether challenged legislation could reasonably be thought to serve legitimate governmental ends. In the case of a government of enumerated powers like the federal government, one might argue that the ends sought are not within those enumerated. But, as the history of the Commerce Clause evidences, the Supreme Court has almost always deferred to Congress's claim to have acted pursuant to one constitutional power or another. Similar deference is given to Congressional and state legislative determinations that the means chosen are reasonably related to the ends sought. Thus, unless you can demonstrate that your rights claim is fundamental or that you are of a suspect class, rational basis review is what you get and that means the law you are challenging will be presumed to be constitutional.

As with many other fundamental principles of judicial review, Chief Justice John Marshall is often cited as authority for the presumption of constitutionality. "The question, whether a law be void for its repugnancy to the constitution," wrote Marshall in the 1810 case of *Fletcher v. Peck*, "is, at all times, a question of much delicacy, which ought seldom, if ever, to be decided in the affirmative, in a doubtful case."[35] Marshall applied that principle in refusing to invalidate a Georgia law widely alleged to have been fraudulently enacted on the strength of many promises of favors to legislators and others of influence. But he then went on to hold that a subsequent Georgia statute designed to remedy the perceived fraud of the earlier law resulted in an unconstitutional impairment of the state's obligation of contracts in violation of Article I, Section 10 of the US Constitution. Would Marshall have explained that the presumption of constitutionality applied to both laws, but that the unconstitutionality of the latter was beyond doubt? Or would he have said that the presumption of constitutionality applies where courts are asked to second guess the legitimacy of legislative motives, but not where legislative action is claimed to have violated individual rights? Of course we cannot know Marshall's meaning with certainty, but he did find that

> the state of Georgia was restrained, either by general principles which are common to our free institutions, or by the particular provisions of the constitution of the United States, from passing a law whereby the estate of the plaintiff in the premises so purchased could be constitutionally and legally impaired and rendered null and void.[36]

This is not a statement suggesting deference to the legislature. Rather it reflects a deep-seated belief in the fundamental importance of the economic liberties of property and contract, whether or not explicitly protected by the Constitution. "All titles would be insecure," said Marshall, "and the intercourse between man and man would be very seriously obstructed, if this principle be overturned."[37]

Notwithstanding Marshall's vigorous assertion of the judicial power to protect the economic liberties of innocent purchasers of fraudulently granted property, the presumption of constitutionality would today, in all probability, lead the Supreme Court to uphold a law like that invalidated in *Fletcher*. "It is well established," said the Court in *Hughes v. Alexandria Scrap*, "that a statutory classification impinging upon no fundamental interest, and *especially one dealing only with economic matters*, need not be drawn so as to fit with precision the legitimate purposes animating it."[38] Legislation dealing with "economic matters" usually involves regulation of economic interests in property and contract, but the assertion of constitutional rights in property and contract does not elevate one's claim above rational basis review. In *Hodel v. Indiana*[39] the Court presumed the constitutionality of a federal land reclamation law in the face of a Commerce Clause challenge, but contrary to Chief Justice Marshall's approach in *Fletcher*, Justice Thurgood Marshall went on to reject equal protection and takings claims based on a "presumption of rationality that can only be overcome by a clear showing of arbitrariness and irrationality."

Although a few recent cases suggested that property rights might rise above the nullifying consequence of the presumption of constitutionality, a majority confirmed in *Kelo* that economic liberties remain entitled to little judicial protection. In *Lucas v. South Carolina Coastal Council*, where the court held that regulation resulting in a total loss of economic value was a per se taking, Justice Blackmun objected that the majority was interfering with the legislative prerogative and that "the presumption of constitutionality must prevail."[40] In *Dolan v. Tigard*, Chief Justice Rehnquist took a weak stab at distancing property rights claims from the rational basis test applied to economic regulations,[41] but Justice Stevens objected that the challenged "exactions associated with the development of a retail business are . . . a species of business regulation that heretofore warranted a strong presumption of constitutional validity."[42] The dissenters again gained the upper hand in *Kelo*. Swing voter Justice Kennedy, like Blackmun in *Lucas* and Stevens in *Dolan*, insisted that the case was governed by the "deferential standard of review [that] echoes the rational-basis test used to review economic regulation under the Due Process and Equal Protection Clauses."[43]

In describing the scope of the presumption of constitutionality leading to rational basis review, the Supreme Court has avoided explicit assertions that infringements of economic liberties are presumed to be constitutional. Rather, the Court has obscured the second-class status of economic liberties by stating, as it did in *Hughes*, that rational basis review applies to challenges to economic and social legislation. There was a time, however, when the Court was explicit in speaking about constitutional protection of economic liberties. That time has come to be called the *Lochner* era, and it is generally remembered today as a period of judicial activism of the worst kind. While *Carolene Products* laid the foundation for modern levels of scrutiny analysis, it was also an important part of the Supreme Court's gradual rejection of *Lochner* era substantive due process, a change in direction that relied on deferential review of the abundant economic legislation of the New Deal.

In *Lochner v. New York* the Supreme Court invalidated a regulation limiting weekly and daily hours of work as an infringement of the right to contract, held to be a liberty protected by the 14th Amendment Due Process Clause.[44] That view, which came to be labeled "substantive due process," was significantly altered 30 years later in *Nebbia v. New York* where, in upholding regulation of the price of milk, the Court stated that "[s]o far as . . . due process is concerned, . . . a state is free to adopt whatever economic policy may reasonably be deemed to promote public welfare."[45] As with the modern cases favoring judicial deference, the *Nebbia* court said nothing to suggest that economic liberties had junior status among constitutional rights, but that was the effect of deferential review of "economic policy" enactments. Over the next several decades *Lochner* was repeatedly repudiated as a worst case example of judicial activism, although in *Griswold v. Connecticut* and subsequent cases substantive due process was revived in service of a right of privacy.[46] The continued rejection of *Lochner* was said to be based upon that court's failure to give proper deference to economic and social legislation. But the court's privacy jurisprudence, including *Roe v. Wade*[47] (abortion) and *Lawrence v. Texas*[48] (sexual privacy), confirms that the Court continues to distinguish between economic and personal liberties behind a facade of deference to economic and social legislation.

Even a cursory review of Supreme Court decisions evidences that social and economic legislation is often subjected to strict scrutiny. Indeed, the legislation challenged in *Griswold*, *Roe*, and *Lawrence* can be described as economic and social—regulating contraceptive use, abortion, and homosexual sodomy in the asserted interests of public health and social welfare. Where free speech, free exercise of religion, or equal protection are denied as a consequence of economic or social legislation, there is no suggestion that the offending laws are presumed to be constitutional. It is true that within the free speech and equal protection doctrine, a lesser standard of review applies in some cases. But those cases do not receive less probing scrutiny because the laws challenged are economic or social. Rather the state gets the benefit of a presumption of constitutionality because of the economic nature of the private interests claimed to be infringed. For example, a regulation intended to avoid disruptions to social and economic intercourse receives a strict scrutiny if political speech is constrained but a less probing review if commercial speech is affected. Similarly under the equal protection doctrine, an economic or social regulation that discriminates is subjected to strict scrutiny if a fundamental right is limited, but only rational basis review if businesses are precluded from contracting with whom and on the terms they choose.

Clearly, it is not economic and social legislation that is presumed to be constitutional. It is any legislation impacting on economic liberties that benefits from a presumption of constitutionality. The Supreme Court may be unwilling to say that economic liberties warrant less judicial protection than political and civil liberties, but that is what the bulk of their case law has held. As noted above, Justice Stewart rejected this distinction in *Lynch v. Household Finance*, but the second-class status of economic liberties persists nonetheless. A brief explanation of where the distinction originated in Supreme Court jurisprudence is instructive.

In the obscure 1939 case of *Hague v. Committee for Industrial Organization*,[49] the Court was faced with determining whether a statutory, jurisdictional requirement that at least $3,000 be at stake precluded federal court review of claimed violations of free speech and assembly that could not be proven to have any particular economic value. Evidencing that an inability to piece together an opinion to which not even a bare majority will agree is not the exclusive province of the modern Court, seven participating justices rendered five opinions with no more than two signing on to any one opinion. Justice Stone, of recent *Caroline Products* fame, wrote one of those opinions with the concurrence of Justice Reed. In an effort to resolve a perceived conflict between two jurisdictional provisions, Stone concluded that "whenever the right or immunity is one of personal liberty, not dependent for its existence upon the infringement of property rights, there is jurisdiction in the district court under §24(14) of the Judicial Code to entertain it without proof that the amount in controversy exceeds $3,000."[50] It appears that Stone meant to suggest that, because property rights are not personal liberties, property claims under the Constitution must satisfy the $3,000 minimum. However, earlier in his opinion he stated that "[s]ince freedom of speech and freedom of assembly are rights secured to persons by the Due Process Clause, all of the individual respondents are plainly authorized by s 1 of the Civil Rights Act of 1871 to maintain the present suit in equity to restrain infringement of their rights."[51] The fact that property rights, both explicitly and by incorporation, are also guaranteed by the Due Process Clause should have given pause if, indeed, Justice Stone did mean to say that property rights are of lesser constitutional import. In any event, Stone's distinction in *Hague* was relied upon in subsequent cases until Justice Stewart pointed out in *Lynch* that there was never a conflict between the jurisdictional provisions and that, more importantly, the distinction was artificial as evidenced by the ongoing difficulty the courts faced with trying to distinguish personal liberty cases in which there was no jurisdictional minimum from property rights cases to which the minimum was said to apply.

From these arcane decisions on the meaning of Congressional legislation, now more than a century and a quarter old, emerged a classification of constitutional liberties that has had significant repercussions for property and contract rights. It is a distinction that has persisted in American constitutional jurisprudence notwithstanding a dearth of persuasive justification and despite the obvious importance of economic liberties in the day-to-day life of every citizen. The impact of the distinction between economic and personal liberties will be evident in the discussion of the takings doctrine that follows. As a preface to that discussion, Justice Stewart's statement from *Lynch* bears repeating:

> [T]he dichotomy between personal liberties and property rights is a false one. Property does not have rights. People have rights. The right to enjoy property without unlawful deprivation, no less than the right to speak or the right to travel, is in truth, a 'personal' right, whether the 'property' in question be a welfare check, a home, or a savings account. In fact, a fundamental interdependence exists between the personal right to liberty and the personal right in property. Neither could have meaning without the other. That rights in property are basic civil rights has long been recognized.[52]

If by "long recognized" Justice Stewart means to say that the framers of the Constitution viewed property rights as civil rights, he is surely correct. But there is little evidence in recent property rights jurisprudence that the view persists in American courts. Although, over the last three decades, there have been occasional indications that property rights might again have the respect of the courts, property rights claimants have generally been abandoned to the twin assumptions noted by Professor Laitos: property rights remain inferior and legislation affecting property rights is presumed to be constitutional.

SEARCHING FOR "TOO FAR"

In the 1978 case of *Penn Central Transportation Co. v. City of New York*,[53] the Court could find no clear guidance in its prior cases to help in deciding whether a historic preservation ordinance that prohibited Penn Central from building in the airspace above Grand Central Terminal resulted in an unconstitutional taking. There is no "set formula to determine where regulation ends and taking begins," said the Court, leaving it to make "essentially ad hoc, factual inquiries."[54] The Court looked at various factors relating to both the economic impacts on Penn Central and the benefits to New York of an unaltered Grand Central Terminal in concluding that there was no unconstitutional taking. In an attempt to provide guidance in future cases, the *Penn Central* court stated that:

> The economic impact of the regulation on the claimant and, particularly, the extent to which the regulation has interfered with reasonable investment-backed expectations are... relevant considerations. So, too, is the character of the governmental action. A "taking" may more readily be found when the interference with property can be characterized as a physical invasion by government than when interference arises from some public program adjusting the benefits and burdens of economic life to promote the common good.[55]

This statement is the basis for what has come to be called the *Penn Central* balancing test, the application of which is supposed to tell a court whether government has gone "too far" in restricting the use of property.

But there is nothing in *Penn Central* to guide the decision of future cases, other than the particular facts of *Penn Central* that are certain to be different from the particular facts of every other case. We do know from earlier cases that the loss of most of the economic value of property does not necessarily mean a taking has occurred. But do the particular economic circumstances of the claimant matter? Did it matter that Penn Central was a very large corporate entity with extensive properties, albeit one having declared bankruptcy less than a decade earlier? Would the result be different if the property on which Grand Central sits previously had been donated to the Salvation Army, which planned to use the revenues from a new high-rise tower to fund programs for the poor? What if Penn Central had donated the air rights to the Salvation Army so that the denial of a permit would compromise the entire value of the property right? The Court had insisted that it must look at the property as a whole, not at individual sticks in the bundle,[56] but if the only stick in a property owner's bundle is air rights, it would then be the whole property. The New York Court of Appeals had noted that Penn Central owned other properties in Manhattan that benefitted from its ownership of Grand Central,[57] so even if the existing use of the terminal property was an economic loser, there was no taking. The Supreme Court did not embrace this wealth-focused idea, but it did not reject it either.

And what about the other side of the "too far" balance—the government's side? If the government builds a road or a school, all agree that it must pay for property taken. *Penn Central* tells us that when government seeks to preserve historic property, it does not have to pay, at least not under the particular facts of that case. Does that mean that roads and schools are less important than historic preservation? That would seem to be the logical conclusion if the point of a balancing test is that greater weight on the side of government's purposes serves to justify uncompensated constraints on property. But where is the logic in saying that government need not pay when its purposes are really important but it must when they are only somewhat or a little bit important. Shouldn't government be most willing and anxious to pay when what it seeks to accomplish is really important? Isn't that when citizens and taxpayers get the most benefit at the expense of others? Not surprisingly, as the *Penn Central* majority noted, among municipal and state governments the preferred method of historic preservation is regulation rather than public acquisition.[58] But why wouldn't it be, if the perceived public benefits, no matter how important, can be realized at the expense of private property owners rather than the public fisc.

Rather than providing guidance in identifying regulations that go too far, the *Penn Central* balancing test, like most constitutional balancing tests, leaves the courts with wide discretion on questions of both policy and law. In stating that historic preservation regulation is an aspect of "adjusting the benefits and burdens of economic life," the *Penn Central* majority confirmed that economic liberties are little more than special interests that must compete in the give and take of politics. In this respect *Penn Central* is consistent with the philosophy espoused in *Carolene Products* and reflected in the Supreme Court's post–New Deal approval of activist government. From the perspective of individual liberty, it is disappointing but not surprising. The compromise of liberty claims is inherent in any constitutional balancing test that pits individual rights against government purposes. As Holmes suggested in *Mahon*, constitutional rights and government purposes do sometimes conflict, and he was not wrong to suggest that "[g]overnment hardly could go on if to some extent values incident to property could not be diminished without paying for every such change in the general law."[59] But values incident to property are not the same thing as rights in property. There may be values in property to which the owner can claim no enforceable right. Drawing that distinction, not balancing rights against public purposes, should be the task of judicial review. But in the tradition of Holmes's "too far" test from *Mahon*, the *Penn Central* majority treated property rights as malleable in the hands of judges.

The idea that economic rights are little more than private interests to be respected (or not) by political majorities, but not protected by the courts, was suggested by Holmes in his dissent in *Lochner*. He described as "a shibboleth for some well-known writers" the claim that every citizen can and should have the liberty "to do as he likes so long as he does not interfere with the liberty of others to do the same." Rather he claimed a position of judicial restraint in asserting "the right of a majority to embody their opinions in law . . . [and to] regulate life in many ways . . . which, equally with this, interfere with the liberty to contract."[60] But in what sense does one have a right if a majority of fellow citizens, no less than a king or potentate, can deny its exercise? A right subject to the will of whomever governs, unless by unanimous consent, is no right at all. This does not mean that liberty has no limits. Well-known writers have made the claim of equal liberty because unequal liberty cannot be justified. American constitutional history is forever blemished by the unjustifiable denial of equal liberty, most notably to blacks and women. But to say that the liberty of one must be the liberty of all is not to claim that liberty is unlimited. Liberty is necessarily limited to assure equal liberty and can be (and often is) limited in the name of the public good. The problem with the *Penn Central* balancing test and Holmes's "too far" test is a failure to recognize that rights, whatever they may be, are trumps on the legislative process, not mere private interests to be balanced against whatever legislatures might seek to accomplish.

A Principled Exception to an Unprincipled Rule

Finally, it should be noted that the *Penn Central* majority also suggested what has become one of two regulatory contexts to which the balancing approach would not apply: "A 'taking' may more readily be found when the interference with property can be characterized as a physical invasion by government."[61] This seemingly obvious proposition was confirmed as a categorical taking four years later in *Loretto v. Teleprompter Manhattan CATV Corp.*[62] Although the impact on property values in *Loretto* was insignificant compared to the losses sustained by Penn Central in not being permitted to build in the valuable New York air space, the Court held that the mandatory installation of television cables on Loretto's property constituted a physical invasion and therefore an unconstitutional taking. Thus the Court recognized a per se rule that a taking occurs whenever private property is physically occupied by the government or at the government's command. This result was not surprising in light of the universally accepted requirement of compensation where property is taken for public uses like roads and schools. Cable connections have become, after all, a critical part of the digital superhighway. Physical occupation of property has the effect of excluding the owner and thereby denying to the owner the most basic right of ownership—the right to exclude others.

But the *Loretto* result was surprising in light of the overarching balancing theme of *Penn Central.* In *Penn Central* the asserted public interest was in preserving what had become a landmark in the City of New York, although it was originally conceived as having a high-rise above it. Indeed at the heart of Grand Central Terminal is located what has come to be called a Schelling point, in honor of Nobel economist Thomas Schelling—it is the place in New York where most people would assume they should meet a friend in the absence of any communication about where to meet. So for many in the city the preservation of Grand Central Terminal, as they had experienced it, was, no doubt, a big deal. But denial of a permit to build wasn't just chickenfeed as far as Penn Central was concerned. They had negotiated an agreement that would bring in $1 million per year during construction and at least $3 million per year thereafter. Even for a big railroad company, but particularly for one recently bankrupt, there was a lot at stake. In *Loretto,* on the other hand, the economic stakes were smaller on both sides, but seemingly insignificant from the perspective of the property owner. The government sought to assure that everyone had access to cable, a reasonably important public purpose even before the launch of the internet. The economic cost to the property owner of allowing a cable to be attached to an external wall of the building was very nearly zero. Had the Court tried to estimate in dollars the public costs of an altered Grand Central Terminal, the amount might well have exceeded the $3 million per year expected by Penn Central, but there was no denying that the costs to the private claimant were nonetheless substantial. In *Loretto* there could be no doubt that the public benefits exceeded the private costs because the latter were virtually nonexistent. Yet it was a taking in *Loretto* and not in *Penn Central.*

The difference, as I have explained, is that *Loretto* escaped balancing on principle—the right to exclude was denied. But if principle governed the outcome in *Loretto*, can it also be said that principle determined the result in *Penn Central*. By what principle do we justify the taking of property rights worth at least $3 million in net annual revenues? Would a determination that the economic value to the public of preserving Grand Central Terminal is greater than the loss to Penn Central be a principled reason for not compensating? If so, wouldn't the same principle justify the uncompensated taking of land for a road providing public benefits in excess of the loss to the property owner? Of course in such a case the property owner can appeal to the principle of *Loretto* and on that basis receive compensation. But isn't the injury to Penn Central every bit as significant as the injury to a landowner to whom the government pays compensation in an eminent domain proceeding equal to the present value of a $3 million annual stream of income? Perhaps there is a sort of Robin Hood principle allowing for uncompensated takings from the wealthy but not from the poor. But the takings cases reflect no systematic method for making such a determination and even with the necessary financial information to make such decisions it would be an approach in direct conflict with the anti-redistribution purposes of the Takings Clause.

We are left to conclude that despite the vastly different economic impacts on the two plaintiffs, *Loretto* is different because it involved a government-mandated physical occupation of property while *Penn Central* involved only the loss of millions of dollars. While some might find the incongruence between financial impact and constitutional result troubling, at least it is a rule of decision that provides reasonable certainty for other property owners. But a clear rule with respect to a narrow category of takings claims does not cure the problems posed by the *Penn Central's* balancing. Absent a physical occupation of property by government or at its command, the task for the judge in a takings case is to determine whether or not a particular regulation has gone "too far" in light of the government purpose and the impact on the property owner. Neither *Mahon* nor *Penn Central*, nor any of the intervening cases, provides standards or guidance sufficient to qualify a judicial decision as based on the rule of law.

AN UNPRINCIPLED EXCEPTION TO AN UNPRINCIPLED RULE

What can be predicted with reasonable certainty is that the property owner is likely to lose in most takings cases to which the categorical exception of physical occupation does not apply. Actually, there has come to be a second categorical taking, but it is a category with little or no content so far as regulatory takings are concerned. In the 1980 case of *Agins v. City of Tiburon* the Court held that a taking occurs when regulation results in the loss of all "economically viable use of [a property owner's] land."[63] This rule, confirmed in the later case of *Lucas v. South Carolina Coastal Commission*,[64] would seem hard to disagree with. But in light of the many cases in which the Court has found no taking where regulation results in the loss of most of the economic value of property, perhaps a categorical rule where there is a total loss of economic value is not so obvious. What is the difference between the total loss of economic value in *Lucas*, where the property owner was precluded from building a home on a beach lot, and the 90 percent loss of economic value in *Hadacheck*, where the property owner was mandated to cease the production of bricks at a long-established brick factory? Ten percent, one might say, but is that, or 5 percent or 25 percent, a difference that can be justified on the basis of a principle worthy of constitutional jurisprudence?

The principle of the first categorical taking rule is clear: a physical occupation of property infringes on the right to exclude, which is an essential attribute of any property right. But what is the principle that explains why a 100 percent loss of economic value is a taking while a 90 percent—or perhaps even 99 percent—loss of economic value is not? Or for that matter, what is the principle that would explain why a 100 percent loss is a taking and just a 10 percent loss is not? In the latter case we might conclude that given the many variables impacting on the economic value of property, it is impossible to know with any degree of certainty whether a particular regulation is the cause of an apparent loss as small as 10 percent. But that is only a problem of proof explained by principles of evidence law, not takings law. What is the principle that allows for most, but not all, property value to be taken by regulation?

It is often commonly argued that no principle is needed—that regulatory impacts are no different from the multitude of other factors influencing property values. An extended drought will reduce the value of land for farming. A hurricane might destroy the farmer's barn and home. A subdivision next door may lead to new costs associated with the inevitable conflicts between urban homes and the sounds and smells of agriculture. These are the risks of investing in property, and there is nothing to distinguish them from the risk that government might impose new or different regulations. But this argument misses the point of constitutional government and the rule of law. The fact of uncertainty does not doom us to our unmitigated fates. We take measures to reduce the risks of drought and hurricane, and we take measures to reduce the risks of social interaction, including between individuals and government. Private contract and constitutional government under the rule of law both serve to reduce the uncertainties inherent in unregulated human interaction. Just because there are risks associated with the ownership of property, there is no principled reason to insist that the particular risk of changing legal rules should be borne entirely by individual property owners rather than government and its taxpaying citizens.

Perhaps an analogy to taxation of property will lead us to a principle that explains the difference between a 100 percent loss of value and some small percentage less than that. In justifying the result in *Penn Central*, Justice Brennan notes that "[e]xercises of the taxing power are one obvious example" of governments' legitimate adverse effects on "recognized economic values."[65] Brennan's point is that routine property taxes that effectively take some of the value of property are clearly constitutional. But certainly a tax equal to 100 percent of the value of property would be viewed as confiscatory and in violation of the Due Process Clause. Surely a tax equal to 90 percent of a property's value would also be considered confiscatory. Indeed, to satisfy due process requirements property taxes must represent no more than the reasonable rents the property might generate in an average year. Otherwise it would be ultimately confiscatory absent other sources of revenue to the property owner. But the reality is that non-discriminatory taxes, like non-discriminatory regulations, are seldom confiscatory in a democratic system. People will not approve taxes or regulations that threaten their personal financial viability. Because democratic majorities will sometimes tax others in a confiscatory manner, most Supreme Court case law on the due process of taxation deals with claims of confiscatory taxation resulting from discriminatory taxes.[66]

If from this we can derive the principle that property taxes will be presumed to be constitutional so long as they are non-discriminatory, it is not helpful to a justification of existing takings doctrine. Much land use regulation is explicitly discriminatory. That is the very purpose of zoning—to allow different uses on otherwise similar parcels. Where such limitations on use of property provide benefits widely shared by those regulated—where there is an "average reciprocity of advantage" in Holmes's terms from *Mahon*—owners of regulated properties are implicitly compensated for their regulatory losses and there is no discrimination that would invite confiscatory regulation.

But the balancing approach of *Penn Central* takes no account of the principle that discriminatory regulation (or taxation) might lead to indefensible confiscation (taking) of private property. Thus, the principle that assures that democratically imposed taxation will comply with the property rights protections of the Constitution is clearly not one that can explain the difference between a taking of 100 percent of the economic value of property from a taking of some amount less than 100 percent. Indeed there appears to be no principle, consistent with the purposes of the Due Process and Takings Clauses, which can explain and justify such disparate outcomes.

It might be suggested that some sort of fairness principle would justify redistribution of wealth through regulatory takings, but that is not consistent with the anti-redistribution purposes of the Takings Clause. Or it might be suggested that a principle of judicial deference based on separation of powers justifies a presumption of constitutionality even where regulations are confiscatory, but that would not explain the almost unlimited judicial discretion inherent in the *Penn Central* balancing test and would represent an approach to judicial review that makes almost meaningless the individual liberties protections of the Constitution. What *Penn Central* represents is a totally unprincipled approach to judicial review, unless simple pragmatism can be considered a principle. The Court itself said in its *Penn Central* opinion, "whether a particular restriction will be rendered invalid by the government's failure to pay for any losses proximately caused by it depends largely 'upon the particular circumstances [in that] case.' "[67] Rather than being a formula for judicial restraint, this ad hoc approach is an open invitation to judicial intervention in the policy-making functions of the legislature and an abandonment of constitutionally guaranteed liberties.

Balancing and Judicial Activism

Judicial takings decisions since *Penn Central* evidence that, for the most part, the courts have not taken up the invitation to intervene in policy making by substituting their balancing of interests for that which is already done by the legislature. But at the same time the courts have generally deferred to legislative determinations that regulations on property do not result in unconstitutional takings in contravention of the 5th Amendment. The conflation of these two very different issues—what is good public policy? and when are constitutional liberties infringed by public policy initiatives?—is an almost inevitable consequence of the balancing approach of *Penn Central.*

An appropriate judicial deference to legislative policy making has morphed into a presumption of constitutionality in the face of rights claims. Inherent in such deference is an almost complete disregard for property rights. Judicial deference to legislative and executive policy judgments is a central principle of separation of powers. But judicial deference to legislative and executive determinations of constitutional liberties is an abandonment of the core judicial role in a constitutional democracy. Indeed rights claims, whether or not labeled "economic," warrant vigilant review in the courts. Absent such careful judicial scrutiny, all constitutional rights are reduced to mere political interests subject to the unconstrained tyranny of the majority.

The muddle of *Penn Central* balancing is part and parcel of the larger confusion in the never ending debate over judicial activism. The reality is that when liberals dominate the courts, conservatives object to an activist judiciary and when conservatives hold sway in the courts, liberals object that judicial activism runs rampant. Conservative objections to what they perceive to be Warren court activism is based largely on the claim that the court manufactured rights to invalidate legislation favored by conservatives. Liberals object that the Rehnquist and Roberts courts have been inappropriately activist in invalidating legislative enactments favored by liberals—usually on the basis of separation of powers or federalism requirements of the constitution. Both sides of this debate make the same fundamental mistake. They equate judicial activism with the invalidation of legislation. They count up the number of cases in which members of the court have voted to invalidate a federal or state law and on that basis rate the justices as more or less activist. But that little exercise in statistics is a charade without pretense of even the slightest understanding of the central judicial review function of the federal courts. Everybody who ever went to law school was required to read *Marbury v. Madison*. It is truly amazing how few seem to understand its central holding that "[i]t is emphatically the province and duty of the judicial department to say what the law is."[68]

In *Marbury* Chief Justice John Marshall wrote:

> Between . . . [two] alternatives there is no middle ground. The constitution is either a superior, paramount law, unchangeable by ordinary means, or it is on a level with ordinary legislative acts, and, like other acts, is alterable when the legislature shall please to alter it.
>
> If the former part of the alternative be true, then a legislative act contrary to the constitution is not law: if the latter part be true, then written constitutions

are absurd attempts, on the part of the people, to limit a power in its own nature illimitable.[69]

At the time the Jeffersonian Republicans objected that the Federalist Supreme Court was improperly activist and seeking to preserve Federalist power lost in the election of 1800. There can be no doubt that Federalist ideas had greater ongoing influence than they would have had in the absence of judicial review, but the core judicial review power and the understanding that the Constitution is "superior, paramount law" have long survived the Federalist–Jeffersonian politics of the early national period. Marshall's point was not that the courts will make the laws or pass judgment on the wisdom of the laws. His point was that the courts have the constitutional duty to interpret the laws, including the law of the constitution, and to invalidate those legislative and executive actions that conflict with the paramount law of the Constitution. If that is judicial activism, then judicial activism is what the Constitution requires.

The *Penn Central* balancing test runs counter to this basic premise of constitutional government in two ways. First, it allows that the courts might judge whether rights have been violated on the basis of their perception of the importance of a law's policy objectives, thus engaging the judiciary inappropriately in the legislative process. This is the sort of judicial activism to which a defender of the Constitution should object. Second, it gives rights an indefinite and malleable content at the discretion of the legislature. This is the sort of judicial restraint to which a defender of constitutional rights should object. In other words, courts should actively and aggressively perform their constitutional role, particularly when it comes to protecting individual liberties from violation by the otherwise all-powerful state. Courts should also restrain themselves from embracing the sometimes powerful temptations to interfere in the legislative and executive functions of government. If the courts are to fulfill their constitutional role as confirmed in *Marbury*, all laws should be presumed to be what the legislature intended them to be, but no laws should be presumed to be constitutional.

Chapter 6

Unconstitutional Takings of Private Property

Since the *Penn Central* decision in 1978, there have been occasional indications that the economic liberties of the constitution might be given a new life. But through it all, the now ageless question of whether a regulation of private property has gone too far has remained the defining issue in property rights jurisprudence. Without a marker to determine when a regulation has gone too far, there is nothing left but "sifting facts and weighing circumstances,"[1] all in service to the *Penn Central* balancing test.

Of course the reality is that such balancing rarely occurs in the courts. For the most part it occurs in the political negotiations surrounding every regulation, with regulators knowing that if they can win the political battle, there is little chance that the affected property owners will prevail should they object in the courts that their property has been taken in contravention of the 5th Amendment. But because there are a few property owners who have the will and resources to challenge government on principle and a network of property rights advocates organized for the same purpose, cases have continued to find their way to the Supreme Court over the last three decades.

How Far Is "Too Far"?

In the term following its *Penn Central* decision, a divided Supreme Court in *Kaiser Aetna v. United States*[2] evidenced the lack of clarity inherent in the balancing approach, even though the majority could have avoided a foray into public policy by ruling on the simple and clear physical invasion principle later confirmed in *Loretto v.*

Teleprompter Manhattan. *Kaiser Aetna* involved an indisputably private pond that had been dredged to create a marina with access to navigable, coastal, waters. The United States subsequently ruled that the pond had been made navigable and that public access must therefore be allowed. The owner of the pond claimed a taking of private property and sought compensation. Writing for the majority and ruling in favor of the property owner, Justice Rehnquist cited *Penn Central* in confirming that the takings doctrine requires the court to engage "in essentially ad hoc, factual inquiries,"[3] notwithstanding the fact that the effect of the government regulation was to deprive the property owner of "one of the most essential sticks in the bundle of rights that are commonly characterized as property—the right to exclude others," and that "the shifting back and forth of the Court in this area . . . bears the sound of 'Old, unhappy, far-off things, and battles long ago,' " and "that the strict logic of the more recent cases . . . might completely swallow up any private claim for 'just compensation' under the Fifth Amendment."[4]

Rehnquist suggested no standard or principle that might guide the Court away from these hazards in future cases. Rather he noted that "as Mr. Justice Holmes observed in a very different context, the life of the law has not been logic, it has been experience."[5] Experience demonstrated to Rehnquist and the *Kaiser Aetna* majority that the government's demand for public access "collides with not merely an 'economic advantage' but an 'economic advantage' that has the law back of it to such an extent that courts may [require compensation]."[6] Although the property owner prevailed, Rehnquist's implication that the law could be "back of" a legal claim but not sufficiently to warrant judicial enforcement and that, in any event, the courts may or may not require compensation, leaves property rights in a precarious position. There is nothing in Rehnquist's statement to give confidence that the law will deliver tomorrow what it promises today. Absent that, balancing, not the rule of law, remains the judicial task. Not surprisingly, Justices Blackmun, Brennan and Marshall "reach[ed] a different balance of interests."[7] Justice Rehnquist could have avoided this tug of war by finding that an unconstitutional taking resulted from the government's effective physical invasion of the plaintiff's property, and saying nothing more.

A year later, the Court faced a similar issue in a challenge to a California Supreme Court finding that no taking resulted when a private shopping center was required to allow political protestors access to shopping center property.[8] Had Rehnquist's *Kaiser Aetna* opinion relied wholly on the fact of physical invasion and the resultant denial of the right to exclude, his opinion in *PruneYard Shopping Center v. Robins* could have easily affirmed the principle that the right to exclude is "one of the essential sticks in the bundle of property rights,"[9] while agreeing with the California court and avoiding another tortured balancing of interests. *PruneYard* was easily distinguishable on the basis that the shopping center, unlike the marina, held itself open to the public. It invited the public in, thereby making the shopping center a public place, while Kaiser Aetna's objective to create an exclusive marina depended on excluding nonmembers. However, Rehnquist went on at some length discussing "the character of the governmental action, its economic impact, and its interference with reasonable investment-backed expectations,"[10] finally distinguishing *PruneYard* from *Kaiser Aetna* on the basis that PruneYard "failed to demonstrate that the 'right to exclude others' is so essential to the use or economic value of their property that the state-authorized limitation of it amounted to a 'taking.' "[11] Although the holding was unanimous, four members of the court found the need to concur in three different opinions by way of clarifying why, in their opinion, the balance came out against the private property claim. But this sort of disagreement is what we should expect from an ad hoc balancing test.

A few years later in *Nollan v. California Coastal Commission*[12] the majority opinion of Justice Scalia went straight to the right to exclude principle in invalidating a requirement that a property owner provide a public easement across his property in return for a permit to remodel and expand an existing home. Stating that "the right to exclude [others is] one of the most essential sticks in the bundle of rights that are commonly characterized as property," and citing to *Kaiser Aetna* and *Loretto v. Teleprompter Manhattan CATV Corp.*[13] (while distinguishing *PruneYard* on the basis suggested above), Justice Scalia noted that "our cases uniformly have found a taking to the extent of the occupation, without regard to whether the action achieves an important public benefit or has only minimal economic impact on the owner."[14]

Once again the Court might have concluded the matter on that clear and simple principle, but regrettably Justice Scalia reverted to the muddle of balancing. Despite having explicitly recognized that a physical occupation would be a taking without regard to the importance of the public benefit or the magnitude of the impact on the property owner, Scalia accepted "that land-use regulation does not effect a taking if it 'substantially advance[s] legitimate state interests,' "[15] even if the regulation mandates or allows physical occupation and a violation of the right to exclude. Acknowledging that the Court had not made clear what constitutes a legitimate state interest or what constitutes substantial advancement of such an interest, and not anticipating that a decade later the Court would unanimously abandon this means–ends test in its takings jurisprudence,[16] Scalia argued that California "unquestionably would be able to deny the Nollans their permit outright if their new house (alone, or by reason of the cumulative impact produced in conjunction with other construction) would substantially impede [such legitimate] purposes," and that if the state has this power it "must surely include the power to condition construction upon some concession by the owner, even a concession of property rights, that serves the same end."[17] Thus, California could not require Nollan to provide a right of way across his property because that advanced not at all the state's purpose of preserving a public vista of the beach, but it could require Nollan to provide a public viewing space on his property. So it turns out there is no right to exclude if a legitimate state interest is substantially advanced by denying that right, and substantial advancement is a matter to be resolved by the courts. This is just balancing by a different name. Granted, the state's having to show substantial advancement of its interests shifts the balance in favor of the property owner (as compared to the state's having to show only a rational basis for its limitation of property rights), but it is nonetheless a formula for judicial balancing with, as Scalia observed, little guidance from the Supreme Court.

In dissent Justice Stevens applauded fellow dissenter Justice Brennan for having seen the light (after siding with the property claimant in an earlier case[18]), but Stevens lamented that Brennan's explicit reliance on the *Penn Central* balancing test, "[e]ven if his position prevailed in this case, . . . would be of little solace to land-use planners who would still be left guessing about how the Court will react to the next case, and the one after that."[19] The statist, anti-libertarian possibilities of Holmesian pragmatism have seldom been more clearly stated. In the context of a claimed infringement of constitutional liberties, Justice Stevens objected that government bureaucrats might be faced with uncertainties.

But what about the uncertainties faced by the property owner? Does the property owner have the right to exclude, or is that right contingent on bureaucratic and judicial discretion? If the latter, then there is no right to exclude. Of course certainty about the scope of their powers and the limitations imposed by individual liberties would be helpful for government officials. It would, among other things, help them avoid the infringement of property rights. As I have argued at various points in this book, there is plenty to object to in making rights contingent on balancing. But when the objection is that the good works of government will be compromised if officials are left to puzzle over what the constitution might next be found to mean, we can rest assured that whatever the proposed remedy for the vagaries of judicial balancing, it will not serve the interest of liberty.

For that reason, it is particularly unfortunate that Justice Scalia did not conclude his opinion in *Nollan* on the simple and obvious principle that a public easement across private property can be constitutionally acquired in one way, and one way only. It can be bought and paid for, either from a willing seller or by eminent domain. The problem for Scalia and the *Nollan* majority was that the conditioning of permits on effective grants to the public of some part of a permittee's property rights had become commonplace across the country. A principled decision on the basis of the right to exclude would have called this practice into question. And well it should have been called into question. As the Supreme Court of New Hampshire observed in an opinion quoted by Justice Scalia, the conditioning of a permit on the applicant's granting to the government title to a portion of his property is "an out-and-out plan of extortion."[20]

CONDITIONAL PERMITS

Two theories seek to justify such conditional permitting, neither of which is consistent with the constitutional protection of property rights. Most troublesome is the view that all property rights are created by the state and subject to alteration, limitation, or obliteration by the state. Legal realists and those who have experienced expropriations of property in other countries might accept this as a pragmatic assertion of reality, but it is not a reality that can be accepted in a regime of constitutionally guaranteed property rights. The point of constitutional protections of individual liberty is to constrain such exercises of raw power—to create a different reality in which government is not allowed to run roughshod over its citizens.

The alternative theory thought to justify conditional permitting is that development of property imposes costs on government or limits the exercise of public or private rights. In the case of government costs resulting from development, the taxation power is adequate to the task of recouping those costs. It is well established that the use of special assessment districts to impose costs on those who directly benefit is consistent with due process. Among those costs in the case of public infrastructure like roads and sewers is the acquisition of land or easements. A property rights purist might demand that the government acquire such property rights through purchase or eminent domain, but the reality is that if the government does not provide the infrastructure, the developer will have to dedicate the necessary land to roads and sewers and bear the costs of their construction and maintenance. It is reasonable to assume that these costs will be roughly similar to the value of property rights granted to government, and the fact that such facilities generally must be open to the public to serve their purposes makes the conditioning of such grants more like *PruneYard* than *Kaiser Aetna*. Thus, a condition that land or an easement be granted for the provision of infrastructure like roads and sewers will allow costs to be fairly distributed to those who benefit (and not be borne by others who receive little or no benefit) while not offending the right to exclude principle.

Some conditional permits, however, are justified in the name of other "public costs." A permit to develop land might be conditioned on the setting aside of open space or the granting of land for parks on the theory that the public suffers costs when open space is eliminated by development. Calling the elimination of open space a public cost implies an existing public right to whatever benefits might be provided by that open space. But there are many external benefits from land to which the beneficiaries have no right. I benefit from the shade of my neighbor's oak tree (or suffer the costs of its shading my vegetable garden), but have no legal complaint if he cuts it down (or duty to pay for newfound sunshine and ripened tomatoes). That is surely the way it is with open space. The government has no basis, beyond bald assertion, to claim that development results in the private taking of public rights to open space. But that is the essence of conditioning a permit to develop on the uncompensated assignment of some portion of the permittee's property rights. That such conditional permitting is blatant "extortion," as the New Hampshire court said, is confirmed by the fact that no American government has yet had the gall to assert a public right to create public parks and open space on private lands for which there are no plans for development. But if a public right to open space exists, it functions as a limitation on the rights of land not intended for development to the same degree as land on which development is planned.

The conditioning of development on the preservation of public or private rights that do in fact exist would be an entirely different matter. Whether such rights exist is a straightforward, though not necessarily simple, question for lawyers and judges to resolve, as the discussion in Chapter 4 demonstrates. If it is determined that public or private rights would be infringed by a proposed development project, the conditioning of a permit on the preservation of those rights is nothing more than a demand that the developer respect the rights of others and undertake only those actions that his property rights allow. As we have observed previously, and as the Court makes clear in the *Lucas* case discussed below, there can be no taking where a regulation or a permit condition prohibits one from doing what he had no right to do in the first place.

Thus, *Nollan* was a simple case made complex by the Court's failure, once again, to extract itself from the muddle of balancing and standards of review. The state of California sought to provide public access to private property without compensation or reliance on eminent domain. Had Justice Scalia stuck with his assertion that neither the nature of the public interest nor the magnitude of the private harm is relevant to finding that government-mandated physical occupation of private property violates the right to exclude resulting in a per se taking of private property, the decision would have been helpful to the development of a coherent takings doctrine. But by suggesting that the uncompensated taking of a public easement is constitutional if the provision of such an easement "substantially advance[s]" a "legitimate state interest," even while acknowledging that the Court had provided definition for neither of those variables, Scalia left property rights to be respected, or not, as regulators and the occasional judge sees fit.

The *Nollan* ruling, and the Court's subsequent invalidation of a permit condition in *Dolan v. City of Tigard*,[21] received renewed attention in the 2013 case of *Koontz v. St. Johns River Water Management District*.[22] Property owner Koontz sought to develop a 3.7-acre portion of a 14.7-acre parcel. Because the land was classified as wetlands under Florida law, Koontz applied to the Water Management District for a required permit and offered to grant the District a conservation easement in the undeveloped 11 acres. The District indicated that Koontz's offer was inadequate and suggested that his project would be approved only if he either reduced the size of the area to be developed and deeded to the District a conservation easement in the resulting larger remainder of the property, or agreed to pay for the improvements to other District-owned wetlands. Koontz challenged the District's action as an unconstitutional taking.

Writing for the majority in a 5–4 ruling, Justice Alito explained that, like in *Nollan* and *Dolan*, the property owner was subjected to an unconstitutional condition. The problem, said Alito, is not that Koontz's property was actually taken, but rather that the proposed conditions "impermissibly burden the right not to have property taken without just compensation."[23] Alito acknowledged that some conditions are permissible, but suggested that those that would have been imposed on Koontz had he proceeded with his project might not satisfy the *Nollan* and *Dolan* requirement that there be "a 'nexus' and 'rough proportionality' between the government's demand and the effects of the proposed land use."[24] That question, said Alito, must be addressed by the Florida courts on remand.

The decision was a clear, if narrow, victory for property owners. No longer must an owner agree to permit conditions before challenging their constitutionality. But the Court's analysis did little to clarify the muddle of takings doctrine. On remand, the Florida courts will presumably determine whether or not there is a "nexus" and "rough proportionality" between the District's suggested conditions and Koontz's proposed land use. That determination will turn on the balancing test of *Penn Central,* which leaves each court with discretion to weigh the uncertain public costs of development against the private costs to the property owner. In the haunting query of Justice Holmes, do the District's conditions go "too far"?

CATEGORICAL TAKINGS

Despite the suggestion in *Nollan* that even a physical occupation of private property might not be a taking, subsequent cases have routinely announced that such physical invasions constitute one of two per se categories of unconstitutional taking. The other per se case is where regulation results in a total loss of economic value. As indicated in Chapter 5, the principle was stated in *Agins v. City of Tiburon*[25] and reaffirmed in *Lucas v. South Carolina Coastal Commission.*[26] Lucas challenged a prohibition on coastal construction that had the effect of making his property of zero value for development. The Court held that "when the owner of real property has been called upon to sacrifice all economically beneficial uses in the name of the common good, that is, to leave his property economically idle, he has suffered a taking."[27] It was a victory for property rights, made all the more satisfying by the state's acquisition and subsequent sale of the property for development by another private owner.

But this new category of per se taking was quickly seen to encompass few cases and to rest upon a puzzling logic. With governments ever wary of enacting regulatory takings, it is a simple matter to assure that at least some modest economic value remains in regulated properties. The logic is puzzling not because a total loss of economic value was held to be a per se taking, but because a nearly total loss of economic value is apparently not a taking. The constitutional difference between a 100 percent loss and a 90 percent loss is not obvious to most property owners. Imagine trying to convince the victim of theft that no crime has been committed because only 90 percent of his money was stolen. But at least this second categorical taking did make clear that at some point the balance between private burden and public benefit would finally tip to the favor of the property owner.

In reaching its decision in *Lucas*, the Court made reference to the *Penn Central* concept of reasonable, investment-backed expectations, suggesting that the time of property acquisition might be relevant to determining whether a particular regulation results in a taking. In the earlier *Nollan* case the Court had stated that "[s]o long as the Commission could not have deprived the prior owners of the [beach access] easement without compensating them, the prior owners must be understood to have transferred their full property rights in conveying the lot."[28] But *Lucas* seemed to suggest that successive owners of a particular property might have to look to regulations in place at the time of their acquisition, rather than the rights of their predecessors in title, to determine the nature and extent of their own rights.

This "notice" concept of property rights has been embraced by some as a compromise position in the property rights debate. A prominent example was Oregon's Measure 37 discussed in Chapter 2 of the companion volume, *Private Property and the State*. That law did not mandate compensation based on the rights of predecessors in title, rather it required compensation only for losses resulting from regulations enacted since the current owner acquired the property. Whether or not this makes sense depends on the expectations of the current owner at the time of purchase. If the current owner relied only upon the deed and a title search, the purchase price might not reflect the impact of regulatory limitations. But it is probably fair to assume that most purchasers, and particularly those contemplating a change of use, will have considered regulatory restrictions and that market prices will, in any event, reflect such limitations on use. This does not mean, however, that no taking occurred when previous regulations were enacted and enforced. Rather it means that losses resulting from regulatory takings are more often than not borne by predecessors in title. If this assumption is generally accurate, the rule suggested in the *Lucas* decision and implemented in the Oregon law would serve to avoid windfall compensation to current owners while leaving predecessors in title to lick their wounds, or turn in their graves. However, the Court later made clear in *Palazzollo v. Rhode Island* that "[t]he State may not put so potent a Hobbesian stick into the Lockean bundle," that purchaser's rights will depend on whatever legislation and regulations the state may have imposed, without regard to the rights of predecessors in title.[29] And as evidenced by the short life of Oregon's Measure 37, enactment of this "notice" concept of property rights did not end the property wars in that state.

While the concept of categorical takings is generally embraced by property rights advocates, it is really an outcome of Holmes' "too far" standard from *Mahon* and the *Penn Central* balancing test. Balancing of public and private interests would become a constitutional farce if public benefits are almost always found to outweigh private costs, as they would be if courts defer to legislative claims of public benefit. Absent at least a few circumstances in which property owners consistently prevail, the Takings Clause would have little consequence. But the existence of categorical takings on the property owner's side of the balance invites categorical non-takings on the government's side. Indeed that was the government's claim in *Arkansas Game & Fish Commission v. United States*.[30] The state sought a categorical exemption from takings resulting from government-induced temporary flooding. Fortunately, a unanimous Supreme Court rejected the argument, but not without reasserting fealty to *Penn Central* balancing.

Background Principles

Although *Lucas* met with dismay by pro-regulation forces and most governments, it has since been found to have a silver lining by those same interests. In holding that a denial of all economically beneficial use of property constitutes a per se taking, Justice Scalia noted that the only exception would be limitations that "inhere in the title itself, in the restrictions that background principles of the State's law of property and nuisance already place upon land ownership."[31] These background principles would be revealed in "the logically antecedent inquiry into the nature of the owner's estate,"[32] that presumably would be central to the consideration of any takings claim, at least if one follows the Epstein approach by asking first whether or not there has been a taking, a question that cannot be answered without determining whether the claimant actually possesses the right claimed to have been taken. In other words, Anglo-American property rights have always been defined by general common law principles as well as by the terms of deeds and instruments of conveyance. Thus, Justice Scalia's reference to background principles was meant to confirm what should be obvious to all property lawyers—that all property rights are defined, in part, by deeply rooted common law principles that the state is free to enforce through regulation as well as by judicial decree. Thus, where principles of nuisance law would preclude a particular use of property, a regulation enforcing that limit is no more a taking than is judicial enforcement in the context of a nuisance lawsuit. The state cannot take what the property owner does not possess.

There is nothing surprising or groundbreaking in this recognition of the relevance of background principles to the resolution of takings claims. Indeed, Scalia's background principles are nothing more than the limitations on property rights that the police power exists to enforce—at least the police power as it was understood in *Mahon* and before. But some advocates for more aggressive and unconstrained regulation of property have suggested that Scalia inadvertently created a potentially massive exemption from takings claims.[33] While historic principles of property and nuisance law have always given definition to property rights in the manner suggested above, the potential for a wide array of "categorical defenses" in future takings claims rests on the view that courts and legislatures are free to adjust those background principles in light of current knowledge, conditions and public concerns.[34] In other words, background principles are not fixed from the time a property interest is acquired, rather they evolve over time meaning that what might have been a taking yesterday could be the legitimate enforcement of new limits on a claimant's property rights today or tomorrow.

This concept of changeable background principles is rooted in Justice Scalia's parenthetical observation that "changed circumstances or new knowledge may make what was previously permissible no longer so,"[35] and in a mistaken understanding of historic common law evolution. The idea that background principles of the common law are infinitely malleable at the discretion of legislatures and courts runs counter to the fundamental values of the rule of law and a constitutional provision clearly designed as a prohibition on such ex post changes to vested property rights.[36] The default rule cannot be that property rights are whatever the government or government official of the moment chooses for them to be. Rather the default rule must reflect, as Justice Scalia stated immediately prior to his parenthetical, "that a particular use . . . long . . . engaged in by similarly situated owners ordinarily imports a lack of any common-law prohibition."[37]

The suggestion that property rights are conditioned on an array of constantly changing background principles leads to the same result as the presumption of constitutional validity for economic and social regulations. The presumption of constitutionality would have us assume that property rights are not violated by government regulation. The changing background principles approach would have us make a lawyer-like investigation of a claimant's property rights only to find that they are newly limited by changed conditions and social concerns as reflected in the challenged regulations.

Although the background principles concept has received little attention from the Supreme Court since its *Lucas* decision, the threat to unconstrained regulation of a less deferential standard of review was clear to the four dissenters in *Dolan v. City of Tigard*,[38] decided two years after *Lucas*. In *Dolan* the majority invalidated two conditions imposed on a property owner in return for a permit to expand her hardware store. The city had conditioned the permit on the dedication of land for a public bike path and for a green way in and adjacent to a bordering flood plain. Citing to *Nollan*, Justice Rehnquist stated that there must be an "'essential nexus'... between the 'legitimate state interest' and the permit condition exacted by the city."[39] He concluded that evidence of increased traffic from a larger store and increased runoff from an expanded and paved parking lot established the necessary nexus. Thus the City of Tigard was not "simply trying to obtain an easement through gimmickry,"[40] as California had tried to do in *Nollan*. But that was not the end of the matter, said Rehnquist. The Court next had "to determine whether the degree of the exactions demanded by the city's permit conditions bears the required relationship to the projected impact of petitioner's proposed development."[41] After reviewing the range of state court approaches to the question, Rehnquist concluded that those states demanding a "reasonable relationship" had it about right, but rejected that language as sounding too much like "rational basis" in favor of a standard of "rough proportionality." Rehnquist found that the City of Tigard had failed to meet that newly minted standard, thus concluding that Dolan's property had been unconstitutionally taken unless the city could meet the standard on remand to the trial court.

Justice Stevens dissented, with concurrences from Justices Blackmun and Ginsburg, on the ground that the majority had abandoned the presumption of constitutionality in takings challenges to economic and social regulation. "The exactions associated with the development of a retail business," wrote Stevens, are "a species of business regulation that heretofore warranted a strong presumption of constitutional validity."[42] Applying such a presumption, according to Stevens, would result in a taking "only if the developer establishes that a concededly germane condition is so grossly disproportionate to the proposed development's adverse effects that it manifests motives other than land use regulation on the part of the city."[43] Stevens even went so far as to suggest that the 5th Amendment Takings Clause does not apply to the states and that the majority was actually engaged in a revival of the much maligned substantive due process of *Lochner*. Despite a century of widespread agreement that the Takings Clause has been incorporated into the 14th Amendment Due Process Clause since the 1897 case of *Chicago, B. & Q.R. Co. v. Chicago*,[44] Stevens argued that that case, and Holmes's opinion in *Mahon* some two decades later, laid the foundation for a regulatory takings doctrine that has no more legitimacy than the substantive due process of the *Lochner* era. It is a remarkable dissent, and one that evidenced, along with Justice Souter's dissent, that even in victory the constitutional protection of property rights hangs by a slender thread.

LINGLE V. CHEVRON—SOME USEFUL HOUSE CLEANING

Since *Dolan*, regulatory takings law, such as it is, has changed little. However, a unanimous court did provide a concise summary of the state of takings law, while jettisoning one piece of the muddle, in its 2005 opinion in *Lingle v. Chevron, U.S.A., Inc.*[45] First, wrote Justice O'Conner for the Court, "the Takings Clause 'does not prohibit the taking of private property, but instead places a condition on the exercise of that power.' "[46] This is an important recognition since it is routine for governments and their pro-regulation allies to argue that important and necessary legislation and regulation will be prevented by active judicial enforcement of property rights. In fact the Takings Clause prohibits no otherwise constitutional government action; it only requires compensation when property is taken in the course of such action. Having recognized this important and fundamental principle, O'Connor then went on to state that "the Court [has] recognized that government regulation of private property may, in some instances, be so onerous that its effect is tantamount to a direct appropriation or ouster—and that such 'regulatory takings' may be compensable under the Fifth Amendment."[47] Her point seemed to be that a regulation of property is a taking when it is like eminent domain in the sense that the government takes effective, if not actual, possession. This happens when the regulation goes "too far," as Holmes said in *Mahon*, but, said O'Connor, "[t]he rub, of course, has been—and remains—how to discern how far is 'too far.' "[48]

O'Connor acknowledges the two per se categories of regulations that go too far: (1) "where government requires an owner to suffer a permanent physical invasion of her property—however minor" and (2) where regulation "completely deprive[s] an owner of '*all* economically beneficial us[e]' of her property."[49] So far this all seems consistent with what has gone before, and makes sense except that a minor physical invasion can hardly be said to be "so onerous that its effect is tantamount to a direct appropriation or ouster."[50] This exception is important because it underscores that, under existing Supreme Court takings law, the existence of a taking does not depend solely on the magnitude of the economic burden on the property owner. The recognition of physical invasion as a per se taking, unlike the total loss of economic value category of cases, is not a mere shifting of the burden of proof on the ground that the balance will in those rare cases generally favor the property owner. Rather it represents a principled recognition that property rights have a constitutional significance apart from whatever economic value they may serve to protect.

Later in the *Lingle* opinion, Justice O'Connor did recognize that physical invasion offends the right to exclude, thus acknowledging the possibility of regulatory takings where the effect is not "tantamount to a direct appropriation or ouster." In *Loretto*, from which the physical invasion principle derives, it could hardly be said that the property has been appropriated or the owner ousted by the mandatory installation of a television cable. Although the physical invasion category is narrow, it represents a recognition by the court that takings occur not only where it can be said that government should have relied upon its eminent domain power, contrary to O'Connor's summary statement about onerous burdens. Even absent a government power of eminent domain with its correlative requirement of compensation, property owners have the right to exclude and a constitutional protection against the deprivation of that right.

Justice O'Connor's restatement of takings law in *Lingle* then acknowledges that the multitude of potential regulatory takings claimants who do not have the benefit of coming within either per se taking category are left to the near Herculean challenge of overcoming the presumption of constitutionality under the *Penn Central* balancing test. While this summation of regulatory takings law is clear and easily recapitulated in casebooks, CLE presentations, lawyers' briefs and judicial opinions, it is unsatisfactory as a definition of property rights or as a guide for private or public decision-makers in the future. It is clear that if one's takings claim involves physical invasion or total loss of economic value, one can usually prevail. But few cases will qualify for per se takings analysis, and legislators can easily design their regulations to avoid these narrow pitfalls. Thus, most regulatory takings claims are left to *Penn Central* balancing where there is an almost insurmountable burden on the property owner to demonstrate that his interests somehow outweigh those of the public. Although logic and experience should lead regulators to conclude that little of what they do is likely to be found in violation of the Takings Clause, they can never be certain that a 'rogue' judge might not decide for the property owner and, in any event, they must be prepared to deal with the costs and delay of possible litigation. The same dim prospect for success, combined with a deeply rooted sense of violated personal autonomy, will keep property owners coming back to the courts, even knowing they are usually tilting at windmills.

Although the *Lingle* decision did accept the presumption of constitutionality and embrace balancing as the method of adjudicating the claims of those sufficiently bold to object to regulations of property, O'Connor's opinion for the Court did eliminate one theoretical difficulty in takings doctrine. In *Agins* a unanimous court had stated that a taking might result if the regulation of property failed to substantially advance a legitimate state interest. This language was repeated with approval by Justice Scalia in his *Nollan* opinion to the effect that even a physical invasion would not be a taking if it substantially advanced a legitimate state interest. The idea that a government regulation of property must have some nexus to a legitimate governmental purpose has deeper roots in property rights jurisprudence. In *Nectow v. City of Cambridge*[51] the Court held that a zoning ordinance would violate the 14th Amendment absent a "substantial relation to the public health, the public morals, the public safety or the public welfare."[52] In *Penn Central* the Court found no taking where "[t]he restrictions imposed are substantially related to the promotion of the general welfare."[53] Together these two cases illustrated the problem O'Connor set out to resolve in *Lingle.* In *Nectow* the Court made reference only to the 14th Amendment Due Process Clause; not stating if it meant to say a substantial relation was required by due process alone or by the Takings Clause whether applied directly to the federal government or to the states as incorporated in the Due Process Clause of the 14th Amendment. In *Penn Central* a nexus was clearly required to satisfy the Takings Clause; as it was in the *Agins* opinion to which there was no dissent.

THREATENING THE PRESUMPTION OF CONSTITUTIONALITY

By the time of the *Nollan* and *Dolan* decisions, four members of the Court who had signed on to *Agins* found reason to object that a majority of the Court had transformed a seemingly innocuous nexus test that would be easily satisfied by any reasonably competent legislature into a heightened standard of review that threatened the presumption of constitutionality in takings cases. Dissenting to the *Nollan* majority's finding of an inadequate nexus between the state's interest in maintaining a beach vista and its requirement that Nollan dedicate a public right of way along the beach, Justice Brennan with Justice Marshall concurring (both of whom had agreed to the *Agins* opinion) objected to the imposition of "a standard of precision for the exercise of a State's police power that has been discredited for the better part of this century."[54] Dissenting to the *Dolan* majority's finding that the required dedication of a bike path and green way was not roughly proportional to the state's interests in traffic and flood control, Justice Stevens with Justice Blackmun concurring (both of whom also agreed to the *Agins* opinion) objected that "[t]he Court has made a serious error by abandoning the traditional presumption of constitutionality and imposing a novel burden of proof on a city."[55]

The dissenting justices in *Nollan* and *Dolan* were clearly distressed that the *Agins* decision, in which they had concurred, was being used to impose on governments a higher burden in justifying regulations of property. It was threatening the seemingly established principle that economic liberties have secondary constitutional importance. But what did all of this have to do with the Takings Clause? That was the question O'Connor posed in *Lingle*, and her answer was that the so-called nexus test had no place in takings jurisprudence. In this conclusion she was surely correct. While regulations that do nothing to advance the end for which they were purportedly enacted or that have a purpose that government has no authority to pursue might be constitutionally suspect, the Takings Clause provides no basis for resolving any suspicion. As O'Connor stated at the outset of her *Lingle* opinion, the Takings Clause is not a prohibition on regulation. It is a condition that otherwise constitutional regulations must satisfy "to bar Government from forcing some people alone to bear public burdens which, in all fairness and justice, should be borne by the public as a whole."[56] As Justice O'Connor clearly explained, the nexus test of *Agins* is irrelevant to assuring that the Takings Clause achieves its purpose.

> A test that tells us nothing about the actual burden imposed on property rights, or how that burden is allocated, cannot tell us when justice might require that the burden be spread among taxpayers through the payment of compensation. The owner of a property subject to a regulation that effectively serves a legitimate state interest may be just as singled out and just as burdened as the owner of a property subject to an ineffective regulation.

It would make little sense to say that the second owner has suffered a taking while the first has not. Likewise, an ineffective regulation may not significantly burden property rights at all, and it may distribute any burden broadly and evenly among property owners. The notion that such a regulation nevertheless "takes" private property for public use merely by virtue of its ineffectiveness or foolishness is untenable.[57]

Furthermore, said O'Connor, the *Agins* nexus requirement "can be read to demand heightened means-ends review of virtually any regulation of private property . . ., [thus] requir[ing] courts to scrutinize the efficacy of a vast array of state and federal regulations—a task for which courts are not well suited."[58]

What Does a Nexus Have to Do with Takings?

This concern for minimizing judicial intervention in clearly legislative functions is well founded, but it falls far short of correcting for the widespread reliance on means–ends standards, or even demonstrating an understanding of why such standards are inappropriate to the enforcement of all constitutional liberties. An assessment of whether regulatory means substantially (or even barely) advance legitimate (or even illegitimate) state ends is as irrelevant to determining whether property is taken in violation of the 5th Amendment as it is to determining whether free speech or equal protection rights are infringed. To paraphrase Justice O'Connor, a person's free speech is no less violated by censorship that is effective in serving its purpose than it is by censorship that totally fails to achieve its objective, and an ineffective regulation that does not constrain communication is no more an affront to free speech than an effective regulation. Furthermore, Justice O'Connor might have said, regulation pursuant to a particularly important governmental purpose is no less a violation of the Takings Clause (or the Free Speech Clause) than a regulation having the same impact on individual liberty but in pursuit of a legitimate but insignificant purpose. Of course O'Connor could not correct the general problem of means–ends tests in a case involving only the Takings Clause, but she might have taken one further step in the direction of appropriate judicial restraint. In the language quoted at the end of the previous paragraph, O'Connor lamented that the nexus test of *Agins* required "heightened means-ends review." Did she mean to suggest that the problem was only a heightened means–ends review, or does any means–ends review involve courts in legislative matters that should be none of their business?

O'Connor pointed out that the *Agins* "substantially advances" test, like all of the Court's means–ends tests, was rooted in the Due Process Clause, "[a]n inquiry . . . [with] some logic in the context of a due process challenge, for a regulation that fails to serve any legitimate governmental objective may be so arbitrary or irrational that it runs afoul of the Due Process Clause."[59] So it seems she does not object to a judicially enforced minimum requirement of regulatory rationality, with due process as the constitutional source of the requirement. Absent a plausible link between means and legitimate ends, it is fair to conclude that the legislature has illegitimate ends. Without such a requirement, there would be no way for the courts to assure that legislative and executive powers are employed only for constitutionally authorized purposes. Accepting that the definition of constitutionally authorized purposes is imprecise at best, particularly with respect to state government police powers, and recognizing that legislative intent is illusive and a mere rationality standard will be easily met by reasonably careful legislators, judicial review for a means–ends nexus will reveal few violations of this minimal requirement of due process. But it is an understanding consistent with the historic foundations of the concept of due process, though not one that requires "heightened judicial scrutiny." Indeed it is the very definition of rational basis review.

O'Connor suggested that the application of the "substantially advances" standard in *Lingle* was "only the tip of the proverbial iceberg . . . [in] foreshadow[ing] the hazards of placing courts in this role."[60] "The reasons for deference to legislative judgments about the need for, and likely effectiveness of, regulatory actions," said O'Connor, "are by now well established."[61] In the latter sentence, O'Connor gets the deference theory exactly right. Determining the "need for and likely effectiveness of, regulatory actions" is clearly the province of the legislature. But that does not mean the courts should defer to legislative or executive judgments about whether or not individual rights are violated by rational efforts to achieve legitimate governmental ends. These are separate and distinct questions, as O'Connor makes clear in *Lingle*, and the courts should be anything but deferential in reviewing claimed violations of constitutional liberties.

While O'Connor effectively jettisons means–ends review from takings doctrine, she fails to recognize that the levels of scrutiny analysis is part and parcel of means–ends review. There are only two reasons that one might employ varying levels of scrutiny to constitutional rights claims: either different rights are of greater and lesser importance—a proposition for which there is no basis in the constitution or its founding history; or different categories of legislation and regulation must satisfy varying levels of rationality—a proposition that violates separation of powers by involving the courts in the legislative and executive functions. O'Connor was correct in asserting that the means–ends requirements of due process call only for rational basis review. She was correct in insisting that a takings claim raises an entirely separate constitutional question. What she failed to state, although it flows directly from these two fundamental conclusions, is that takings claims, like all constitutional rights claims, warrant strict judicial scrutiny and have nothing to do with the importance of the governmental purpose or the court's perception of the significance of the particular claim of right.

By failing to understand or make clear that levels of scrutiny analysis is nothing more than the judicial ranking of individual liberties and public purposes for application to the balancing inherent in all but minimum rationality, means–ends, review, the *Lingle* decision will likely be detrimental to the interests of property owners. Indicative of this unfortunate result from an otherwise potentially helpful opinion was the Court's reliance on *Lingle* in its notorious *Kelo* decision. Rather than recognize O'Connor's central point that means–ends analysis has nothing to do with takings law, Justice Stevens's opinion in *Kelo* emphasized "[t]he disadvantages of a heightened form of review" where "[o]rderly implementation of a comprehensive redevelopment plan obviously requires that the legal rights of all interested parties be established before new construction can be commenced."[62] The problem with heightened scrutiny in the establishment of such rights is that it would "require[] postponement of the judicial approval of every condemnation until the likelihood of success of the plan had been assured,"[63] meaning all needed properties could be successfully acquired. This, said Stevens, "would unquestionably impose a significant impediment to the successful consummation of many such plans."[64] Thus the majority in *Kelo* was happy to abandon the heightened scrutiny of the *Agins* "substantially advances" test, but they were not prepared to jettison means–ends review where it would be helpful to discounting the importance of 5th Amendment property rights claims.

While concise in its summary of takings doctrine and helpful in its abandonment of the *Agins* nexus requirement, O'Connor's opinion in *Lingle* makes clear, and *Kelo* confirms, that the Supreme Court's takings jurisprudence remains, though under different nominal labels, a replication of its equal protection and due process reliance on a pre-weighted (by judges) balancing system. As noted above, equal protection and due process balancing tilt the scales in favor of particular claimants and particular types of claims (not including economic liberties) through a levels of scrutiny analysis ranging from strict (the rights claimant wins) to rational basis (government wins). The broadest category of cases calling for rational basis review are those involving economic and social legislation. Except for the rare cases where regulators have been so careless as to offend the right to exclude, takings doctrine treats all regulation impacting on property rights as economic and social, thus assuring that *Penn Central* balancing will be in the tradition of rational basis review. Only by demonstrating a total loss of economic value, in an all or nothing assessment, will a takings claimant have any hope of overcoming a strong bias against property rights and a heavy presumption that the government can do no constitutional wrong.

RECURRENT ISSUES IN TAKINGS LAW

Exactions

One other aspect of the *Lingle* decision bears mention and underscores yet another serious problem in takings jurisprudence. O'Connor notes that exactions cases like *Nollan* and *Dolan* do not fit neatly in the tripartite approach of two categories of per se taking and *Penn Central* balancing. While the property owners prevailed in both *Nollan* and *Dolan*, the Court affirmed that exactions do not violate the Takings Clause so long as an appropriate nexus exists. In *Nollan*, for example, Justice Scalia allowed that an exaction in the form of a mandated dedication of land as a viewing site would not offend the Takings Clause. In *Dolan* Justice Rehnquist held that the exactions would have been valid if the city had demonstrated a rough proportionality in their nexus to the public purposes sought to be promoted. In abandoning the nexus requirement as an aspect of takings law, Justice O'Connor might have effectively rejected the analysis in both *Nollan* and *Dolan*. But in an effort to demonstrate that abandonment of the *Agins* nexus test did not require the overruling of any of the Court's takings cases, O'Connor insisted that exactions are a special case to which a nexus requirement is relevant within takings law.

In *Nollan* and *Dolan*, said O'Connor, "the Court [did not] question whether the exaction would substantially advance *some* legitimate state interest," rather it questioned "whether the exactions substantially advanced the *same* interests that land-use authorities asserted would allow them to deny the permit altogether."[65] These are "worlds apart," said O'Connor, which may be true but does not explain why the Takings Clause makes a nexus relevant to the latter but not the former. O'Connor acknowledged that *Nollan* and *Dolan* "both involved dedications of property so onerous that, outside the exactions context, they would be deemed per se physical takings."[66] Thus, the only way the state could mandate the dedications of property was by providing just compensation. The fact that the property owners sought permits that could be granted or denied at the state's discretion could not alter the conclusion that the mandated dedications were takings. The only plausible relevance of the state's granting a discretionary permit is if it can be said to serve as compensation for the taken property. But if that is the point of Rehnquist's rough proportionality requirement in *Dolan*, there is no reason to require a nexus between discretionary benefit provided by the state and the property taken. If the state can pay cash to compensate for a taking, there is no constitutional reason that it cannot offer some other benefit acceptable to the property owner. Whether or not there is a nexus between the permit to be granted and the property to be dedicated is likely irrelevant to the property owner's judgment about the adequacy of the compensation. A permit to develop a totally separate parcel of land might serve as well as a permit to develop the parcel from which land is to be exacted.

This does not suggest that the state can willy-nilly demand exactions as conditions for the granting of permits or that a property owner's willingness to accept conditional exactions evidences that no taking has occurred. If the granting of a permit is discretionary in the sense that the state can deny the permit for any reason or no reason, then the applicant has nothing to complain of when a permit is denied and therefore no basis to object to whatever exactions the state may demand. If an approved permit is not adequate compensation for property to be dedicated, the applicant can decline to accept the permit. But few if any regulatory regimes grant such unlimited discretion to the state. Generally a permit is required to allow the state to assure that private action will not impose harm or costs on the public or on neighbors (or that offsetting benefits are provided) that the applicant has no right to impose. If it is determined that no such costs or harm will result (or that offsetting benefits will be produced), an applicant will generally have a right to the issuance of a permit. Thus the state cannot arbitrarily deny and grant permits, but it does have discretion in the sense of exercising reasonable judgment about the likely impacts of a permitted action on the private and public rights at stake. In the interest of facilitating development, the state might reasonably require that the applicant agree to dedicate some part of his property in return for the issuance of a permit to which he is not otherwise entitled. From the perspective of the state's responsibilities to the public, it might be argued that such a dedication must offset or compensate for the harm or costs borne by the public as a consequence of the permitted development, although it is not apparent that this connection is required in any legally enforceable sense. But from the perspective of the Takings Clause, the only question is whether the approved permit is just compensation for the property dedicated.

The answer to this question is not as simple as may appear on the surface. Defenders of exactions will, no doubt, suggest that a property owner's decision to dedicate demanded property interests demonstrates that the permit is just compensation for those interests. This would assure that all exactions are found to be just compensation for required dedications. But the willingness of a developer to accept particular exactions has no relation to the market value of the dedicated property interests. Rather it evidences only what the developer is willing to give up in return for a permit granted by a monopoly supplier of such permits. In fact it is not difficult to determine the market value of dedicated property interests relying on the usual methods of property valuation in eminent domain and inverse condemnation cases. The challenge is in determining the value of the permit in the absence of a market. Buried within *Dolan*'s rough proportionality standard is an approach that can protect against governmental extortion while avoiding windfalls to property owners whose activities require the government's blessings.

Exactions designed to offset the harms or costs a permitted development will impose on the public are similar to development or impact fees that serve the same purpose. Both must be roughly proportional to public harm resulting from development. In a sense, both function as compensation to the public for rights taken by private development. As suggested above, the risk in this practice is that more than fair compensation will be demanded—that the state will use its permitting power to extort property dedications and cash payments from property owners seeking permits to develop. The fact that a property owner might be willing to bear extortionate costs in return for a permit because the expected gains from development will exceed even extortionate permitting costs surely cannot justify the state's use of its coercive powers in this manner. Exacting property with value far in excess of harms or costs resulting from development is no different from special assessment taxation significantly in excess of the benefits to the taxpayer from the public services funded by the special assessment. Both offend the fundamental fairness required by due process. If exactions and development fees are understood to be compensation for private takings of public rights, then exactions and fees in excess of the value of those public rights can no more be justified than can compensation to property owners in excess of the value of property taken by eminent domain. The rough proportionality standard of *Dolan* is thus a recognition that the state can fairly demand compensation for public rights compromised by the granting of a permit, just as government can impose taxes for public benefits provided and just as property owners are entitled to compensation when their property is taken by the government.

Thus, it should be clear that exactions do present a special case, but not one relevant to the determination of whether or not a taking has occurred. Every exaction is a taking. By definition, exactions involve a transfer of title, even if only to an easement, from a property owner to the state. This is a categorical taking under the physical invasion principle and can only be accomplished by eminent domain or by voluntary transfer. When government demands the dedication of property in the course of its regulatory function, it has engaged in inverse condemnation and the only question is whether any discretionary benefit conferred on the property owner is just compensation. That is what *Dolan's* rough proportionality standard is meant to assure. To the extent Chief Justice Rehnquist suggested that there must also be a nexus linking the state's regulatory objective to the property exacted, as O'Connor suggests in her *Lingle* opinion, then *Dolan* does contradict O'Connor's claim that the nexus test can be abandoned without upsetting any existing case law. Because O'Connor was correct in finding no nexus requirement in the Takings Clause, courts must recognize in future exactions cases that all exactions are takings, whether or not there is a nexus between the dedicated property and the public harm sought to be avoided.

Whether a dedication is private payment for acquisition of a public right or the public taking of a private right for which government owes compensation, there is a transfer of private property to the state. Because dedications occur in the context of permitting some regulated use of private property, they are, in their nature, transfers of a severable portion of an existing property interest. Sometimes this will be in the nature of an easement and other times it will constitute fee simple title to some physical portion of a previously private parcel. Its adequacy as compensation for the acquisition of a public right or as just compensation for a public taking of a private right will depend on the market value of the severed portion. This can be more or less easily determined through established methods of property valuation.

One issue in the recent *Koontz* case was whether exactions of money, as opposed to portions of parcels for which permits are sought, are subject to the heightened scrutiny of *Nollan* and *Dolan*. In her dissent, Justice Kagan insists that mandated payments or expenditures of money in return for the granting of a permit are indistinguishable from the "impos[ition] of…[the] general financial obligation[s]" of taxation, which all agree are not takings.[57] Alito acknowledges the difference between the taxation and eminent domain powers of government, but argues that where money exactions are tied to a particular piece of property, nexus and proportionality requirements of *Nollan* and *Dolan* apply. Alito is surely correct, as far as he goes. If the state is prohibited from exacting land for its public purposes but free to exact financial payments sufficient to purchase land or services of equivalent value, it will happily take the latter course and the economic impact on the permit applicant will be the same. As the Court's *Penn Central* balancing test confirms, economic impact on property owners is relevant to takings analysis and there is no reason it should matter by what means that impact is imposed. Contrary to Kagan's claim that a money exaction is indistinguishable from the general financial obligations of taxation, the reality is that the money exaction proposed to Koontz in return for his permit has no relation to general financial obligations of citizens. The exaction would be a 'one-off' based on the particulars of Koontz's proposed development and its public impacts as perceived by the officials with discretion to grant or deny the permit.

Thus, there is a more fundamental flaw in both Kagan's and Alilto's arguments. Alito struggles to show that the money exaction is somehow linked to Koontz's 14.7 acre parcel, but that should have no relevance to determining whether his constitutional rights have been violated. Whether or not linked, the economic impact on Koontz is the same. How can an exaction of land for a particular public purpose violate Koontz's constitutional rights while an exaction of money equivalent to the value of the land for the same public purpose not violate his rights? The fact that both Alito and Kagan accept that the government can do to its citizens pursuant to one power what it cannot do to them exercising another power—that constitutional rights vary with the government power being exercised—underscores the Court's general failure to recognize the integral connections among takings, due process, and equal protection. Those connections should be apparent from Justice Black's oft-quoted statement in *Armstrong v.*

United States that the takings clause is "designed to bar Government from forcing some people alone to bear public burdens which in all fairness and justice, should be borne by the public as a whole."[68] The same could be said of the Equal Protection Clause, and the Due Process Clause. In the pseudo-scientific tradition of the nineteenth-century Harvard Law School Dean Christopher Columbus Langdell, the Court has constructed a taxonomy of constitutional doctrine that neglects and ultimately disserves the liberty-preserving function of the Constitution. Rather than disputing whether *Koontz* is a takings or an unconstitutional conditions case, the Court should be doing its best to protect liberties however they may be categorized in the case books and treatises.

PARTIAL TAKINGS

Accepting that at least some dedications result in a taking and that all dedications involve the transfer of a portion of an existing property interest, another issue in takings jurisprudence comes into focus. When, if ever, is a partial taking an unconstitutional taking? Or, one naive in the mysteries of takings law might ask, why is a partial taking not always a taking? Given that a dedication mandated in return for a permit to which a property owner is entitled is a taking, it is clear that at least some partial takings are unconstitutional takings. But what about a regulation prohibiting all economic use of a portion of one's property? If that is not a taking, how is it different from the mandated dedication of the same portion of the same property? In *Dolan*, the court found a taking where the property owner was required to dedicate land for a greenway in and adjacent to the flood plain. Would it not be a taking if the City of Tigard had simply regulated to preclude any economic use of the flood plain? If so, what conceivable principle might explain the difference, and why would any government choose to mandate a dedication when it could avoid the expenses of compensating by regulating the property to the same effect?

This conundrum, like others in takings jurisprudence, is rooted in the "too far" standard from *Mahon*. If the regulation of an entire property is not a taking until it goes "too far," it seems to follow that a prohibition on all economic use of a portion of that property is not a taking unless it affects too much of the total property. If it was not a taking in *Hadachek* for regulation affecting the entire property to reduce the value of that property by over 90 percent, why would it be a taking if all economic use is prohibited on 90 percent of the same property, assuming that the remaining unregulated portion of the property has roughly 10 percent of the value of the whole? The economic impact on the property owner is the same, and the property owner retains the right to exclude, in both cases. If there is no taking in the former case, there surely can be no taking in the latter case. But the property owner might object that in advance of the regulation the portion on which all economic use is prohibited could have been severed and sold for good value. As suggested above, the airspace above Grand Central Terminal could have been sold to a developer for millions of dollars if only it had been done before the city imposed its historic preservation regulations. Had airspace been conveyed, a prohibition on building would then result in a total loss of economic value to the owner of the airspace. How can the deprivation of that valuable property interest be a taking in the latter case but not in the former just because Penn Central retains the right to use the surface and a bit of the airspace for its existing train station?

Among aficionados of takings jurisprudence, this is known as the "relevant parcel" or the "denominator" problem. To determine whether regulation has destroyed all economic value (resulting in a categorical taking under *Lucas*) or the extent to which it has diminished economic value (for *Penn Central* balancing purposes), we must define what the relevant whole is. The problem can be illustrated most easily in the context of the physical dimensions of property in land. For example, assume that all economic use is prohibited on 10 acres of a 100 acre parcel. If the relevant whole (the denominator) is the 10 regulated acres, then 10/10ths or 100 percent of the relevant property is restricted from use and we have a categorical taking. But if the relevant whole is 100 acres only 10/100ths or 10 percent of the property is lost to economic use so there is no categorical taking. As we have seen in *Penn Central*, however, there are other ways to describe the whole and fractional parts of property. Pursuant to the classic sticks-in-a-bundle metaphor, the various possible uses of a parcel of land are described as fractional parts of the whole. So in *Penn Central*, the right to use of the airspace was one stick in a bundle of rights that also included the surface, the subsurface, possible easements for specific uses in each of those strata, and so forth. Had the denominator in *Penn Central* been viewed as the unutilized airspace, the historic preservation regulation would have resulted in a total loss of economic use. But the Court made clear in that case that it must look at the "parcel as a whole," meaning the combination of all of these fractional parts:

> "Taking" jurisprudence does not divide a single parcel into discrete segments to determine whether rights in a particular segment have been entirely

abrogated. In deciding whether a particular government action has effected a taking, this Court focuses rather... on the nature of the interference with rights in the parcel as a whole.[69]

That would seem to have settled the matter whether the fractional parts of a property interest are defined in terms of use, horizontal strata, surface acreage, or some other factor, but in *Lucas* the Court hedged, or at least admitted that there remained confusion in the case law.

Regrettably, the rhetorical force of our "deprivation of all economically feasible use" rule is greater than its precision, since the rule does not make clear the "property interest" against which the loss of value is to be measured. When, for example, a regulation requires a developer to leave 90 percent of a rural tract in its natural state, it is unclear whether we would analyze the situation as one in which the owner has been deprived of all economically beneficial use of the burdened portion of the tract, or as one in which the owner has suffered a mere diminution in value of the tract as a whole.[70]

Although the Court declined to resolve the question in the context of *Lucas* where the plaintiff "pleaded (a fee simple interest) in an estate with a rich tradition of protection at common law," it did describe as "unsupportable" the lower court's consideration in *Penn Central* of the "total value of the takings claimant's other holdings in the vicinity."[71] Unless takings doctrine is to become a means for, rather than an obstacle to, wealth redistribution, this bit of clarification had to be uncontroversial. But the Court did suggest a promising path to defining the relevant parcel in the way it described the claimant's interest in *Lucas*—"an estate with a rich tradition of protection at common law." The Court went on to suggest that

[t]he answer to this difficult question may lie in how the owner's reasonable expectations have been shaped by the State's law of property—*i.e.*, whether and to what degree the State's law has accorded legal recognition and protection to the particular interest in land with respect to which the takings claimant alleges a diminution in (or elimination of) value.[72]

This is not the so-called "investment-backed" expectations to which the Court has often referred. Rather it is the expectations that reasonably arise from the law of property. Investment-backed expectations have little to do with the occurrence of a taking, if we understand a taking to be the deprivation by the state of a vested right in property. The expectations of which Justice Scalia wrote have everything to do with determining whether the state has taken a property interest the owner could have reasonably expected to use or convey.

The *Lucas* court's rejection of the extreme position of the state court in *Penn Central* should help us to understand why the less extreme position of the Supreme Court in that same case is also unsupportable. If the extent of diminution in value resulting from regulation is determined with reference to the value of all Manhattan properties held by Penn Central, as the state court urged, then the existence of a taking depends upon the current circumstances and wealth of the claimant. If the same regulation is applied with the same effect to identical properties owned by A, who owns no other properties in the jurisdiction, and B, who owns several other properties, this approach would require a court to find a taking with respect to A but not B. There can be no justification for such a result other than redistribution of wealth (by a most ham fisted method). Indeed, if ownership of other properties within the jurisdiction is relevant, there is no reason to exclude from consideration properties held in other jurisdictions since all relate to the claimant's economic capacity to bear the costs of uncompensated regulation. But pursuant to no plausible theory or account of constitutional history can the Takings Clause be understood to excuse takings where circumstances suggest that the property owner has the ability to bear the costs of regulation.

The aforementioned possibilities—multiple properties anywhere and multiple properties within the jurisdiction—can be viewed as points on a continuum of possible combinations of property interests. Other points on the continuum might include a single parcel of X acres *usque ad caelum et ad inferos* (from the heavens to the center of the earth), a single parcel of x minus y acres, a surface estate from which the mineral rights have been severed, air rights held separately from the surface estate and an easement for passage across the surface estate of another, just to name a few "estate[s] with a rich tradition of protection at common law." See Figure 6.1.

Easement	Surface with severed air or minerals	Divided surface	Single parcel *caelum a inferos*	Multiple parcels in jurisdiction	Multiple parcels anywhere

Figure 6.1 Possible Descriptions of the Parcel as a Whole.

What the foregoing figure makes clear is the difficulty of establishing the relevant parcel(s) for the purpose of calculating the degree of loss resulting from regulation. If one owns only an easement, its regulatory obliteration would be a total diminution in value and thus a taking. But the owner of a mere easement may have multiple other properties, which, if included in the accounting, would make the loss of the easement not a taking. This unsupportable result could be avoided by excluding other properties from the denominator, but the challenges posed by the *Penn Central* and *Keystone* facts remain. Properties can be severed horizontally or vertically. In *Penn Central* that means a prohibition on high-rise construction is a taking if the claimant owns only the air rights but not if he owns the air and the surface. In *Keystone*, it is a taking if the mineral estate is severed, but not if the surface and subsurface estates remain in a single ownership.

From the preceding it should be clear that the concept of a whole or relevant parcel against the value of which the extent of a regulatory induced diminution in value is to be compared is elusive of principled definition. To date it has been so elusive as to make the total loss of economic value test anything but categorical and the related extent of diminution factor in *Penn Central* balancing a source of unlimited judicial discretion. Unless our courts are meant to be in the business of upholding or rejecting rights claims on the basis of the wealth of the claimant, there is no principled basis on which a defensible line can be drawn on the continuum of circumstances in which takings claims might arise.

Of course this so-called relevant parcel or denominator problem is ultimately rooted in the unfortunate foundation of sand laid by Justice Holmes's "too far" test nearly a century ago. So long as that remains the Supreme Court's mantra in takings cases, there is little prospect for the sort of clarity one expects in a rule of law system. Making matters worse, the Supreme Court seems bent on preserving the mystery. Rather than struggle with the challenge of articulating reasonably clear standards or guidelines, a majority of the Court has "generally eschewed" any set formula for determining how far is too far, choosing instead to engage in "essentially ad hoc, factual inquiries."[73] "Indeed," said the Court in *Tahoe–Sierra Preservation Council v. Tahoe Regional Planning Agency*, "we still resist the temptation to adopt per se rules in our cases involving partial regulatory takings, preferring to examine 'a number of factors' rather than a simple 'mathematically precise' formula."[74] Why the Court resists the temptation to provide greater certainty to both property owners and governments is anybody's guess.

From its existing case law, the Court's best prospect for bringing order worthy of the rule of law to this fundamental issue is to follow the logical implications of Justice Scalia's reference in *Lucas* to "estate[s] with a rich tradition of protection at common law." A central purpose of a constitutional, rule of law system is to define legal expectations and to give citizen's reason to rely on those expectations by respecting and enforcing the rules on which they depend. As Scalia observed, expectations with respect to property are "shaped by the State's law of property," which has nothing to say about how much property one owns and a lot to say about "whether and to what degree the State's law has accorded legal recognition and protection to [a] particular interest in land." Although *Penn Central* balancing dooms property owners to the uncertainties inherent in unbridled judicial discretion, those uncertainties would be reduced by, and the rule of law would benefit from, a definition of the relevant parcel as any interest in land to which state law has "accorded legal recognition and protection." When such an interest loses all economic value as a result of regulation, there is no principled reason to conclude that it is taken if it is the only interest held by the claimant, but not if the claimant holds other sticks in the proverbial bundle.[75] Nor, in the context of *Penn Central* balancing, is there a principled reason to find that the diminution in value is great in the former case and slight in the latter.

TEMPORARY TAKINGS

Accepting that at least a few regulations of property will be found to be regulatory takings either because they result in physical invasion of property or because they render property without economic value, it was not settled until 1987 whether government had the option of rescinding such regulations and thus avoiding the payment of compensation. In other words, on the rare occasion when a court held that a taking had occurred, did governments have the option of saying: "Oops, we didn't mean it. No harm, no foul." In *First English Evangelical Lutheran Church of Glendale v. Los Angeles*, the Supreme Court effectively held that repeal of a regulatory taking does not eliminate the harm, so there is a constitutional foul to be remedied by compensation. While recognizing that government can amend or withdraw a regulation found to result in a taking, Chief Justice Rehnquist held "that where the government's activities have already worked a taking of all use of property, no subsequent action by the government can relieve it of the duty to provide compensation for the period during which the taking was effective."[76]

Justice Stevens objected in dissent that "[c]autious local officials and land-use planners may avoid taking any action that might later be challenged," that "[m]uch important regulation will never be enacted, even perhaps in the health and safety area," and that the majority decision would ignite a "litigation explosion."[77] Whatever the merits of his objections to the concept of temporary takings, Justice Stevens certainly got it wrong in predicting a future of cautious regulators and rampant litigation. Because temporary takings would result only in circumstances where permanent regulation would be found to impose a taking, and because the Court had effectively limited takings to the two narrow categories of physical invasion and total loss of economic value, the *First English* case did little to alter the prospects for potential takings claimants. To the contrary, the rule Stevens preferred, one that would allow governments to avoid takings liability by amending or repealing an offending regulation, invited regulators to have little or no concern for the risks of such liability. In an earlier case in which a dissenting Justice Brennan proposed (with three concurrences)

> [t]he constitutional rule . . . that, once a court finds a police power regulation has effected a "taking," the government entity must pay just compensation for the period commencing on the date the regulation first effected the "taking," and ending on the date the government entity chooses to rescind or otherwise amend the regulation.[78]

Brennan quoted the following from a California city attorney's presentation to other city attorneys:

> If legal preventive maintenance does not work, and you still receive a claim attacking the land use regulation, or if you try the case and lose, don't worry about it. All is not lost. One of the extra "goodies" contained in the recent [California] Supreme Court case of *Selby v. City of San Buenaventura*, 10 C.3d 110, [109 Cal.Rptr. 799, 514 P.2d 111] appears to allow the City to change the regulation in question, even after trial and judgment, make it more reasonable, more restrictive, or whatever, and everybody starts over again.[79]

Rather than leave property owners victim to such bait and switch tactics by government lawyers, Justice Brennan suggested that "liability [for temporary takings] might . . . encourage municipalities to err on the constitutional side of police power regulations, and to develop internal rules and operating procedures to minimize overzealous regulatory attempts."[80]

When a majority of the court finally embraced Brennan's position in *First English*, it served to underscore, perhaps inadvertently, some of the theoretical flaws of the Court's overall approach to takings doctrine. The procedural posture of the case led the majority to assume that a taking had occurred while recognizing that the California courts might find differently on remand.[81] In making this assumption the Court effectively separated the takings issue from the compensation question as Richard Epstein's approach recommends, but the Court's regulatory takings doctrine fails to do. Justice Stevens's dissent points out this departure from the *Penn Central* balancing test under which the severity of the burden on the property owner is a critical factor in establishing a taking. "[R]epeal will, in virtually all cases," said Stevens, "mitigate the overall effect of the regulation so substantially that the slight diminution in value that the regulation caused while in effect cannot be classified as a taking of property."[82] Stevens was surely correct, if we take the *Penn Central* test at face value. Even accepting that total loss of economic value results in a per se taking, a temporary regulation can deprive property of all economic value only while in effect. Repeal unavoidably means that over time there is not a total loss of value and the extent of the diminution becomes less and less.

The lesson to be drawn from this, however, is not that Stevens has the better argument on temporary takings. Rather the lesson is, once again, that the *Penn Central* balancing approach is fundamentally flawed. In finding a temporary taking in *First English*, Chief Justice Rehnquist and the majority side-stepped *Penn Central* by assuming that a taking had occurred. By thus separating the taking and compensation issues, the Court was left to determine only whether a taking can be remedied by repeal of the offending regulation. In answering that question in the negative, the Court effectively held that a taking does not depend on the magnitude of the economic injury to the property owner or on the extent of the diminution of total property value. A pragmatic acceptance of the delays inherent in bureaucratic process might serve to justify some uncompensated, temporary constraints on the exercise of property rights. But where the explicit purpose of a regulation is to constrain property use in a manner that would be a taking if permanent (as was assumed in *First English*), the only plausible justification for refusing to compensate for a temporary restraint is the lesser economic burden imposed on the property owner. Under *Penn Central* balancing that would be an acceptable outcome—but not under *First English*.

Separation of the taking and compensation questions also led the court to recognize that property interests can be severed on a temporal basis as well as on physical or functional bases. This should be news to no one. Undeveloped land is subdivided for suburban housing.

Mineral rights are severed from the surface estate with the mineral owner acquiring a right to use the surface to the extent reasonably necessary to extract the minerals. And property is leased for a period of months or years. All of these severed property interests have a value that in the latter case is represented by rent. In *First English* the Court simply recognized that if the government forbids the use of property for a period of time, it should pay rent. Although the California court subsequently held that no rent was due because no taking had occurred, that in no way altered the Supreme Court's holding that when a property right is taken, even if only temporarily, compensation, or rent, is owing. Whether the California court got it right on the taking question is important, but beside the point. The use of property for a period of time, just like its use for a particular function or the use of a physical portion can be "an estate with a rich tradition of protection at common law." When that is the case, deprivation of that use by the government is a taking for which just compensation is due.[83]

While the distinction between temporary and permanent takings comports with popular usage and proved useful in further elucidating the shortcomings of the *Penn Central* balancing approach, it is a distinction without a difference if one thinks seriously about the regulatory process. The *Lucas* case, for example, has always been analyzed as a garden variety, permanent taking case. The state of South Carolina sought to permanently prohibit building in the coastal zone. The Court said it was a per se taking because it deprived Lucas of all beneficial economic use of his property. But as we saw in the aftermath of the Supreme Court decision, the regulation was not actually permanent. The state acquired the property from Lucas, removed the regulatory restriction, and sold it to another developer. So Lucas was really compensated for a temporary taking. Indeed all regulatory takings hold the possibility of being temporary. The legislature can always amend or repeal a regulation, if not in an effort to avoid paying compensation as in *First English*, then at a later time when it has a change of heart or mind. What the Court confronted in *First English* was the reality of real economic loss to the property owner whether or not the regulation was repealed. Because they had already assumed that a taking had occurred, the various factors of the *Penn Central* test, including the wealth and circumstances of the claimant, had no relevance. It became crystal clear that the loss suffered by the property owner had nothing to do with whatever value his property would have if the regulation were repealed (as Justice Stevens would have it) or with the importance of whatever interests the state might claim to have. In the interpretation of a constitutional provision meant to spread the costs of government and restrict rather than facilitate the redistribution of wealth, this is a far more defensible result than the *Penn Central* balancing approach preferred by Justice Stevens. Unfortunately, a few years later, the Court reverted to its muddled approach in finding that a three-year moratorium on all economic use of property on the shore of Lake Tahoe was not a categorical taking and was thus subject to *Penn Central* balancing.[84] The opinion, not surprisingly, was written by Justice Stevens.

A Theoretical Conundrum

All of the cases discussed in the preceding sections of this chapter relate to what is generally described as regulatory takings law. A separate line of cases, examined in Chapter 3, relates to the 5th Amendment's Public Use Clause. As the term "public use" is used in the 5th Amendment, it would seem to function as a limit on the purposes for which government can constitutionally take property. In other words, even if compensation is paid, property can be taken only when it is for a public use. As we have seen, however, the Supreme Court has effectively written the Public Use Clause out of the Constitution by holding repeatedly that a public use is whatever the relevant legislative body says it is. In fact, a legislature does not even need to declare something a public use. The courts will presume that any legislative resort to the eminent domain power is in service to a public use, public purpose, the public good, whatever.

But there was a time when property owners and governments took very different views of the meaning of public use. Illustrative is an 1872 Wisconsin case. In an effort to promote economic expansion and development, many nineteenth-century states, including Wisconsin, authorized the private construction of dams in public waters that resulted in the flooding of nearby properties. One such flooded property owner sought compensation under the Wisconsin constitution for a state-authorized taking.[85] (At the time the 5th Amendment did not apply to the states, but the Wisconsin provision was nearly identical and thought by the Supreme Court to have the same meaning.) It was argued in defense that the flooding was "a remote and consequential injury"[86] and therefore not a public use for which compensation was due. In rejecting the defense's narrow definition of public use and ruling in favor of the property owner, Justice Miller wrote:

> It would be a very curious and unsatisfactory result, if in construing a provision of constitutional law, always understood to have been adopted for

protection and security to the rights of the individual as against the government,... it shall be held that if the government refrains from the absolute conversion of real property to the uses of the public it can destroy its value entirely, can inflict irreparable and permanent injury to any extent, can, in effect, subject it to total destruction without making any compensation, because, in the narrowest sense of that word, it is not *taken* for the public use. Such a construction would pervert the constitutional provision into a restriction upon the rights of the citizen, as those rights stood at the common law, instead of the government, and make it an authority for invasion of private right under the pretext of the public good, which had no warrant in the laws or practices of our ancestors.[87]

In effect, Justice Miller was asserting an expansive definition of public use that would include government-induced or -authorized impacts on private property well beyond government occupation and acquisition of title. But his purpose was not to expand the scope of government power as Justice Stevens sought to do in *Kelo*. Rather his purpose was to acknowledge the breadth of constitutional protection of private property.

What explains the apparent contradiction in the positions of Justices Miller and Stevens? In the nineteenth century property rights were the equal of any constitutional liberty and it was clear that their protection against government interference required either a narrow definition of the police power or a broad definition of public use. By the time of *Kelo*, property rights had acquired second-class standing at best, government initiatives were presumed to be constitutional, and regulatory takings claims were treated as barely related to eminent domain and public use. The result is a theoretically incoherent combination of doctrines that have left both property owners and governments to make self-contradictory arguments depending on whether the case at hand involves eminent domain or a regulatory taking claim.

Consider, first, the property owner's perspective. In *Kelo*, *Midkiff*, and other cases in which government seeks to use its eminent domain power to reallocate land among private owners, the logical argument in opposition is that, while such reallocations of property might advance a public purpose, they do not provide for a public use. If we understand the term public use to require literal use by the public, if not public ownership, then the eminent domain power cannot be used to pursue public purposes like those in *Kelo* and *Midkiff*. But if the government cannot employ the eminent domain power for the many public purposes it can pursue under its police powers, how does one justify a regulatory takings claim? By its nature regulation limits the use of property for a public purpose, but it does not, in most circumstances, require the property owner to allow public access to and use of the property. If the Public Use Clause is understood to limit the eminent domain power to acquisitions for actual public use, how can the Takings Clause be understood to require government to pay for the effects of regulations mandating no public use? When a court holds that a particular regulation has resulted in a taking, the implication is that government has authority to impose the regulation, but only if it pays compensation for the taking. Presumably the government could have avoided the lawsuit by including in the regulation provision for compensation. But how would that not be an illegitimate use of the eminent domain power under the narrow interpretation of the Public Use Clause? Can property rights advocates have it both ways? Can they claim an exemption from public purpose condemnations while also claiming a right to compensation for public purpose regulations?

Defenders of unconstrained government power to limit property rights face the mirror image of the same theoretical problem. On the public use question, the logical argument for government is that public use encompasses any public purpose, thus giving broad scope to the eminent domain power. As Justice O'Connor stated it in *Midkiff*, "The 'public use' requirement is thus coterminous with the scope of a sovereign's police powers."[88] But if the Public Use Clause is understood to permit the condemnation of private property for any public purpose, why doesn't it also require the government to compensate when the regulatory power is used to achieve the same public purposes? Like the property owner, government wants it both ways. The only difference is that government gets to have it both ways while property owners come up short whether claiming a regulatory taking or an abuse of the eminent domain power. When governments are prepared to pay compensation for the economic losses imposed on property owners, they are not limited to purposes involving only actual public use. But because they rarely are required to pay compensation when regulating for the same purposes, governments seldom resort to eminent domain if regulation will achieve the same end. So for them, theoretical difficulties are of little note since both public use and regulatory takings law work in their favor. Of course this means that property rights claimants lose most of the time whether their claim is based on regulatory takings or public use theory. A sad irony is that property rights advocates have helped to construct the flawed theoretical framework on which their claims falter.

To reiterate, property claimants find themselves arguing for a narrow definition of public use when government seeks to take property by eminent domain, but an expansive understanding when regulation is claimed to result in a taking. Because regulation seldom is undertaken to provide an actual public use, and when it is, a per se taking is found to result from the resultant abridgement of the right to exclude, regulatory takings claims generally require the property owners to argue that compensation is due where there is no public use, narrowly conceived. Yet in resisting eminent domain condemnation, property advocates must argue that a compensated eminent domain taking is not permitted except where there is a narrowly defined public use. They want courts to mandate compensation where government regulates for a public purpose, but to forbid the government from voluntarily compensating when pursuing the same public purpose by eminent domain. Within the existing takings and eminent domain jurisprudence, property owners have no alternative but to make these inconsistent arguments. Not surprisingly, the theoretical problem faced by property owners is grounded in the "too far" test from *Mahon*.

Re-linking Regulatory Takings and Eminent Domain

The "too far" test and its modern articulation in the *Penn Central* balancing test might be understood as explaining when a police power regulation is a taking and when it is not. But the idea that a police power regulation can result in an unconstitutional taking is inconsistent with the traditional distinction between the police and eminent domain powers, and with Holmes's analysis in *Mahon*. Holmes made clear that compensation was due because the state had exercised its eminent domain power, not because some police power regulations result in takings while others do not.[89] This position was consistent with the longstanding distinction, for Takings Clause purposes, between the police power and the eminent domain power.[90] As explained in depth in Chapter 2, in the nineteenth century it was generally understood that pursuant to the police power, the state had authority to prevent people from doing harm to others through infringement of their personal rights. The police power thus served to enforce preexisting limits on personal liberties of action, including in the use of property—the background principles mentioned by Justice Scalia in *Lucas*. Pursuant to this understanding of the police power, there could be no police power takings because property rights did not extend to actions subject to police power regulation—there could be no right to do that which the state had authority to prohibit or, stated differently, there is no right to use one's property in a way that violates the rights of others.

Takings for which compensation was due under the 5th Amendment were, therefore, the result of the exercise of some other government power—namely eminent domain. Because nineteenth-century American governments were concerned largely with the prevention of harm and the provision of public benefits in the form of public facilities and improvements to transportation and navigation, the dual categories of police power and eminent domain covered everything government did in relation to private property. Based on this neat categorization of government functions, takings cases were easily resolved. Regulations of property pursuant to the police power never resulted in a taking, while government exercise of the eminent domain power was a taking, by definition. Thus, Holmes's point in *Mahon* was that when regulation goes "too far" it must be either invalidated or treated as an exercise of the eminent domain power for which compensation is due. This understanding of Holmes's argument does not overcome the unfortunate vagaries of his "too far" test, but it does comport with a logical and historically accurate account of the police and eminent domain powers.

Holmes's statement with respect to eminent domain was quoted with approval in *Penn Central*,[91] but that Court's validation of the several cases in which regulatory limitations on vested property rights had been upheld in the face of takings challenges belied an acceptance of the traditional distinction between the police and eminent domain powers. No longer were police power regulations concerned with enforcing existing rights. Under *Penn Central* the police power is a source of authority to provide public benefits at the expense of vested property rights. By embracing this fundamental change in the nature of police power while also accepting the traditional understanding that exercises of the eminent domain, but not the police power, require compensation, the Court exempted the state from virtually all regulatory takings claims. By embracing a broad view of public use allowing expansive application of the eminent domain power, while limiting regulatory takings to two narrow categories and the dim possibility that some regulations might just go too far, the Supreme Court has placed property claimants in a theoretical and practical bind. When government chooses to rely on eminent domain, defenders of property must argue that government lacks the authority to compensate for takings in service of a public purpose. When government chooses to rely on police power, defenders of property must argue that government is required to compensate for takings in service of a public purpose. And both arguments must rely upon the same constitutional provision.

RECAPITULATION AND RENEWAL

Despite repeated academic and professional commentary on the incoherence of takings law, the history since *Mahon* suggests that the Court will continue to muddle through with *Penn Central* balancing as its core takings "principle." To bring coherence to takings jurisprudence the Court will have to jettison much of the existing case law and that is difficult for any court that adheres to *stare decisis* as a basic rule of law principle. But if the court can be persuaded that uncertainty, not the predictability meant to be served by *stare decisis*, results from its continuing efforts to make sense of existing case law, reason and liberty might yet prevail.

In summary, modern takings jurisprudence took its first wrong turn in *Pennsylvania Coal Co. v. Mahon*. While Justice Holmes acknowledged that regulation can result in a taking and made the important observation that many regulations have an average reciprocity of advantage, he offered no useful standard for determining what regulatory impacts on property are, in fact, unconstitutional takings. In stating that "government hardly could go on if to some extent values incident to property could not be diminished without paying for every such change in the general law"[92] but that "if regulation goes too far it will be recognized as a taking,"[93] Holmes inadvertently laid the groundwork for a balancing test. Implicit, though not intended, was that on one side of the balance would be whatever public benefits resulted from the regulation. The values to be weighed on the other side (the property owner's side) of the balance were finally summarized in *Penn Central* as (1) the "economic impact of the regulation on the claimant," (2) "the extent to which the regulation has interfered with distinct investment-backed expectations," and (3) "the character of the governmental action."[94] The first and third factors anticipated, respectively, the Court's later recognition of categorical takings where regulation resulted in a total loss of economic value and a physical invasion. But the vast majority of regulatory takings claims were left to be subjected to this balancing of public and private interests. The courts, thus, found themselves in the position of evaluating the public importance of challenged regulations—seemingly a legislative function. Given the general presumption of constitutionality, the balance was weighted in favor of the government, but there was no guidance as to when the balance might finally tip in the property owner's direction.

Implicit in the task of weighing the public benefits arising from any particular regulation is the need to assess whether and to what extent the regulation actually delivers public benefits. In considering the relationship between the means and ends of regulation, the courts were, at best, looking to principles of due process and, at worst, intruding even farther upon the legislative role. The reliance on due process further confused takings law by treating the Takings Clause as a test of legislative validity rather than a condition imposed on otherwise valid legislation. Although Justice O'Connor made clear in *Lingle,* that a taking is a taking whether or not the means serve the end and whether or not the end is legitimate, the persistence of the *Penn Central* balancing test did not allow the courts to escape the need to make some assessment of the extent to which the means actually produced public benefits.

In the interest of assuring that government can go on, reliance on the courts to "engag[e]...in these essentially ad hoc, factual inquiries" that "depend[] largely 'upon the particular circumstances [of each] case' "[95] is clearly a plausible approach. After all, the courts have been relying on it for nearly a century. But is it a constitutional approach? It might be suggested that, rather than legislating, the courts are merely clarifying the police power's implied limitation on property rights, but as Holmes, himself, observed, this "implied limitation must have its limits or the Contract and Due Process Clauses are gone."[96] Gone, also, would be the Takings Clause. That is why Holmes took a broad view of the eminent domain power and the public use requirement of the 5th Amendment. Had he insisted on a narrow definition of public use he could not have found that a taking resulted from the regulatory reassignment of rights from the subsurface to the surface owner. Had it been a regulation of general application providing an "average reciprocity of advantage" to those affected, there is little doubt that Holmes would have found against the property owner—not because there was no taking but because there was implicit compensation. But the regulation at issue in *Mahon* was not one of general application and it had the effect of "mak[ing] it commercially impracticable to mine certain coal [which] has very nearly the same effect for constitutional purposes as appropriating or destroying it."[97] Had Holmes continued to think more like a practitioner of the common law and less like a public policy pragmatist, he might have thought better of describing the case before him as one in which government regulation had gone "too far." He might have been concerned that a prescription so vague would supply none of the predictability that marks a rule of law system like the common law. He might have observed that the interest effectively appropriated or destroyed is "an estate with a rich tradition of protection at common law," and for that reason entitled to compensation under the 5th Amendment.

Unless we are intent on protecting the public fisc without regard to fairness or redistributing wealth through the ham-fisted methods of regulation, the letter and spirit of the Takings Clause can be interpreted in a straightforward way that is both protective of property rights and respectful of the needs of government. Using the approach suggested below, there would be more compensation expenses for government and less government regulation, but regulation would be more cost effective and the public fisc would benefit from the greater productivity that would result from heightened respect for private property rights. In other words, when government, like any private interest, is required to pay for what it acquires, it will have incentive to assure that net social benefits of regulation exceed net social costs. At the same time private property owners will have the security of rights necessary to the social wealth maximizing investment and trade of the free market.

In a nutshell, the Supreme Court should construct a new takings doctrine around the sequential consideration of the four questions implicit in the Takings Clause:

1) Does the plaintiff have the property interest claimed to have been taken? If no, there is no case under the Takings Clause. If yes,
2) Has that property interest been taken by government action? If no, there is no case under the Takings Clause. If yes,
3) Is the taking for a public use? If no, the property owner's consent is required (there can be no forced sale). If yes,
4) Has just compensation been paid? If no, compensation for the full value of the property taken is due or the government may rescind the taking with compensation due for the period of temporary taking. If yes, the government has complied with the requirements of the 5th Amendment Takings Clause.

Because all of the trouble started with *Pennsylvania Coal Co. v. Mahon*, it is appropriate and useful to illustrate the rationale and application of this approach in that context. The answer to the first question rests in property law, not constitutional law. The law of property is ancient and complex. It covers a wide array of interests in addition to land

and its associated resources. Although determination of the parameters of a particular property right can be difficult and complicated, it is not mysterious. It is the day-to-day work of real estate lawyers, trusts and estates lawyers, patent and copyright lawyers, commercial lawyers, and anyone else providing legal advice on the purchase, sale, and protection of interests in property. These property rights experts look to common law, statutory law, and private agreements to determine the scope and content of particular rights in property. From these sources they will discover the extent of exclusivity, permitted and prohibited uses, and any constraints on disposition.

Thus, in *Mahon*, the analysis would proceed as follows. Did the claimant have a property right to the coal the regulation required him to leave in place as a support for the surface estate? By private agreement Pennsylvania Coal had conveyed the surface estate with an express reservation of the right to remove all of the coal and with the owner of the surface estate to bear the risks of resulting damage to the surface. Neither the common law nor statutory law prohibited such private agreement. Indeed, absent evidence to the contrary, the common law recognized a general right (a background principle in Scalia's words) in mineral estates to use the surface to the extent reasonably necessary to extract the mineral resources. So there was clearly a property right, unless that right expired with the enactment of the Pennsylvania statute. But if the state has the authority to thus curtail what was thought to be a right recognized by the common law and retained by private agreement, then it cannot be said that any such right exists.

The second question then is, has that property right been taken? The answer has to be yes, unless we are prepared to accept either that the state has the authority to alter vested rights by statute or that the right to mine the coal does not mean all of the coal. But in either case we would really be saying that Pennsylvania Coal did not have the property right claimed to have been taken. We would be back to the first question. If we are convinced that Pennsylvania Coal did have a right to extract all of the coal, the second question is purely one of fact. Has the coal Company been prohibited by the state from exercising its right to extract all of the coal? The answer is clearly yes, so there must be a taking. But wait a minute, says the state of Pennsylvania, a taking for constitutional purposes is not the same thing as a taking for common law purposes. It is certainly the case that the surface owner or some other private party cannot take the coal, but the state has the authority to regulate for public health and safety under the police power. The coal company may have a right in relation to other private parties but, says the state, it is a right limited by the police power. In other words, the right, at least in relation to the state, is contingent on the state's altering it for the public benefit. But the Pennsylvania statute altered more than Pennsylvania Coal's relation to the state. The Pennsylvania statute had the effect of giving the surface estate owner a right in coal that had been expressly reserved to the coal company. The statute affected a transfer of right from one private party to another. That which is a common law taking must also be a constitutional taking, because every state-imposed constraint on property rights will have the effect of transferring that right to other private parties, though they may also be part of what the state likes to think of as the public.

This recognition gets us to the heart of the matter. The *Mahon* court concluded that the Pennsylvania statute resulted in a taking because it went "too far." The clear implication was that a regulation having less impact, but still limiting the right to mine coal, would not be a taking. Or, as it turns out, that the same regulation with greater public benefits would not be a taking, as the court held in *Keystone*. In either case, Pennsylvania Coal's property right would exist only so long as there is not less than an undefined ratio of private benefit from mining coal to public benefit (meaning benefit to other private parties) from not mining coal. There is nothing in the common law, its statutory refinements or the history of the 5th Amendment to justify treating property rights as so contingent, but if there were it would be relevant to the existence of a property right, not the existence of a taking. This may seem a trivial distinction, but it is not. Introducing vague contingencies into the definition of a taking buries them in the muddle of constitutional balancing. But in the context of defining rights in property, those contingencies stand in stark contrast to the history and deeply rooted principles of property law. Justice Holmes could have (and should have) reached the same result in *Mahon* by finding that Pennsylvania Coal proved a taking simply by demonstrating that the Pennsylvania statute deprived the property owner of its exclusive right to possess, use, and dispose of some of its coal. That right is, as Justice Scalia wrote in *Lucas*, "an estate with a rich tradition of protection at common law." Proof of the regulatory deprivation of such an estate, or of a severable portion of such an estate, is all that should be required to establish a taking.

Having established that a property right has been taken, the third question is whether it has been taken for a public use. As the earlier discussion of public uses demonstrates, a narrow understanding that public use requires acquisition of public title or mandating of public access leads to an even narrower understanding of what constitutes a regulatory taking. Although the language of public use invites the narrow interpretation in eminent domain, that same understanding applied to regulatory takings leads to a result inconsistent with the underlying purpose of the Takings Clause. Thus, a better understanding of public use is public purpose, with the result that regulatory takings are far broader than the Supreme Court has recognized while the constitutional scope of the eminent domain power was correctly determined in *Kelo*. This final conclusion will not sit well with most property rights advocates, but the reality is that the constitutional remedy for discrimination against property owners is compensation, not judicial second-guessing of legislation. The good news is that the political remedy, as Justice Stevens said in *Kelo* and as over 30 states have demonstrated, is a powerful one.

That does not mean that government is thereby prohibited from undertaking discriminatory regulations of property. Although such regulations might be precluded by the Equal Protection Clause or some other constitutional limitation on government power, the Takings Clause poses no prohibition. It requires only that compensation be paid when such discrimination occurs. Of course the most common and blatant example of discrimination against particular property owners is the exercise of the eminent domain power. There, the third question inherent in the Takings Clause is posed explicitly—is there a public use? Because takings jurisprudence has long separated eminent domain from regulatory takings, we are not accustomed to asking the public use question in a case like *Mahon*. But there is only one 5th Amendment compensation provision, even if we choose sometimes to call it the Eminent Domain Clause and other times the Takings Clause. If compensation is to be paid in *Mahon*, as Holmes said it must be, then there has to be a public use justifying the regulatory taking. By accepting that the State of Pennsylvania has police power authority to regulate subsurface estates for the purpose of protecting the health and safety of occupiers of overlying surface estates, Holmes implicitly found that the public use requirement was satisfied. Otherwise, Pennsylvania had no authority to impose the regulation, an unconstitutional act that could not be remedied by compensation for a taking. The state, no more than a private individual, cannot make illegal conduct legal simply by paying for the harm done.

One might conclude from Holmes's opinion in *Mahon* that the foregoing approach is not practical. Holmes did say, after all, that "[g]overnment hardly could go on if to some extent values incident to property could not be diminished without paying for every such change in the general law."[98] It was this pragmatic recognition that led Holmes to the "too far" test. But the reality is that government could readily go on if required to pay its way, and Holmes explained why in the very same opinion. Most laws of general application provide an average reciprocity of advantage, meaning that the burdens and benefits of regulation are generally shared. This gets us to the question of compensation. The fact that a particular regulation provides offsetting benefits for burdens imposed does not mean there is no taking. It means there has been a taking for which just compensation is paid implicitly. The vast majority of police power regulations will satisfy this test and government will go on just fine. The exceptions will be those regulations that do not have general application, but apply only to one or a few property owners. In other words, average reciprocity of advantage will exist except where there is discrimination in application, and it is precisely those cases the Takings Clause is meant to rectify. The remedy is not invalidation of the discriminatory regulation, rather the remedy is just compensation. In *Mahon* there could be no reciprocity of advantage because those burdened by the regulation were all owners of property interests in anthracite coal while the beneficiaries were all owners of residential structures.

It is not surprising that many takings claims have involved zoning and other regulations of land and resource use. Zoning laws are not, by their nature, of general application. They create zones in which uses are permitted, limited, or forbidden. Properties in different zones are subjected to different rules. The point of zoning is discrimination and discrimination is what the Takings Clause prohibits. But the fact that zoning and land-use regulation pose frequent takings issues is not evidence that government in general could hardly go on under a strict takings regime. Most health and safety regulations are of general application and thus provide implicit compensation in the form of improved health and safety.

In the case of regulations of general application, there is no acceptable way for the courts to assess whether the shared benefits outweigh or equal the shared burdens. If burdens exceed benefits, on average, it is likely that some property owners will experience a larger disparity between benefit and burden than others, but those disparities will tend to even out over the course of time. Judicial intervention to assure that every discreet regulation of general application provides average reciprocity of advantage would involve the courts in a fundamentally legislative function, whereas judicial intervention in cases of discriminatory regulation involves the courts in their familiar and essential judicial review function. One of the great risks of democratic government is the tyranny of the majority. The Takings Clause is an important part of the constitutional shield against majoritarian excesses. By requiring government to pay its way in every case, either by implicit or explicit compensation, discrimination against random or disfavored individuals will be avoided and government will be forced to account for all of the costs of its initiatives.

Under the Supreme Court's existing takings doctrine, property owners have no real protection under the Public Use Clause of the 5th Amendment, though when government invokes its eminent domain powers the property owners do get just compensation. But where regulations impact on private property values, even where the government's purpose might have been pursued by eminent domain, property owners get little protection from the Takings Clause. Although the property owners prevailed in *Nollan*, *Lucas*, and *Dolan v. City of Tigard*, the prospects for property owners seeking to recover compensation under the Takings Clause of the 5th Amendment remain distant. A property owner is likely to prevail under two circumstances: (1) where there is a physical occupation of his property by the government or by someone else at the government's command, and (2) where there is a total diminution in the economic value of his property. Otherwise the question is whether the government regulation goes too far—a sort of balancing of the property owner's interests (investment back expectations) against the government's interests. In such a balancing test it is very unlikely that the property owner will prevail since the government purports to act on behalf of the entire public and the property owner can claim only his own interests. If the balancing test also took account of the importance of secure property rights to economic prosperity, not to mention public confidence in government, the balance may shift in the property owner's direction. But the idea that there is a strong public interest in the protection of private property rights—that a core function of government is the preservation of property rights as foundational to other liberties—is seldom a part of the Supreme Court's property rights jurisprudence.

Chapter 7

Conclusion

In 1952 the US Supreme Court held that President Harry Truman's seizure of the nation's steel mills during the Korean War was an unconstitutional abuse of executive power. Concurring in that judgment, Justice Felix Frankfurter observed that the "long-headed statesmen" who drafted and ratified the Constitution "had no illusion that our people enjoyed biological or psychological or sociological immunities from the hazards of concentrated power."[1] Barely a decade before the Philadelphia convention and the constitution's ratification by the states, such naiveté may have influenced the rebellious colonials to believe that their liberties would be restored by the simple expedient of replacing monarchical rule with democratic governance. The founders of the new nation learned quickly, however, that elected officials and popular majorities would also abuse the awesome powers of government unless constrained. The Constitution of 1787, though partly an effort to make government power more effective, was designed to provide those constraints.

The Awesome Powers of Government

In the United States, government power is separated vertically, from local to national, and horizontally, among the three branches of government. In drafting the constitution the framers gave little thought to local governments, which were presumed to exist as creatures of the state. A century and a half of colonial history guaranteed that state governments were presumed to exist as well. But not everything was taken for granted. The division of powers among the levels of government was by careful design. In parallel with the horizontal separation of powers among the executive, legislative, and judicial branches, the vertical separation between the state and national governments was instituted as a protection of liberty. By separating the awesome powers of government into multiple hands, the framers believed they could discourage the abuse of power.

The national government was to be one of limited powers. Those powers are enumerated in the constitution, and the 10th Amendment makes clear that "powers not delegated to the United States by the Constitution, nor prohibited by it to the States, are reserved to the States respectively, or to the people." Reserved to the people are the power of the ballot box, inherent to popular sovereignty, and those inalienable rights that function as limits on the powers of government. Reserved to the states are the powers inherent in all governments minus those exclusively delegated to the national government or reserved to the people by state constitutions.

Although the US Constitution says nothing about the nature or scope of state power beyond a few express limits, it has always been understood that the states have four basic powers: taxation, spending on public services, eminent domain, and police. The principal limit on the powers to tax and spend is the ballot box. So long as taxes do not discriminate against particular individuals or groups, or burden constitutional liberties, it is assumed, with reason, that the people will not vote to tax themselves excessively. It is also assumed, though with less good reason, that spending will be restrained because voters know the difference between public goods, that will generally not be supplied privately, and private goods, supplied by the voters themselves.

The eminent domain power is constrained by the dual requirements of just compensation and public use. Although there are disagreements on the margins, just compensation is generally understood to be fair market value. However, there are disagreements at the core of the meaning of public use. Traditionally property taken by eminent domain had to be open to free access by the public, if not actually owned by the state. Supreme Court doctrine today gives total deference to legislatures to declare that any public purpose constitutes a public use. In response, most states have imposed a more demanding standard designed to prevent eminent domain takings from one private party for transfer to another private party.

Historically, government had the power to police the private relations among its citizens. Common law courts enforced criminal, tort, property, and contract rules defining the relative rights of individuals. Many of these rules were subsequently adopted and amended by legislative bodies as statutes and ordinances, but the concept of the police power remained unchanged. In the case of property rights, the state's police function was the interpretation and enforcement of vested property rights consistent with background principles necessary to protect the rights of others.

The modern concept of the police power is much changed and expanded from its rights protection role of common law history. Today the police power is widely understood to encompass anything and everything governments aspire to do. Indeed many modern cases suggest that the police power encompasses the eminent domain power as well as spending on traditionally private goods like health care and housing. This greatly expanded notion of the police power poses threats to private property rights the framers could not have anticipated.

When the police power was the enforcement of private rights, it did not threaten private property. To the contrary, its function was to protect property rights and could not therefore be exercised to violate those rights through unconstitutional takings. But with today's much expanded police power, many regulations do have the effect of altering vested property rights. The historic principle that exercise of the police power could not result in an unconstitutional taking because it was merely the enforcement of existing rights is no longer valid when the police power is said to encompass state and local government actions that require the redefinition and redistribution of those vested rights.

Although it is generally understood that the police power rests with the states and not with the national government, the greatly expanded role of the federal government since the New Deal looks a lot like the modern version of the police power. Most of that expansion has been justified as an exercise of the enumerated power to regulate commerce among the states. Although this expansion of federal power into something resembling the states' police powers is clearly contrary to the division of powers contemplated by the framers, the Supreme Court has, with rare exceptions, interpreted the commerce clause to authorize regulations and programs affecting virtually every aspect of American life.

The Demise of Economic Liberties

In abandoning the division of powers between Congress and the states as a significant restraint on abuses of government power, the Supreme Court opened a large chink in the liberty protecting armor of the Constitution. With respect to private property rights, this forsaking of the shield of constitutional structure left only the 4th, 5th and

14th Amendments standing guard against the vastly expanded police powers of both state and federal governments. The 4th Amendment's prohibition on unreasonable searches and seizures has stood relatively firm in defense of personal privacy and the sanctity of the home, but the 5th and 14th Amendment protections of private property have been severely eroded.

The erosion of these constitutional guarantees has resulted from a combination of judicial deference to the other two branches of government and reliance on balancing tests weighted heavily against the private property claimant. Ironically, conservatives have played a leading, if inadvertent, role in this steady erosion of property rights. In reaction to the Supreme Court's recognition of a constitutionally guaranteed right of privacy and its aggressive defense of the individual liberty claims of those accused of crime, conservatives in the courts and legal academy pressed the argument that an activist judiciary was riding roughshod over the will of the democratic majority. The solution to the problem of judicial activism, they concluded, was deference by the courts to the will of the majority. Judicial activism was to be measured by the frequency of judicial invalidations of legislative acts, without regard for the rationale of a particular finding of unconstitutionality. Unfortunately this argument from the right ignored a fundamental reason the framers of the constitution included both structural and substantive safeguards of liberty—the prospect of a tyrannous majority.

While the liberals on the Supreme Court stuck to their guns on privacy and the rights of the accused, they were more than happy to defer to legislatures on the constitutionality of regulations and other actions affecting property and contract rights. The often stated explanation for the resultant two-tiered system of constitutional rights was that regulations affecting economic liberties are social and economic in character. But this is no explanation at all. The reality is that almost all government regulations can be described as social and economic. The difference is not in the character of the government action but in a perceived difference between the types of rights affected. Despite Justice Potter Stewart's protestation in *Lynch v. Household Finance* that "[t]he dichotomy between personal liberties and property rights is a false one,"[2] economic liberties have become second-class rights in Supreme Court doctrine. Although conservative judges usually agree with Justice Stewart in principle, most remain firmly committed to the view that the solution to liberal judicial activism is deference to the elected branches of government. As a result they usually are unwilling to come to the defense of economic liberties.

As a general matter, the Supreme Court has implemented its deference doctrine through a system of varying levels of review. At the most deferential level of judicial review, the question for the court is whether the legislature had a rational basis for concluding that the means it has employed will serve a legitimate state purpose. Given that in applying this test courts are to defer to the legislature on both what constitutes a public purpose and whether the means are rationally related to that purpose, virtually every legislative act subjected to rational basis review is found to be constitutional. Elevated levels of review apply only where the affected rights are at least really important, if not fundamental, or where a previously discriminated against class of people has been singled out. Owners of property rights do not meet the latter requirement and, despite nothing in the constitution supporting the conclusion, economic liberties are not fundamental or even really important. As a result economic liberty claims seldom prevail in court.

Implicit in the levels of review doctrine is a full embrace of the increasingly pervasive balancing approach that has gradually overtaken Supreme Court jurisprudence. The approach had its constitutional roots in progressive era judicial pragmatism. When Justice Holmes held in ***Pennsylvania Coal v. Mahon*** that a regulation of private property is not a taking unless it goes "too far,"[3] he helped lay the groundwork for transforming property rights from trumps on government action into mere interests that must compete in the political arena as well as in the increasingly politicized courts. Even at the level of strict scrutiny, where courts must find a compelling state interest to validate limitations on constitutional liberties, rights are occasionally compromised based on a judicial determination of the importance of the state's asserted interest. At the rational basis level of review, with courts deferring to the balance of interests already declared by the legislature, rights can become meaningless. For the most part, the rights compromised under rational basis review are economic liberties.

Taking Economic Liberties Seriously

For the very reasons that the framers of our various constitutions established structural constraints on government power, enumerated limited powers for the federal government, and provided explicit constitutional guarantees for individual liberties, we cannot expect our elected officials and hired bureaucrats to suddenly exercise restraint in their impositions on property rights and other economic liberties. The incentives for empire building on the part of government officials and rent seeking by their special interest constituents are powerful. And the Supreme Court's jurisprudence of balancing has made it all too easy to rationalize impositions on private rights as limitations necessary to achieving the greater public good. If economic liberties are to regain a constitutional status equal to the so-called personal and civil liberties, it will only happen in the courts.

But, as we have seen in several of the foregoing chapters, the courts face most of a century of precedent validating legislative and executive constraints on property rights. An unyielding and unthinking commitment to the principle of *stare decisis* (let the prior decision stand) leads most courts to conclude that there is nothing they can do to restore meaningful constitutional protections for economic liberties. That is generally a prudent posture for lower courts. However, the core purpose of *stare decisis*—to provide legal certainty in an otherwise uncertain world, argues for the Supreme Court and the high courts of the various states to reconsider legal doctrines that have yielded growing uncertainty for property owners. While property rights in relation to other private parties have remained secure and predictable, property rights in relation to government have become ever less certain.

Courts can restore to property rights the certainty and predictability that *stare decisis* is meant to promote in several straightforward ways.

- They can clarify that the police power is the power to encourage respect for private rights and to prosecute violations of those rights. Thus understood, the police power poses no threat to private property rights. Other legitimate government functions that result in explicit or effective alteration of vested property rights should be required to employ the eminent domain power. While it will be objected that the foregoing prescription will incapacitate governments because they would be buried in compensation costs, the reality is that most such "takings" are implicitly compensated consistent with Justice Holmes's average reciprocity of advantage concept. Where they are not and compensation is required, governments will be forced to account for the true costs of their actions.
- Courts can be clear that the only public rights claims that function as true limits on private property rights are those rooted in background principles of the common law, like nuisance and public trust. The declaration of new public rights and the conflation of public rights with the public interest are simply glorified assertions that government has the discretion and authority to alter vested property rights without compensation.

- Courts can revise and restate takings doctrine as suggested in Chapter VI. By addressing, in order, whether a property right exists, whether it has been taken, whether there is a legitimate public use, and whether there has been implicit or explicit compensation, courts can develop a coherent takings doctrine that will provide certainty to property owners, prospective property owners, and government.
- Courts can be clear, as was Justice Stewart in *Lynch v. Household Finance,* that there is no logical distinction between economic and personal or civil liberties. While some will dispute whether property rights are truly the foundation of all liberties, it is certainly true that property rights often facilitate the exercise of other liberties and that in every person's life not a day goes by without reliance (usually subconsciously) on the security of their property rights.
- Courts can recognize that their mistaken, two-tiered concept of liberty is part and parcel of their ever more pervasive and equally mistaken reliance on balancing tests in the adjudication of rights claims against government. Where existing law has failed to provide a clear boundary between private rights claims, balancing has long been an effective and fair judicial method for resolving disputes. Neither party is clearly in the right, so a compromise of their claims is the best solution consistent with individual liberty. Not so when liberty conflicts with government power. Government (purportedly public) interests will almost always outweigh the liberty interests of an individual. That is why rights must be viewed as trumps if our governments really were created to secure those rights.
- Finally, the foregoing point makes clear that courts must reconsider their general presumption that legislative and executive actions are constitutional. This presumption reflects a legitimate concern on the part of the courts not to intrude upon the powers of the other two branches of government. But a respect for the constitutional separation of powers and a concern to avoid judicial activism should not deter the courts from performing their central responsibility of protecting liberty from the inevitable abuses of executive and legislative power. The courts should leave policy making to the other branches, but must be activist in their defense of liberty.

In his concurring opinion in the steel seizure case, Justice Frankfurter acknowledged that "[i]t is absurd to see a dictator in a representative product of the sturdy democratic traditions of the Mississippi Valley."[4] So too it seems absurd to imagine elected officials and legislative majorities purposely violating the trust and rights of their constituents. But as the revolutionary generation learned, in the wake of their victory over a tyrannous king, trust is sometimes breached and rights infringed even by those elected to exercise the awesome powers of government. As Frankfurter reminded us, "[t]he accretion of dangerous power does not come in a day. It does come, however slowly, from the generative force of unchecked disregard of the restrictions that fence in even the most disinterested assertion of authority."[5]

Notes

Chapter 1

1. Berman v. Parker, 348 U.S. 26 (1954).
2. 545 U.S. 469 (2005).
3. Pennsylvania Coal Co. v. Mahon, 260 U.S. 393 (1922).

Chapter 2

1. Hawaii Housing Authority v. Midkiff, 467 U.S. 229, 240 (1984).
2. "The powers not delegated to the United States by the Constitution, nor prohibited by it to the States, are reserved to the States respectively, or to the people." U.S. Const. amend. X.
3. "The Constitution, and the Laws of the United States which shall be made in Pursuance thereof; and all Treaties made, or which shall be made, under the Authority of the United States, shall be the supreme Law of the Land . . . ." U.S. Const. art. VI, cl. 2.
4. See 61 Mass. (7 Cush.) 53 (1851).
5. *Id.* at 70.
6. *Id.* at 71.
7. *Id.* at 85.
8. *Id.*
9. *Id.* at 82 ("This right of dominion and controlling power over the sea and its coasts, shores, and tide waters, when relinquished by the parent country, must vest somewhere; and, as between the several states and the United States, whatever may have been the doubts on the subject, it is settled that it vested in the several states, in their sovereign capacity, respectively, and was not transferred to the United States by the adoption of the constitution intended to form a more perfect union.").
10. *Id.* at 81 and see quotation at note 6 *supra*.
11. *Id.* at 85–86.
12. *Id.* at 85.
13. *Id.* at 96.
14. *Id.* at 104.
15. *Id.*
16. *Id.* at 81.

17. *Id.* at 96–97.
18. *Id.* at 103.
19. *Id.* at 103–04.
20. Munn v. Illinois, 94 U.S. 113, 124 (1876).
21. *Id.*
22. *Id.*
23. *Id.* at 125 (first omission added) (quoting *The License Cases*, 46 U.S. (5 How.) 504, 583 (1847)).
24. *Id.* at 126 (quoting Matthew Hale, *De Portibus Maris*, reprinted in 1 A Collection of Tracts Relative to the Law of England 72, 78 (Francis Hargrave ed., 1787) (1670)).
25. *Id.*
26. *Id.* at 148 (Field, J., dissenting).
27. See *id.* at 149–51; *see also id.* at 129 (majority opinion) (quoting *Ex parte* Jennings, 6 Cow. 518, 536 (N.Y. Sup. Ct. 1826)).
28. 2 Denio 461, 487 (N.Y. 1845).
29. Opinions of the Court of Exchequer in Bates' Case, 1606. II State Trials, 30–32., Prothero, 340–342), reprinted in Select Documents of English Constitutional History 329, 330–331 (George Burton Adams and H. Morse Stephens eds., Macmillan & Co. 1920).
30. Joseph Chitty, The Prerogatives of the Crown 4 (1820).
31. 4 Edward Coke, Institutes of the Laws of England 36 (William S. Hein Co. 1986) (1628).
32. 1 William Blackstone, Commentaries *156.
33. Marbury v. Madison, 5 U.S. (1 Cranch) 137, 177 (1803).
34. Observations Leading to a Fair Examination of the System of Government Proposed by the Late Convention, Letters from the Federal Farmer, Letter no. 16, January 20, 1788, reprinted in 2 The Complete Antifederalist 323, 323–324 (Herbert J. Storing ed. 1981).
35. Thomas M. Cooley, *A Treatise on the Constitutional Limitations 22* (Boston, Little, Brown & Co. 1868).
36. 4 Blackstone, *supra* note 32, at *162.
37. *Id.* at *133.
38. *Id.* at *160.
39. *Id.* at *154.
40. *Id.* at *160.
41. McMullen v. City Council of Charleston, 1 S.C.L. (1 Bay) 46 (1787).
42. Johns v. Nichols, 2 U.S. (2 Dall.) 184, 187 (1792).
43. State v.—, 2 N.C. (1 Hawy.) 28, 32 (1794).
44. *Id.* at 34.
45. *Id.* at 33.
46. *Id.* at 31.
47. *Id.* at 37.

48. The Federalist No. 10 (James Madison).
49. In *Calder v. Bull*, 3 U.S. (3. Dall.) 386 (1798), the Supreme Court held that the Ex Post Facto Clause of Article I, Section 10, of the US Constitution applies to criminal, but not civil, matters. Although that holding has remained the law ever since, it has not gone without challenge. As recently as 1998, exactly two centuries later, Justice Thomas expressed his willingness to reconsider the *Calder* holding in an appropriate case. Eastern Enterprises v. Apfel, 524 U.S. 498, 538–39 (1998) (Thomas, J. concurring).
50. State v.—, 2 N.C. (1 Hawy.) at 39.
51. *Id.* at 33.
52. *Id.*
53. Zylstra v. Corp. of Charleston, 1 S.C.L. (1 Bay) 382 (1794).
54. State v. Wheeler, 44. N.J.L. 88, 91 (N.J. 1882). The same maxim was expressed as "*sic uit suo ut non laedat alienum*" in the famous case of *Rylands v Fletcher*, (1868) 3 L.R.E. & I. App. 330 (H.L.).
55. Oliver Wendell Holmes, Jr., Privilege, Malice and Intent, 8 *Harv. L. Rev.* 1, 3 (1894).
56. Lochner v. New York, 198 U.S. 45, 75 (1905).
57. See Justinian, De Cloacis, *in* 4 *The Digest of Justinian* 601, 601–02 (Theodor Mommsen & Paul Krueger eds., Alan Watson trans., University of Pennsylvania Press, 1985).
58. The first clause of Lord Coke's expanded maxim makes explicit reference to the use of property. Although the more frequently quoted second clause states a more general principle of not doing harm to others, it is generally translated as having application to property.
59. Aldred's Case, (1611) 77 *Eng. Rep.* 818, 820 (K.B.).
60. 3 Blackstone, *supra* note 32, at *217.
61. 1 Blackstone, *supra* note 32, at *295–96.
62. George P. Smith, II, Nuisance Law: The Morphogenesis of an Historical Revisionist Theory of Contemporary Economic Jurisprudence, 74 *Neb. L. Rev.* 658, 680 (1995).
63. J. R. Spencer, Public Nuisance—A Critical Examination, 48 *Cambridge L.J.* 55, 57 (1989).
64. 3 *Bracton on the Laws and Customs of England 164* (George E. Woodbine ed., Samuel E. Thorne trans., Harvard University Press 1977).
65. J.R. Spencer, Public Nuisance—A Critical Examination, 48 *Cambridge L.J.* 55, 60 (quoting William Sheppard, The Court-Keeper's Guide (5th ed. 1662)).
66. *Id.* at 65–66.
67. Morgan v. Banta, 4 Ky. (1 Bibb) 579, 582 (Ky 1809).
68. Shackelford v. Hendley's Ex'ors, 8 Ky. (1 A.K. Marsh.) 496, 500 (Ky. 1819).

69. Shepherd v. Hees, 12 Johns. 433, 433 (N.Y. 1815) (emphasis omitted).
70. Mahony v. Township of Hampton, 651 A.2d 525, 527 (Pa. 1994).
71. Thomas M. Cooley, A Treatise on the Constitutional Limitations which Rest upon the Legislative Power of the States of the American Union 574 (1868).
72. 180,000 ($270,000) today.
73. Mouse's Case, (1608) 77 Eng. Rep. 1341 (K.B.).
74. See, e.g., Regina v. Dudley and Stephens, 14 Q.B.D. 273 (1884) (a cabin boy was killed and eaten by three other starving survivors of a shipwreck at sea) and United States v. Holmes, 26 F.Cas. 360 (1842) (passengers in lifeboat were thrown overboard to prevent the lifeboat from sinking and save the lives of those remaining); see also A.W. Brian Simpson, *Cannibalism and the Common Law* (1984).
75. Khalid Ghanayim, Excused Necessity in Western Legal Philosophy, 19 *Canadian J.L. & Juris.* 31, 32 (2006).
76. *Id.* at 33.
77. Francis Bacon, Maxims of the Law, *in* 3 *The Works of Francis Bacon* 229 (A. Hart 1850).
78. John Alan Cohan, Two Men and a Plank: The Argument from a State of Nature, 29 *Whittier L. Rev.* 333, 344 n.87 (2007).
79. 4 Blackstone, *supra* note 32, at *31.
80. Supra note 74.
81. Cooley, *supra* note 35, at 594.
82. *E.g.*, Harrison v. Wisdom, 54 Tenn. (7 Heisk.) 99, 114 (1872).
83. 4 Blackstone, *supra* note 32, at *31–32.
84. *Wisdom*, 54 Tenn. at 114.
85. *Saltpetre Case*, 77 Eng. Rep. 1294, 1294, 12 Co. 12 (1606).
86. Stone v. City of New York, 25 Wend. 157 (1840).
87. *Saltpetre Case*, 77 Eng. Rep. at 1295.
88. *Stone*, 25 Wend. at 175–76.
89. Willard Hurst, Law and the Conditions of Freedom in the Nineteenth-Century United States (1956).
90. W.P. Prentice, Police Powers Arising Under the Law of Overruling Necessity 1 (1894).
91. *Id.* at 4.
92. *Id.* at 1.
93. Later in the same treatise Prentice would contradict this conclusion, stating the self-defense is "one of the bases of police laws upon the side of society organized in the State." *Id.* at 473.
94. *Id.* at 5.
95. Prentice makes specific reference to *sic utere tuo ut alienum non lædas* in explaining why police power regulation does not require compensation. "The police power of the State, which authorizes the legislature to pass laws for the protection of the health and safety of

the public, and which is a power sufficient to warrant the destruction of property for the protection of the public health without compensation, is, in this particular, founded upon the rule of law which requires one person so to use his property as not to interfere with the rights of his neighbors." *Id.* at 467.

96. *Id.* at 69–70.
97. Munn v. Illinois, 94 U.S. 113 (1876).
98. Mugler v. Kansas, 123 U.S. 623, 669 (1887).
99. Budd v. People, 143 U.S. 517, 534 (1892).
100. *Id.*
101. *Id.* at 549 (Brewer, J., dissenting).
102. Holden v. Hardy, 169 U.S. 366, 391–92 (1898).
103. Chicago, B. & Q. Ry. Co. v. Illinois, 200 U.S. 561, 592 (1906).
104. *Id.* at 600 (Brewer, J., dissenting). Ironically, this was the very same case in which the Supreme Court first held that the 5th Amendment Takings Clause was incorporated into the 14th Amendment Due Process Clause and therefore a limit on state governments. Said Brewer, "And after a declaration by this court that a state may not, through any of its departments, take private property for public use without just compensation, I cannot assent to a judgment which, in effect, permits that to be done."
105. Hudson Cnty. Water Co. v. McCarter, 209 U.S. 349, 355 (1908).
106. United States v. Ohio Oil Co., 234 U.S. 548 (1914).
107. Block v. Hirsh, 256 U.S. 135, 156 (1921).
108. *Id.* at 155.
109. *Id.* at 165 (McKenna, J., dissenting).
110. Eubank v. City of Richmond, 226 U.S. 137, 142 (1912).
111. Miller v. Schoene, 276 U.S. 272 (1928).
112. *Id.* at 279–80.
113. New State Ice Co. v. Liebmann, 285 U.S. 262 (1932).
114. *Id.* at 302 (Brandeis, J., dissenting).
115. Home Bldg. & Loan Ass'n v. Blaisdell, 290 U.S. 398, 442 (1934).
116. *Id.* at 448 (Sutherland, J., dissenting).
117. Euclid v. Ambler Realty Co., 272 U.S. 365 (1926).
118. Berman v. Parker, 348 U.S. 26, 32 (1954).
119. Chongris v. Corrigan, 409 U.S. 919, 920 (1972).
120. *Id.* at 920 (quoting Pennsylvania Coal Co. v. Mahon, 260 U.S. 393, 415–416 (1922).

CHAPTER 3

1. Although the dominant view is that the power of eminent domain is inherent in sovereignty, it was not assumed to be inherent in the powers of the federal government, presumably because that government was meant by the framers to be one of enumerated (delegated)

powers only. It was not until 1875 that the Supreme Court recognized the power of eminent domain in the U.S. government. Kohl v. United States, 910 U.S. 367, 371–72 (1875).

2. 1 *Kings* 21.
3. *In re* New Orleans Draining Co., 11 La. Ann. 338, 358 (1856).
4. William D. McNulty, Eminent Domain in Continental Europe, 21 *Yale L.J.* 555, 556 (1912).
5. W. W. Buckland, *A Text-Book of Roman Law from Augustus to Justinian 188* (3d ed. 1966).
6. Richard Tuck, *Natural Rights Theories: Their Origin and Development 10* (1979).
7. *Id.* at 11.
8. See e.g., J. Walter Jones, Expropriation in Roman Law, 45 *L. Q. Rev.* 512 (1929); McNulty, *supra* note 4.
9. Nathan Matthews, The Valuation of Property in the Roman Law, 34 *Harv. L. Rev.* 229, 253–54 (1921).
10. Jones, *supra* note 8, at 526.
11. See *id.* at 526 (translating and quoting Rudolf von Ihering, Geist 1, 7 (1906)).
12. Hugo Grotius, *On the Law of War and Peace* 50 (Stephen C. Neff ed., W. Kelsey trans., Cambridge Univ. Press, Student ed. 2012) (1625).
13. *Id.* at 226.
14. *Id.* at 428.
15. Samuel Pufendorf, De Officio Hominis et Civis, bk. II, ch. 15, § 4 (1682).
16. Montesquieu, *The Spirit of the Laws*, bk. 26, ch. XV (1748).
17. 8 Christian Wolff, Jus Naturae, ch. I, §§ 110–19 (1748).
18. Emerich de Vattel, Law of Nations, bk. I, ch. XX (1773).
19. "Since property is an inviolable and sacred right, no one shall be deprived thereof except where public necessity, legally determined, shall clearly demand it, and then only on condition that the owner shall have been previously and equitably indemnified." Declaration of the Rights of Man, Art. 17 (Aug. 26, 1789).
20. See McNulty, *supra* note 4, at 563–64.
21. *Id.* (citing Bousquet, Explication du Code Civil (1805)).
22. Other terms used in English law include "compulsory acquisition" and "expropriation."
23. William B. Stoebuck, A General Theory of Eminent Domain, 47 *Wash. L. Rev.* 553 (1972).
24. 1 William Blackstone, Commentaries *232.
25. 1 Frederick Pollock and Frederic William Maitland, 1 *The History of English Law* 512 (Cambridge Univ. Press 1895).
26. In McCulloch v. Maryland, 17 U.S. (4 Wheat.) 316 (1819), Chief Justice Marshall upheld Congress's establishment of a national bank

as "necessary and proper" to the exercise of its power to regulate commerce. On the same basis, the vast array of modern federal regulation is found to come within the enumerated powers of Congress.

27. 1 Julius L. Sackman, Nichols's The Law of Eminent Domain §§ 1–71, 1–72 (Rev. 3d ed. 2012).
28. 3 Blackstone, *supra* note 24 at *259.
29. Stoebuck, *supra* note 23 at 554.
30. 1 Blackstone, *supra* note 24 at *135.
31. In reporting the early American foundations of eminent domain law, I have relied on the leading treatise on the subject, published a century later, Nichols's The Law of Eminent Domain, *supra* note 27 at 1–71 through 1–86.
32. See The Compact with the Charter and Laws of Colony of New Plymouth 277–78 (Boston, Dutton & Wentworth 1836).
33. New Hampshire, Massachusetts, Rhode Island, Delaware, Maryland, Virginia and North Carolina.
34. See II Statutes at Large: Being a Collection of all the Laws of Virginia from the First session of the Legislaturwe 260 (William Waller Hening ed., New York, W & G. Bartow 1823).
35. Following the example of J. A. C. Grant in his article The "Higher Law" Background of the Law of Eminent Domain, 6 *Wis. L. Rev.* 67, 69 (1930), I have included Vermont among the original constitutions because it was enacted in 1777, although Vermont was not admitted as a state until 1791.
36. Bowman v. Middleton, 1 S.C.L. (1 Bay) 252, 252 (1792).
37. Vanhorne's Lessee v. Dorrance, 28 F.Cas 1012 (C.C.D. Pa. 1795) (No. 16,875).
38. Gardner v. Vill. of Newburgh, 2 Johns. Ch. 162, 166 (N.Y. Ch. 1816).
39. Bradshaw v. Rodgers, 20 Johns. 103, 106 (N.Y. 1822).
40. I James Kent, *Commentaries on American Law* 420 (New York, O. Halsted, 1826).
41. Lindsay v. Commissioners, 2 S.C.L. (2 Bay) 38, 56 (1796).
42. *Bradshaw*, 20 Johns. at 104.
43. Kohl v. United States, 91 U.S. 367, 372 (1875).
44. Miss. & Rum River Boom Co. v. Patterson, 98 U.S. 403, 406 (1878).
45. 2 James Kent, Commentaries on American Law 276 (New York, O. Halsted 1827).
46. John Locke, Second Treatise on Government ch. 11, § 138, *in Two Treatises of Government* 360–61, 286 (Peter Laslett ed., Student ed., Cambridge University Press 1988) (1690).
47. Lindsay v. Commissioners, 2 S.C.L. (2 Bay) 38, 59 (1796).
48. Vanhorne's Lessee v. Dorrance, 28 F.Cas 1012 (C.C.D. Pa. 1795) (No. 16,875).

49. Aldridge v. Tuscumbia, Courtland & Decatur R.R. Co., 2 Stew. & P. 199, 213–14 (Ala. 1832).
50. Boston & Roxbury Mill Corp. v. Newman, 29 Mass. (12 Pick.) 467, 476 (1832).
51. Scudder v. Trenton Del. Falls Co., 1 N.J. Eq. 694, 728 (N.J.Ch. 1832).
52. *Id.* at 729.
53. Bloodgood v. Mohawk & Hudson R.R. Co., 18 Wend. 9, 56–57 (N.Y. 1837).
54. *Id.* at 60–61.
55. Beekman v. Saratoga & Schenectady R.R. Co., 3 Paige Ch. 45, 73 (N.Y. Ch. 1831).
56. Gilmer v. Lime Point, 18 Cal. 229, 252 (1861).
57. Bankhead v. Brown, 25 Iowa 540, 548 (1868).
58. Twelfth St. Market Co. v. Philadelphia & R. T. R. Co., 21 A. 989, 990 (Pa. 1891).
59. Lowell v. Boston, 111 Mass. 454 (1873).
60. Philip Nichols, Jr., The Meaning of Public Use in the Law of Eminent Domain, 20 *B.U. L. Rev.* 615, 626 (1940).
61. John Lewis, 1 A Treatise on the Law of Eminent Domain in the United States 507 (3d ed. 1909).
62. Salisbury Land & Improvement Co. v. Commonwealth, 102 N.E. 619, 622 (Mass. 1913).
63. Pa. Mut. Life Ins. Co. v. Philadelphia, 88 A. 904 (Pa. 1913).
64. Frelinghuysen v. State Highway Comm'n, 107 N.J.L. 218 (N.J. 1930).
65. Fountain Park Co. v. Hensler, 155 N.E. 465, 470 (Ind. 1927).
66. *Id.*
67. Comment, The Public Use Limitation on Eminent Domain: An Advance Requiem, 58 *Yale L.J.* 599, 605–06 (1949).
68. Int'l Paper Co. v. United States, 282 U.S. 399 (1931).
69. Mt. Vernon-Woodberry Cotton Duck Co. v. Ala. Interstate Power Co., 240 U.S. 30, 32 (1916).
70. For example, in *A.L.A. Schechter Poultry Corp. V. United States*, 295 U.S. 495 (1935) the Supreme Court held that the Commerce Clause did not empower Congress to regulate the live poultry business in metropolitan New York. In *Railroad Retirement Board v. Alton R. Co.*, 295 U.S. 330 (1935) the Court invalidated as beyond Congress's commerce regulation powers the uniform national pension system for railroad employees created by the Railroad Retirement Act. In *Carter v. Carter Coal Co.*, 298 U.S. 238 (1936) the Court held that the regulation of the coal mining industry pursuant to the Bituminous Coal Conservation Act of 1935 was not within Congress's Commerce Clause powers.
71. 297 U.S. 1 (1936).

72. 301 U.S. 548 (1937).
73. 301 U.S. 619 (1937).
74. Green v. Frazier, 176 N.W. 11 (N.D. 1920).
75. 253 U.S. 233 (1920).
76. *Id.* at 242.
77. *Id.* at 240.
78. 9 F. Supp. 137 (D.C. Ky. 1935).
79. *Id.* at 140.
80. *Id.* at 138–39.
81. 71 U.S. (4 Wall.) 2 (1866).
82. United States v. Certain Lands in Louisville, 78 F.2d 684 (Sixth Cir. 1935).
83. Oklahoma City v. Sanders, 94 F.2d 323 (C.A.10 1938).
84. N.Y.C. Hous. Auth. v. Muller, 1 N.E. 2d 153, 155, 156 (N.Y. 1936).
85. *Id.* at 155.
86. Dornan v. Phila. Hous. Auth., 200 A. 834, 842 (Pa. 1938).
87. See Comment, *supra* note 67, at 608.
88. Allydonn Realty Corp. v. Holyoke Hous. Auth., 23 N.E. 2d 665 (Mass. 1939).
89. Nichols, *supra* note 60, at 633.
90. Hairston v. Danville & W. Ry. Co., 208 U.S. 598, 607 (1908). In fact there was at least one such case. In *Missouri Pacific Railway Co. v. Nebraska*, 164 U.S. 403 (1896), the court had invalidated a taking of railroad property for the construction of a grain elevator as in violation of the Due Process Clause of the 14th Amendment.
91. Mt. Vernon-Woodberry Cotton Duck Co. v. Ala. Interstate Power Co., 240 U.S. 30 (1916).
92. Cherokee Nation v. S. Kan. Ry. Co., 135 U.S. 641, 657 (1890).
93. United States v. Gettysburg Electric Ry. Co., 160 U.S. 668, 681–83 (1896).
94. United States v. Eighty Acres of Land in Williamson County, 26 F. Supp. 315 (E.D. Ill. 1939).
95. Shoemaker v. United States, 147 U.S. 282 (1893).
96. Berman v. Parker, 348 U.S. 26 (1954).
97. District of Columbia Redevelopment Act of 1945, ch. 736, § 2, 60 Stat. 790, 790 (1946).
98. *Berman*, 348 U.S. at 33.
99. *Id.* at 35–36.
100. 272 U.S. 365, 395 (1926).
101. 341 P.2d 171 (Wash. 1959).
102. *Id.* at 193.
103. 190 N.E.2d 402 (N.Y. 1963).
104. *Id.* at 405.
105. United States *ex rel.* Tenn. Valley Auth. v. Welch, 150 F.2d 613 (4th Cir. 1945), *rev'd*, United States *ex rel.* Tenn. Valley Auth. v. Welch, 327 U.S. 546 (1946).

106. Judge Parker was appointed to the Fourth Circuit Court of Appeals in 1925 and served as chief judge from 1948 to 1958. He was nominated to the Supreme Court in 1930 by President Herbert Hoover, but was rejected by the US Senate by one vote.
107. *Welch*, 327 U.S. at 553.
108. Black was quoting from *Old Dominion Land Co. v. United States*, 269 U.S. 55, 66 (1925).
109. *Welch*, 327 U.S. at 556 (Reed, J., concurring).
110. *Id.* at 557 (Frankfurter, J., concurring).
111. Marbury v. Madison, 5 U.S. (1 Cranch) 137, 177 (1803).
112. Midkiff v. Tom, 702 F.2d 788, 806 (9th Cir. 1983), *reversed by* Hawaii Housing Authority v. Midkiff, 467 U.S. 229 (1984).
113. *Id.* at 808.
114. *Midkiff*, 467 U.S. at 240 (1984) (quoting *Berman v. Parker*, 348 U.S. 26, 33 (1954)).
115. *Id.* at 239.
116. *Id.* at 241.

CHAPTER 4

1. W.W. Buckland, A Text-Book of Roman Law from Augustus to Justinian 182–83 (3d ed., 1966).
2. *Id.* at 205 *et seq.*
3. See Hughes v. Oklahoma, 441 U.S. 322 (1979).
4. For a brief summary of Magna Carta chapters 16 and 23, see James L. Huffman, Speaking of Inconvenient Truths—A History of the Public Trust Doctrine, 18 *Duke Envtl. L. & Pol'y F.* 1, 19–23 (2007).
5. Magna Carta, ch. 13 (1215).
6. *Id.* ch. 41.
7. See, e.g., Davidson v. New Orleans, 96 U.S. (6 Otto) 97, 99 (1877).
8. Magna Carta, ch. 29 (1225).
9. 110 U.S. 516, 531 (1884).
10. *Id.*
11. *Id.* at 553 (Harlan, J., dissenting).
12. *Id.* at 550.
13. 1 Thomas Paine, The Writings of Thomas Paine 382–88 (1774).
14. Gordon Wood, The Creation of the American Republic: 1776–1787, at 601 (1969).
15. *Id.* at 24.
16. 3 William Blackstone, Commentaries *2.
17. The Federalist No. 43 (James Madison).
18. U.S. Const. art. IV, § 4.
19. See Wood, *supra* note 14, at 63.
20. Proprietors of Charles River Bridge v. Proprietors of Warren Bridge, 36 U.S. (111 Pet.) 420 (1837).

21. *Id.* at 557 (1837) (McLean, J.).
22. United States v. Hoar, 26 F.Cas. 329, 331 (C.C. Mass. 1821) (No. 15,373) (citations omitted).
23. See Dodge v. Woolsey, 59 U.S. (18 How.) 331 (1855).
24. See Wilson v. New, 243 U.S. 332 (1917); Mugler v. Kansas, 123 U.S. 623 (1887).
25. See Schenck v. Pro-Choice Network of W. N.Y., 519 U.S. 357 (1997); Thomas v. Union Carbide Agric. Products Co., 473 U.S. 568 (1985); Buckley v. Valeo, 424 U.S. 1 (1976).
26. See Hodges v. Snyder, 261 U.S. 600 (1923).
27. See Nati'l Licorice v. NLRB, 309 U.S. 350 (1940).
28. Munn v. Illinois, 94 U.S. 113, 126 (1876) (upholding state regulation of the rates charged by grain storage warehouses).
29. See Leonard W. Levy, The Law of the Commonwealth and Chief Justice Shaw 255–59 (1957).
30. See, e.g., Nebbia v. New York, 291 U.S. 502 (1934) (upholding state regulation of the price of milk).
31. Yellin v. United States, 374 U.S. 109, 135 n.9 (1963).
32. Washington v. Wash. State Commercial Passenger Fishing Vessel Ass'n, 443 U.S. 658 (1979).
33. Garner v. Teamsters, Chauffeurs & Helpers Local Union No. 776 (A. F. L.), 346 U.S. 485, 49596 (1953).
34. State of Georgia v. Stanton, 73 U.S. (6 Wall.) 50, 60 (1867).
35. 1 Alexis de Tocqueville, Democracy in America 106 (Vintage Books ed. 1945) (1835).
36. Hohfeld developed a theory of what he called jural opposites and jural correlatives to explain the nature of all private legal relationships. See Wesley Newcomb Hohfeld, Fundamental Legal Conceptions as Applied in Judicial Reasoning and Other Legal Essays (1919).
37. Flast v. Cohen, 392 U.S. 83, 119–20 (1968) (Harlan, J., dissenting) (footnotes omitted).
38. Stark v. Wickard, 321 U.S. 288, 309–10 (1944).
39. Lujan v. Defenders of Wildlife, 504 U.S. 555, 578 (1992).
40. U.S. v. Students Challenging Regulatory Agency Procedures, 412 U.S. 669 (1973).
41. Anthony Randazzo and John M. Palatiello, Reason Found., Knowing What You Own: An Efficient Government How-To Guide for Managing State and Local Property Inventories (2010), *available at* http://reason.org/files/how_to_manage_or_sell_state_local_property.pdf.
42. Hoboken v. Pa. R.R. Co., 124 U.S. 656, 681 (1888).
43. U.S. Const. art. IV, § 3.
44. An Act Granting the Right of Way to Ditch and Canal Owners over the Public Lands, and for Other Purposes, ch. 262, 14 Stat. 251 (1866).
45. Taylor Grazing Act, ch. 865, 48 Stat. 1269 (1934) (codified at 43 U.S.C. §§ 315–316o).

46. First Morrill Act, ch. 130, 12 Stat. 503 (1862) (codified at 7 U.S.C. § 301 et seq.) (provided land grants for the establishment of agricultural colleges).
47. 505 U.S. 1003, 1029 (1992).
48. Restatement (Second) of Torts § 821B.
49. See Huffman, *supra* note 4.
50. Ill. Cent. R. Co. v. Illinois, 146 U.S. 387 (1892).
51. See Joseph L Sax, The Public Trust Doctrine in Natural Resource Law: Effective Judicial Intervention, *68 Mich. L. Rev.* 471, 509–46 (1970).
52. Joseph L. Sax, Liberating the Public Trust Doctrine from Its Historical Shackles, 14 *U.C. Davis L. Rev* 185 (1980).

CHAPTER 5

1. I The Records of the Federal Convention of 1787, at 147 (Max Farrand ed., 1966).
2. *Id.* at 302.
3. *Id.* at 605.
4. See Forrest Mcdonald, Novus Ordo Seclorum: The Intellectual Origins Of The Constitution 1–5 (1985).
5. Charles A. Beard, An Economic Interpretation of the Constitution of the United States (1913).
6. Woody Holton, Unruly Americans and the Origins of the Constitution (2007).
7. McDonald, *supra* note 4, at 154.
8. *Id.* at 22.
9. There were contemporary voices raised in opposition on moral grounds, but most participants in the framing process were sympathetic with the property rights of slave owners, if not the moral foundation of the peculiar institution. The initial proposal to include the Fugitive Slave Clause was challenged by James Wilson of Pennsylvania on the ground that it "would oblige the Executive of the State to do it, at the public expense." No further mention was made until September 15 when "the term 'legally' was struck out, and 'under the laws thereof' inserted after the word 'State,' in compliance with the wish of some who thought the term legal equivocal, and favoring the idea that slavery was legal in a moral view." II The Records of the Federal Convention of 1787, *supra* note 1, at 628.
10. Lincoln proposed to compensate slave owners in his annual message to Congress, December 1, 1862. V Abraham Lincoln, Collected Works 518–37 (Roy P. Basler ed. 1953). The absence of a compensation provision in the final version of the Emancipation Proclamation had less to do with principle than with the realities of expense to the government.

11. The proposal for compensation was also influenced by a hope that support for the war among slaveholders might be weakened.
12. I The Records of the Federal Convention of 1787, *supra* note 1, at 134.
13. III The Records of the Federal Convention of 1787, *supra* note 1, at 143.
14. *Id.* at 144.
15. 32 U.S. (7 Pet.) 243 (1833).
16. Bernard Siegan, Economic Liberties and the Constitution 42 (1980).
17. Wilkinson v. Leland, 27 U.S. (2 Pet.) 627, 658 (1829).
18. 166 U.S. 226 (1897).
19. 405 U.S. 538, 552 (1972).
20. Lucas v. S.C. Coastal Council, 505 U.S. 1003 (1992).
21. 123 U.S. 623 (1887).
22. 239 U.S. 394 (1915).
23. 260 U.S. 393, 413 (1922).
24. 480 U.S. 470 (1987).
25. *Mahon*, 260 U.S. at 415.
26. 276 U.S. 272 (1928).
27. 272 U.S. 365 (1926).
28. 277 U.S. 183 (1928).
29. Jan Laitos, Law of Property Rights Protection 1–18 (2007 Supp).
30. 304 U.S. 144, 152 (1938).
31. *Id.* at n.4.
32. *Id.*
33. Ronald Dworkin, Taking Rights Seriously 269 (1977).
34. See John Hart Ely, Democracy and Distrust (1980).
35. 10 U.S. (6 Cranch) 87, 128 (1810).
36. *Id.* at 139.
37. *Id.* at 133–34.
38. 426 U.S. 794, 813 (1976) (emphasis added).
39. 452 U.S. 314, 331–32 (1981).
40. 505 U.S. 1003, 1046 (1992) (quoting O'Gorman & Young, Inc. v. Hartford Fire Ins. Co., 282 U.S. 251, 257 (1931)).
41. 512 U.S. 374, 391 (1994).
42. *Id.* at 402 (Stevens, J., dissenting).
43. Kelo v. City of New London, 545 U.S. 469, 490 (2005) (Kennedy, J., concurring).
44. 198 U.S. 45 (1905).
45. 291 U.S. 502, 537 (1934).
46. See 381 U.S. 479 (1965).
47. 410 U.S. 113 (1973).
48. 539 U.S. 558 (2003).
49. 307 U.S. 496 (1939).
50. *Id.* at 531–32.

51. *Id.* at 527.
52. Lynch v. Household Fin. Corp., 405 U.S. 538, 552 (1972).
53. 438 U.S. 104 (1978).
54. *Id.* at 124.
55. *Id.* (citations omitted).
56. *Id.* at 130–31.
57. Penn Cent. Transp. Co. v. City of New York, 386 N.E.2d 1271, 1276 (1977).
58. *Penn Cent.*, 438 U.S. at 110.
59. Pa. Coal Co. v. Mahon, 260 U.S. 393, 413 (1922).
60. Lochner v. New York, 198 U.S. 45, 75 (1905) (Holmes, J., dissenting).
61. *Penn Cent.*, 438 U.S. at 124.
62. 458 U.S. 419 (1982).
63. 447 U.S. 255, 260 (1980).
64. 505 U.S. 1003 (1992).
65. *Penn Cent.*, 438 U.S. at 124.
66. See, e.g., Greene v. Louisville & I.R. Co., 244 U.S. 499, 507 (1917); Raymond v. Chi. Union Traction Co., 207 U.S. 20, 37–38 (1907).
67. *Penn Cent.*, 438 U.S. at 124 (quoting United States v. Cent. Eureka Mining Co., 357 U.S. 155, 168 (1958)).
68. 5 U.S. (1 Cranch) 137, 177 (1803).
69. *Id.*

CHAPTER 6

1. Burton v. Wilmington Parking Auth., 365 U.S. 715, 722 (1961). The phrase was used in the context of assessing whether state action can be attributed to discriminatory private conduct for equal protection purposes. In *Burton* the balancing led to the conclusion that the state had violated a constitutional right, but a different court with different judges could just as well decide it the other way.
2. 444 U.S. 164 (1979).
3. *Id.* at 175.
4. *Id.* at 176–77.
5. *Id.* at 177.
6. *Id.* at 178.
7. *Id.* at 181.
8. Robins v. PruneYard Shopping Ct., 592 P.2d 341 (Cal. 1979).
9. 447 U.S. 74, 82 (1980).
10. *Id.* at 83.
11. *Id.* at 84.
12. 483 U.S. 825 (1987).
13. 458 U.S. 419 (1982).
14. *Nollan*, 483 U.S. at 831–32 (quoting *id.* at 433).

15. *Id.* at 834.
16. See discussion *infra* at note 56, *et seq.*
17. *Nollan*, 483 U.S. at 836–37 (footnote omitted).
18. San Diego Gas & Electric Co. v. City of San Diego, 450 U.S. 621 (1981). Justice Brennan dissented from a majority finding that the lower court decision was not final, and then went on to conclude that an unconstitutional taking resulted from the down-zoning of land even where the offending regulation was subsequently repealed. The concept of a temporary taking was embraced by a majority of the court in *First English Evangelical Lutheran Church of Glendale v. Los Angeles*, 482 U.S. 304 (1987).
19. *Nollan*, 483 U.S. at 867 (Stevens, J., dissenting).
20. *Id.* at 837 (quoting J.E.D. Assocs., Inc. V. Atkinson, 432 A.2d 12, 14 (N.H. 1981)).
21. 512 U.S. 374 (1994).
22. 133 S. Ct. 2586 (2013).
23. *Id.* at 2596.
24. *Id.* at 2591.
25. 447 U.S. 255 (1980).
26. 505 U.S. 1003 (1992).
27. *Id.* at 1020.
28. *Nollan*, 483 U.S. at 833 n.2.
29. 533 U.S. 606, 626 (2001).
30. 133 U.S. 511 (2012).
31. *Lucas*, 505 U.S. at 1029.
32. *Id.* at 1027.
33. See, e.g., Michael C. Blumm & Lucas Ritchie, Lucas's Unlikely Legacy: The Rise of Background Principles as Categorical Takings Defenses, 29 *Harv. Envtl. L. Rev.* 321, 367 (2005); J.B. Ruhl, Making Nuisance Ecological, 58 *Case W. Res. L. Rev.* 753, 759 (2008).
34. The term "categorical defenses" is used by Blumm & Ritchie, *Id.*
35. *Lucas*, 505 U.S. at 1031.
36. For in-depth explanations of the historic and theoretical errors in the arguments of Ruhl, Blumm and Ritchie, see James L. Huffman, Background Principles and the Rule of Law: Fifteen Years after Lucas, 35 *Ecology L.Q.* 1 (2008), and James L. Huffman, Beware of Greens in Praise of the Common Law, 58 *Case W. Res. L. Rev.* 813 (2008).
37. *Lucas*, 505 U.S. at 1031.
38. 512 U.S. 374 (1994).
39. *Id.* at 386.
40. *Id.* at 387.
41. *Id.* at 388.
42. *Id.* at 402 (Stevens, J., dissenting).
43. *Id.* at 403.
44. 166 U.S. 226 (1897).

45. 544 U.S. 528 (2005).
46. *Id.* at 536 (quoting First English Evangelical Lutheran Church of Glendale v. County of Los Angeles, 482 U.S. 304, 314 (1987)).
47. *Id.* at 537.
48. *Id.* at 538.
49. *Id.*
50. *Id.* at 537.
51. 277 U.S. 183 (1928).
52. *Id.* (citing Euclid v. Ambler Co., 272 U.S. 365, 395 (1926)).
53. Penn. Cent. Transp. Co. v. City of N.Y., 438 U.S. 104, 138 (1978).
54. Nollan v. Cal. Coastal Comm'n, 483 U.S. 825, 842 (1987) (Brennan, J., dissenting).
55. Dolan v. City of Tigard, 512 U.S. 374, 405 (1994) (Stevens, J., dissenting).
56. Lingle v. Chevron U.S.A., Inc., 544 U.S. 528, 542 (2005). Justice O'Connor is here quoting Chevron's brief, which is in turn quoting *Armstong v. United States*, 364 U.S. 40, 49 (1960).
57. *Id.* at 543.
58. *Id.* at 544.
59. *Id.* at 542.
60. *Id.* at 544.
61. *Id.* at 545.
62. Kelo v. City of New London, 545 U.S. 469, 488 (2005).
63. *Id.*
64. *Id.*
65. *Lingle*, 544 U.S. at 547.
66. *Id.*
67. *Koontz*, 133 S. Ct. at 2609 (Kagan, J., dissenting).
68. 364 U.S. 40, 49 (1960).
69. Penn. Cent. Transp. Co. v. City of N.Y., 438 U.S. 104, 130–31 (1978).
70. Lucas v. S.C. Coastal Council, 505 US 1003, 1016 n.7 (1992).
71. *Id.*
72. *Id.*
73. *Id.* at 1015 (quoting *Penn Central*, 438 U.S. at 124.).
74. 535 U.S. 302, 326 (2002).
75. The bundle of sticks metaphor was relied upon in *Andrus v. Allard*, 444 U.S. 51 (1979), but the Court offered no principled justification beyond asserting that "the aggregate must be viewed in its entirety." *Id.* at 66.
76. First English Evangelical Lutheran Church of Glendale v. Los Angeles Cnty., 482 U.S. 304, 321 (1987).
77. *Id.* at 340–41 (Stevens, J., dissenting) (footnote omitted).
78. San Diego Gas & Electric Co. v. City of San Diego, 450 U.S. 621, 658 (1981).

79. *Id.* at 655 n.22.
80. *Id.* at 661 n.26.
81. In fact the California court did find that no taking had occurred, a decision the Supreme Court declined to review. See First English Evangelical Church of Glendale v. County of Los Angeles, 258 Cal.Rptr. 893 (1989), *cert denied* 493 U.S. 1056 (1990).
82. *First English*, 482 U.S. at 328.
83. There was a time when the Court understood that temporary or partial obstructions of the use of property had the effect of taking a severable interest. In *Jacobs v. United States*, 290 U.S. 13, 16 (1933), Justice Hughes held that "[a] servitude was created by reason of intermittent overflows [from a government dam] which impaired the use of the lands for agricultural purposes.... There was thus a partial taking of the lands for which the government was bound to make just compensation under the Fifth Amendment."
84. Tahoe–Sierra Preservation Council, Inc. v. Tahoe Reg'l Planning Agency, 535 U.S. 302 (2002).
85. Pumpelly v. Green Bay Co., 80 U.S. (13 Wall.) 166 (1872).
86. *Id.* at 172.
87. *Id.* at 177–78 (emphasis in original).
88. Haw. Hous. Auth. V. Midkiff, 467 U.S. 229, 240 (1984).
89. Holmes wrote that "the act cannot be sustained as an exercise of the police power. [T]here must be an exercise of eminent domain and compensation to sustain the act." Pa. Coal. Co. v. Mahon, 260 U.S. 393, 413–14 (1922).
90. In the 1887 case of *Mugler v. Kansas*, 123 U.S. 623 (1997), Justice Harlan relied on this distinction in rejecting a claim that a prohibition of the manufacture or sale of intoxicating liquors resulted in a taking for which compensation was due. The case did "not involve the power of eminent domain, in the exercise of which property may not be taken for public use without compensation," said Harlan. *Id.* at 668. Rather it was a police power "prohibition simply upon the use of property for purposes that are declared, by valid legislation, to be injurious to the health, morals, or safety of the community, [which] cannot, in any just sense, be deemed a taking or an appropriation of property for the public benefit." *Id.* at 668–69.
91. Penn Cent. Transp. Co. v. City of N.Y., 438 U.S. 104, 136 (1978).
92. *Mahon*, 260 U.S. at 413.
93. *Id.* at 415.
94. *Penn Cent. Transp. Co.*, 438 U.S. at 124.
95. *Id.* (quoting United States v. Cent. Eureka Mining Co., 357 U.S. 155, 168 (1958)).
96. *Mahon*, 260 U.S. at 413.
97. *Id.* at 414.
98. *Id.* at 413.

CHAPTER 7

1. Youngstown Sheet & Tube v. Sawyer, 342 U.S. 579, 593 (1952).
2. 405 U.S. 538, 552 (1972).
3. Pennsylvania Coal Co. v. Mahon, 260 U.S. 393, 415 (1922).
4. *Id.* at 593.
5. *Id.* at 594.

Table of Cases Volume II

Index

Printed in the United States of America